#1 BESTSELLING AUTHOR

THE BUSINESS SALE PARADOX

Before and Beyond The Exit to Maximize Value & Live Richer

ROBERT PAGLIARINI, PH.D., CFP®

OTHER BOOKS BY ROBERT PAGLIARINI

BADASS RETIREMENT

GET MONEY SMART

THE SUDDEN WEALTH SOLUTION

THE OTHER 8 HOURS

THE SIX-DAY FINANCIAL MAKEOVER

Hardcover ISBN: 978-0-9905715-6-8

Paperback ISBN: 978-0-9905715-7-5

Library of Congress Control Number: 2026900029

CONTENTS

QUICK START GUIDE:
WHERE TO BEGIN

If You're Two to Three Years From Selling. Your mission: Build maximum value and prepare emotionally. Your biggest risks: Waiting too long. Not cleaning up valuation-killing issues. Failing to make the business transferable. Start with Chapters 1 and 2. Write your Why Letter and assess the Four Pillars.

If You're Actively Marketing or Talking to Buyers. Your mission: Execute a competitive process and negotiate the best terms. Your biggest risks: Losing leverage by showing desperation. Accepting the highest price without understanding structure. Start with Chapters 3, 4, and 5. Review the Three Pillars of Deal Structure.

If You Just Signed a Letter of Intent (LOI). Your mission: Survive due diligence and protect your terms. Your biggest risks: Due diligence fatigue. Allowing the buyer to re-trade terms. Taking your eye off operations. Start with Chapters 4, 5, and 6. Reread your Why Letter.

If the Wire Just Hit. Your mission: Avoid wealth-destroying mistakes and design a life worth the money. Your biggest risks: Making major decisions before you're ready. Drifting without purpose. Damaging relationships. Start with Chapters 6, 7, and 8. Implement the Green, Yellow, and Red framework immediately.

If You're Struggling Post-Sale. Your mission: Rebuild meaning intentionally. Your biggest challenges: Feeling lost despite success. Missing structure and validation. Questioning whether selling was right. Start with Chapters 7 and 8. Read "The Grief You Didn't Expect."

If You're not Sure Where You Are. You are exactly where you need to be. Turn the page…

INTRODUCTION:

THE BUSINESS SALE PARADOX

Most business owners approach selling their company exactly backwards.

A successful sale requires equal focus on three distinct phases—BEFORE, DURING, and AFTER. Most sellers obsess over the transaction. They clean up financials, pitch to buyers, negotiate terms, and manage due diligence. Business owners spend 98% of their focus and energy on the transaction itself and maybe 1% each on preparing before and planning for after. That's the business sale paradox. The imbalance is staggering, and so are the consequences.

When you neglect the before, you enter the sale reactive instead of ready. You haven't clarified your goals, optimized the business for maximum value, or prepared your team. This lack of preparation leads to lower valuations, difficult negotiations, and unnecessary stress. Worse, it forces you into defensive decisions—accepting unfavorable terms or rushing the process just to get it done. You're negotiating from weakness when you could have been negotiating from strength.

When you neglect the after, the fallout can be equally devastating. I've watched owners wake up the morning after closing feeling completely unmoored. They spent years, sometimes decades, defining themselves by their business. Now that it's gone, they don't know who they are. The deal created financial success but emotional emptiness because they never defined what came next. They assumed the sale would deliver meaning, but meaning doesn't come with the wire transfer.

Make no mistake, the during is where everything culminates. This is where deals are won or lost, where small mistakes cost millions, where leverage shifts and negotiations determine your real payout. But you can't win the transaction if you haven't prepared before it.

And even a flawless deal that maximizes every dollar means nothing if you wake up six months later wealthy, free, and completely lost.

After nearly thirty years helping business owners sell their companies, I've watched gifted entrepreneurs succeed and fail at every stage. Some nail the preparation but crumble during negotiations. Others execute flawless deals but implode six months later. The rare few who master all three phases walk away with exceptional outcomes on every level.

What You'll Learn

BEFORE is where you build power. You prepare your mindset, strengthen your structure, and optimize your numbers so you enter the sale from a position of strength, not desperation.

DURING is where you convert that power into results. You'll assemble your Core Four deal team, create competition among buyers, structure offers that maximize real value, and navigate due diligence without bleeding control.

AFTER is where you protect what you've built and design what comes next. You'll manage sudden wealth without losing it, rebuild purpose and identity beyond your business, and create a life that's as rich and intentional as the company you sold.

I'll share real-world stories from clients who've been through it all—deals that closed at record valuations, negotiations that went sideways, and everything in between.

When the deal closes, you'll have new wealth, new freedom, and new questions you never expected. Who are you without your business? What's next? How do you turn financial success into a life that actually feels successful?

The Business Sale Paradox is about how to sell your business for maximum value AND create a life afterward that's as rewarding as what you built.

Why I Wrote This

You're about to enter a world filled with new language, unfamiliar players, and emotions you've probably never experienced. You'll be asked to make once-in-a-lifetime decisions that could change your financial future, your family's future, and your sense of identity.

I've spent nearly thirty years working with business owners through the most consequential financial events of their lives. With a Ph.D. in retirement planning, a master's degree in psychology, and six books including *The Sudden Wealth Solution*, I've become a nationally recognized expert in sudden wealth management. I help clients assemble their teams, interpret LOIs, navigate due diligence, and manage the financial and personal transition after the sale.

I've seen entrepreneurs negotiate brilliant deals, and I've watched others leave millions on the table or spiral after closing because no one prepared them. My goal is to help you avoid the pitfalls, capture the upside, and walk away not only richer, but freer.

Your Next Step

Before we dive into the mechanics of selling, we need to talk about something more important. Your mindset.

Selling your company isn't like selling a product or signing a big client. It's not just another deal. It's a fundamental identity shift from builder to seller. And that shift starts now, long before you ever sign an LOI.

Chapter 1 begins by getting *you* ready to sell.

Because selling your business isn't simply a transaction. When it's done right, it's a transformation.

Yours starts now.

STAGE ONE:
BEFORE

Most business owners skip this part. They decide they're ready to sell, and immediately start calling investment bankers. But the work begins right now—before anyone knows you're considering a sale, before the first buyer meeting, and before due diligence. This is the BEFORE stage, the quiet work that separates sellers who negotiate from a position of strength from those who negotiate out of desperation. You can't fake readiness. Buyers can sense when a company isn't truly sellable, or when the business can't function without its founder. This stage is where you fix that, and where you build the mental foundation and transform your company into something someone else can buy. Everything that happens after—your valuation, your leverage, your ability to walk away—will be determined by how you approach BEFORE. The race hasn't started yet. That's exactly why this moment matters...

CHAPTER 1:

GET YOURSELF READY

Discover the Mindset
Behind Maximum Value

I t was late when John called me.

"Robert," he said quietly.

His voice had that thin edge of exhaustion that only comes from months of strain. For three decades, he'd built his business from the ground up. He'd led hundreds of employees, managed thousands of decisions, and never once hesitated when the pressure was on. But that night, he sounded defeated.

"Why am I even doing this?"

For a moment, I didn't answer because that's the question almost every owner eventually asks when the sale process strips away their certainty.

John had always been in control. He could read a balance sheet in seconds, negotiate with suppliers in his sleep, and motivate his team like a coach at halftime. But now, surrounded by attorneys, accountants, and investment bankers, John felt like a spectator. The process that was supposed to reward him for his decades of sacrifice had turned into something that made him feel powerless.

That's the paradox of selling your business. The very mindset that built your success can work against you when you try to let it go. It isn't just financial — it's emotional, psychological, and existential. It forces you to examine who you are, what you've built, and what your life will look like when the thing that's defined you for years is no longer yours. The money, the contracts, the negotiations — those are the tangible parts. What's harder to measure is the emotional toll of letting go of something that has shaped your identity.

The Business Sale Mindset

Most entrepreneurs live in a constant state of forward motion. They're doers, fixers, and improvisers. When something breaks, they fix it. When there's risk, they embrace it. That bias toward action is why they succeed in business. But the sale of a business demands a completely different skill set.

A business sale rewards patience, not speed. It demands humility, not certainty. It values letting go more than taking charge.

That's a foreign concept to the founder mind. You've spent decades conditioning yourself to believe that control equals safety. You *earned* your success by steering every decision, managing every detail, and keeping the ship steady. But now, to maximize value, you must begin to *release* control.

John's problem wasn't a lack of intelligence; it was a lack of endurance for a different kind of race. The sale process is a marathon disguised as a sprint. The early stage (choosing bankers, cleaning up financials, and gathering data) feels fast. Then, suddenly, everything slows. You wait for responses. You wait for diligence requests. You wait for the next draft of the purchase agreement.

That waiting drives entrepreneurs insane. They've spent their careers solving problems immediately. Waiting feels like failure.

The best preparation transcends operational reflection. You need to train like an athlete for this process. Sleep well, exercise daily, and delegate aggressively. Protect your energy like you protect your equity, because you'll need both.

I've seen countless deals fall apart because the seller burned out. They got tired of the grind, snapped at a buyer, or refused a reasonable compromise out of frustration. Fatigue kills deals faster than bad numbers.

The first step in preparing to sell isn't cleaning up your books or hiring an investment banker; it's getting your head and heart aligned.

You'll need to confront conflicting emotions. Excitement and anxiety. Pride and fear. Relief and grief. You'll question whether it's the right time, whether you're getting enough, and whether you'll be happy afterward. That's normal. The more self-aware you are, the smoother this process will be.

That mental, emotional, and even physical shift, is what I call the Business Sale Mindset. It's the ability to think like the buyer, seller, *and* the successor. To be able to step out of the driver's seat and view your company as an asset that someone else must eventually run.

The Skill Shift Paradox

You got here through confidence, quick decisions, and a deep sense of control. You trusted your instincts, moved fast, and made tough calls when others froze. Those traits made you a great builder, but they can also make you a difficult seller.

The sale process rewards a different skill set: patience, collaboration, and the ability to let others lead. It requires trust in your advisors, restraint in negotiation, and the humility to accept that you're no longer the expert in the room. You're used to being the one who drives outcomes. Now, you must sit back and let the process drive itself.

It's hard to do, but it's critical. The founder mindset and the seller mindset are two entirely different playbooks. What made you indispensable to your company can make you expendable in the deal. The Skill Shift Paradox is a test of evolution, and the sellers who adapt fastest are the ones who get the best outcomes.

What got you here won't get you there.

Mind(set) Over Money?

One of the most honest interactions I've had with a client occurred early in the process. After I explained that we needed to get him ready for the sale, he shot back, "I don't need all that mindset crap. I just want to sell my company for as much money as possible!"

I get it. You didn't build your business by meditating on your feelings; you built it by grinding, solving problems, and focusing relentlessly on results.

And now you want to get as much as you possibly can from the sale. Believe me, I want that for you as well.

But here's the truth that surprises even the most hard-nosed, numbers-driven founders. When you focus on the before, you dramatically increase the odds of a successful sale, and often the financial outcome itself. On the company side, it's about clarity and control. Positioning your team, tightening financials, strengthening systems, and documenting everything so buyers see consistency and confidence instead of chaos and key-person risk. When a buyer reviews your materials and sees order rather than noise, it communicates that your company is not dependent on you. It runs on process and discipline, not personality and improvisation. This lowers risk and raises multiples greatly. Preparation sends a powerful signal to buyers. This is a business they can trust.

But the other half of preparation is personal readiness. Battle scars notwithstanding, selling a business is a gauntlet. There will be stress, pressure, second-guessing, and moments when the deal feels like it's slipping away. The owners who thrive through that process are the ones that prepared, defined their goals, and visualized their post-sale life beforehand. When you know who you are, what you want, and what truly matters, you're far less likely to make reactive, fear-based decisions in the heat of negotiation. You'll stay grounded when tensions rise, confident when buyers push, and clear when tough tradeoffs emerge. The more you prepare internally, the more leverage you gain externally.

When you take the time to think about your after (what life will look like post-sale), you put yourself in a far stronger position to negotiate. Most owners assume they'll figure it out later, but that's exactly how they end up negotiating for things they don't even care about while ignoring what matters most. I've watched it happen countless times. Owners get caught up in the heat of the deal, fighting for a slightly higher earnout multiple or obsessing over valuation points. Meanwhile, they totally overlook the lifestyle implications, such as when they'll actually be free to leave, what kind of role they'll play post-sale, or how their payout is structured for tax efficiency.

The result? They win the battle over numbers, but lose the war over meaning.

When you've defined your after, you gain clarity. You come to know exactly what you need from the deal and what's noise. Maybe you don't want to stick around for three years under someone else's leadership. Maybe you value more cash up front, rather than a potentially higher, riskier earnout. Or maybe you care deeply about keeping your name on the door or preserving your team's culture. You can't know what to ask for, or what to walk away from, unless you've done the work to visualize life after the deal closes.

The most successful sellers are the ones who negotiate with intention. They understand that the after isn't some distant phase. Instead it's the filter through which every big decision must be examined.

So, if you believe mindset is "woo-woo," think again. This isn't about spiritual introspection; it's about leverage. The more self-aware, prepared, and emotionally grounded you are, the better decisions you make, the more confidence you project, and the stronger your negotiating position becomes. Getting yourself ready before and after the sale isn't a distraction; it's the ultimate multiplier. Owners who embrace the full arc—before, during, and after—are far more likely to maximize the deal value, build greater wealth, claim the freedom they desire, and create real peace of mind.

This chapter will help you build the mindset of a successful seller, one who's calm, prepared, and in control of their feelings. Because, in the end, the deal that matters most is the one you make with *yourself.*

If you're like many business owners I've worked with over the years, you may be experiencing apprehension and insecurity about the process of selling your company. Well, consider this little fact. Everyone involved in your deal is a mergers and acquisitions (M&A) expert. Your investment banker, your attorney, your tax advisors, and even the buyer have all done this dozens or (hopefully!) hundreds of times. You haven't. If you're fortunate, you will sell one company in your lifetime, but everyone else working on your deal will do hundreds of transactions throughout their careers.

Does that cause some trepidation? You bet. And that's exactly why preparing yourself is so very important.

The Emotional Reality of Selling

By the time a business owner calls me to say they're "thinking about selling," the idea has usually been simmering for years. The thought always starts the same way. "There has to be more than this."

But turning that whisper into action is hard, because selling your business is an identity earthquake. You're not just changing jobs, you're changing who you are.

Before you talk to a banker or sign an NDA, you need to understand that you're about to enter a psychological minefield. Every part of the sale process will test your patience, your ego, and your sense of self-worth.

You will feel second-guessed. You will feel exposed. You will have moments when you doubt your own numbers, your team, and your decisions. It will seem like the questions during due diligence never stop. You will feel like you want to scream.

That's normal—but it's dangerous if you don't expect it.

The goal here is to prepare you, not scare you for the sale process. Selling your business is an emotional rollercoaster. There are moments of excitement and pride (hiring the investment bank and signing the LOI), followed by stretches of frustration (endless requests and late-night debates over working capital). At times, you'll wonder if it's worth it. You'll curse the process. You might even curse yourself for getting into it in the first place.

One of my clients was living it in real time as I was writing this book. He was running and growing his company while also taking on the brand-new, full-time job of selling it. After signing the LOI, he was deep in the trenches of due diligence, buried in spreadsheets and calls. Then, my phone rang.

"Uh, Robert...you'll never guess what I just did."

He sounded half exasperated, half amused. "Well," he said, "I've had so much on my mind lately that I got distracted. I just filled my truck with gas."

I paused. "Okay…so what's the problem?"

"My truck takes diesel."

That's what selling your company can do to you. It consumes your focus, drains your energy, and tests your patience. But that's not a reason to avoid it. Instead, it's a reason to be ready for it.

It's also the reason you need to have a strong why for what you're doing. A strong why can get you through almost anything. Even an Ironman….

In 2016, I finished an Ironman triathlon. When I say finished, I mean *barely* finished. They give you eighteen hours, and I did it in seventeen hours and fifty-two minutes.

There were many challenges, but the swim was the most brutal. It was in the Gulf off of the Florida coast, and the waves were rough. I'm sensitive to motion sickness and threw up no less than twenty times during the swim. The lifeguards in the water pleaded with me to quit, and to let them help me. But there was only one thought going through my mind. My daughter. I had told her I was going to finish, and I couldn't bear the thought of disappointing her. I kept telling myself I had to keep going.

As I started the bike, I was in *last* place. I was still dizzy and sick from the swim, but I kept spinning my feet, just trying not to stop. The only thing that kept me going that long day was thinking about my daughter and the look on her face when I could tell her I did it. Having a strong why is what got me through it.

Create Your "Why Letter"

This is why I have every client write what I call the *Why Letter* before they start the process.

It's a simple but powerful exercise. Here's how it works. Sit down (without your advisors, without your phone, and without any distractions) and write yourself a letter explaining why you've decided to sell. Be brutally honest. Write about your motivations, your goals, your fears, and what you hope this next chapter of life will look like.

Don't write what you think sounds good on paper. Write what's true. Maybe you're tired. Maybe you want to de-risk and diversify. Maybe you want to travel, spend more time with family, or start something new. Maybe you want to cash out while the market's strong.

Whatever it is, put it down on paper.

Otherwise, six months from now, you're likely to forget. You'll be tired, frustrated, and ready to walk away, and you'll need to remind yourself why you started this journey.

The Why Letter becomes your anchor. When the process tests you, go back and read your own handwriting. That version of you (the calm, clear, rational version) will help guide the stressed version you'll become.

I can't tell you how many times a client has called me mid-sale, saying, "I can't take this anymore. I'm done." I tell them, "Go read your letter." They always come back calmer, because it reconnects them to their purpose.

Remember John, from the beginning of this chapter? Reminding him of his why is what got him reconnected to the deal, and the transaction closed.

Write to Your Future Self

When you write your Why Letter, think of it as speaking to your future self—the one who will be stressed, tired, and questioning everything. That future version of you will need perspective and encouragement from the present you who made this decision with clarity and purpose.

Include three things in your letter:

1. **Your motivation.** Why now? What are you hoping to achieve? What will selling allow you to do or become?

2. **Your vision.** What will life after the sale look like? What will fill your days, challenge you, and excite you?

3. **Your promise.** What will you commit to remembering when things get hard (e.g., integrity, patience, long-term focus)?

Keep the letter somewhere private but accessible. Pull it out when you feel frustrated, or when a deal term makes you want to throw your laptop across the room. It's a recalibration tool and grounds you back in intention.

Craft a Mantra

Once you're clear on your *why*, condense it into something simple. One word. One phrase. Something you can repeat to yourself when things get hard.

It might be *Freedom*. It might be *Legacy*. It might be *Next*.

Choose a word that reflects what this sale represents to you. The best mantras are short, emotional, and directional. They remind you of where you're going, not what you're leaving behind.

Write it on a Post-it note and stick it to your computer monitor. Put it on the lock screen of your phone. Make it your password, if you have to. During this process, you'll need constant reminders of what matters most.

A simple mantra keeps you centered when stress spikes. When you're in a heated negotiation or your attorney just sent you a seventy-page markup, or you're staring at another document request list at midnight, pause, breathe, and repeat it to yourself.

This isn't New Age fluff. It's performance management. It's how you maintain focus when your brain is flooded with stress hormones and your patience is wearing thin. Professional athletes do it. Special Forces operators do it. High-stakes performers know that their mindset determines their outcome when they are under pressure.

Building an Emotional Support System

Surround yourself with people who understand what you're going through, not just technically, but emotionally. Your advisors, banker, attorney, tax advisor, and wealth planner are your tactical team. They'll guide the process, protect your interests, and keep the deal on track. That said, you also need people who can help you process the stress, uncertainty, and identity loss that come with letting go.

If you're married, talk early and often with your spouse about what life after the sale looks like. Selling affects them, too. Their routines, security, and sense of partnership will shift. The more united you are, the smoother the transition will be.

If you don't have peers who've sold a business, find some. Other founders who've been through it can offer perspective that no book or banker can. They'll tell you what surprised, hurt, and ultimately freed them. Hearing their stories can help you normalize the emotions you'll inevitably face.

Feeling Guilty?

After years and sometimes decades of leading the same group of people through challenges, growth, and uncertainty, the idea of selling can feel like walking away from family. These are the people who stayed late, solved problems, and believed in the vision, even when times were tough. They celebrated wins and weathered losses together. So, when an owner finally decides to sell, the excitement of a big payday can be mixed with a heavy dose of guilt. It's not uncommon to hear, "I feel like I'm abandoning them."

That sense of guilt is understandable. In many ways, a business owner isn't just the founder; they're the caretaker of a community. Selling the company can feel like breaking an unspoken promise to protect that community. Even if the new buyer is capable and well-intentioned, there's still uncertainty. What if the culture changes? What if people lose their jobs? What if the buyer doesn't value them the way you did? Those questions linger long after the deal closes. For owners who've built strong personal relationships with their teams, the emotional weight can be immense. Remember, it's not only a business transaction; it's a personal transition.

I often remind owners that feeling guilty is a sign of how deeply they cared, and that's a good thing. It means they've built something worth caring about. Don't suppress that guilt, but channel it productively. That might mean communicating openly with your team, advocating for their well-being in the terms of the sale, or choosing a buyer who shares your values and will honor your people. You can't guarantee that everything will stay the same, but you can influence the kind of legacy you leave behind. Selling your company doesn't have to mean abandoning your team; it can mean ensuring they're part of something that continues to grow long after you've stepped away.

Go Pro: Copy Elite Athletes and Performers

If you've ever run a marathon, climbed a mountain, or even pushed yourself through an intense season in business, you know that success isn't just about skill, it's also about stamina. Selling your company is no different. It's not a sprint; it's an ultra-endurance event disguised as a financial transaction.

You'll be tested mentally, physically and emotionally, in ways you can't fully anticipate. There will be weeks of long nights, tense negotiations, and emotional whiplash. One day, you'll feel on top of the world; the next, you'll wonder if the deal will even happen.

This is why I call selling your business a performance. And like any elite performance, it requires conditioning.

You wouldn't show up to a marathon without training, and you shouldn't show up to a business sale without preparation. That means taking care of your body, mind, and emotions before the process begins. Your business has thrived because you've been the engine behind it, and now that same engine needs to run at its best through one of the most grueling stretches of your career.

Start treating yourself like an athlete in training. Get serious about sleep, nutrition, and exercise. The better you feel physically, the sharper your decision-making will be. Keep your stress under control through meditation, time in nature, journaling, or unplugging for short breaks each day. A calm mind makes better strategic choices.

Mental conditioning also means building resilience, the ability to keep going when you're exhausted and the finish line still feels far away. During the sale process, there will be moments when you're tempted to settle, to stop pushing for one more term, or to give in so you can make it all end. But those final negotiations are often where the difference between a good deal and a great one is made.

Don't get me wrong: You should rely on your advisors, talk to your spouse, and consult your peers. But if you want a real edge, "go pro." Guess what all elite professional athletes use? A mental coach. The top athletes around the world all have access to the best nutritionists, physical trainers, and strength and conditioning coaches money can buy—but they don't just focus on the physical. The best and most successful spend a lot of time on the mental, too.

The "Performance Coach" Advantage

I distinctly remember working with one of my clients. Early in the sales process, he was already feeling the pressure from the negotiations, the competing buyer interests, and the constant flow of due diligence requests. I recommended he talk with someone once a week to keep his emotional footing. I did not use the word "therapist," as most driven founders recoil when they hear it. They are wired to power through, not to process feelings. Instead, I framed it as working with a coach. In his case, it landed immediately. He was a high-performance endurance athlete with strength coaches, nutrition coaches, and training plans for every race, so a "performance coach" fit his identity. It felt like preparation, not vulnerability, and that made all the difference. Months later, after his sale closed, he told me it was the best money and time he spent each week. It gave him perspective, helped him separate emotion from strategy, and ultimately made him a better negotiator and leader during the process.

Selling your company will test you in ways that running it never did. You don't need to go through that test alone. Having someone to help you manage your mind is just as essential as having an investment banker to manage your deal. For many people, working with a therapist or executive coach is one of the smartest investments they make.

Preparing for the Loss of Identity

For most founders, the company is who they are. It gives structure to their days, meaning to their work, and identity to their lives. When it's gone, that sense of purpose can suddenly vanish.

I've seen it time and again. The first few weeks after a sale feel like a honeymoon. Relief. Celebration. Freedom. And then the stillness comes.

You wake up and realize you have no calls to lead, no fires to put out, no one needing your approval. The pace slows, but your brain doesn't. You're still wired for urgency, and the same intensity that built your business has nowhere to go.

That's where many sellers hit what I call the Post-Exit Void. It's the identity gap between who you were as a business owner and who you are without your company—without employees, responsibility, and a reason to get up on a Monday morning. I wrote extensively about this in my book *Badass Retirement*. It can happen whether you retire from your career or sell your company.

And this doesn't only hit sellers who walk away clean. Even if you're staying on for a transition period or working toward an earnout, the shift begins the moment you're no longer the owner. You may still be showing up, but the company isn't yours anymore. That realization can be just as disorienting.

Some try to fill the void by jumping into a new venture too quickly. Others distract themselves with travel, toys, or hobbies. But unless you've done the emotional work beforehand, the transition can feel hollow and even depressing.

Emotional readiness isn't optional. It's strategic. You don't have to go through this alone. In fact, you shouldn't.

When Is the Right Time to Sell?

Many business owners begin thinking about selling years, and sometimes decades before they actually do. It starts as a quiet thought. What would life look like without the business? Then, over time, that thought grows into curiosity, conversations, and eventually action.

One of my clients, an adventurer at heart and a wildly successful entrepreneur, began having those thoughts long before he ever took a meeting with an investment banker. I still remember hiking with him through Patagonia, with towering peaks, roaring winds, and endless stretches of open wilderness. At 40,000 feet, flying over the Andes on the way home, we spent hours talking about what a sale might look like. What kind of buyer would make sense? What would he do next? What would life after look like?

Ten years later, he called me and said, "I'm ready." The business had grown beyond what either of us imagined that day in the mountains. But what struck me wasn't how much the company had evolved, it was how much he had. The conversation we'd had in Patagonia had planted a seed, and over the next decade he had slowly grown into the mindset of someone ready to let go.

That's the reality of selling a business. It's often less about timing the market and more about timing yourself.

The Exit Timing Matrix

Perfect timing is more art than science. You'll never have absolute clarity. Instead, you have to balance three forces that I call the Exit Timing Matrix:

- **Personal timing** – Your readiness, energy, and what's pulling you forward

- **Business strength** – How transferable and valuable your company is to buyers

- **Market environment** – Whether conditions are working for or against you

When two of these align, it's time to start preparing. When all three converge, you're standing in one of those rare windows where opportunity meets readiness.

Personal Timing: The Internal Equation

The right time to sell often starts as a whisper. It's a sense of fatigue that doesn't go away after a vacation. The creeping thought that you've climbed this mountain as high as you can. The realization that you're ready for something new, and your company isn't giving you the same energy it once did.

Maybe it's burnout. Maybe it's health. Maybe it's the realization that your kids are grown and you've missed too many moments. Whatever form it takes, internal timing is about being prepared emotionally and psychologically, not just financially.

I've witnessed owners ignore these signs for years. They tell themselves, "Just one more year" or "One more strategic hire." But here's the problem. The longer you wait when your heart's no longer in it, the more likely you are to plateau or even decline. Your team can sense when your passion fades. Your leadership starts shifting from offense to defense—protecting what you've built instead of growing it. And that subtle shift can quietly erode value.

Here's the test. If you can look at your business objectively and say, "I've taken it as far as I can or want to," it might be time. If you're spending more time maintaining than creating, that's another sign. And if the thought of doing the same thing for another five years makes you tired instead of excited, that's your body and mind telling you something your ego doesn't want to admit.

The best exits often happen when founders are inspired by the next chapter, not just exhausted by the current one. When curiosity starts to outweigh obligation, the clock begins quietly ticking.

Business Strength: The Operational Equation

Buyers don't pay for your history. They pay for what they believe your business will become without you.

A transferable business is one supported by systems, leadership depth, and a culture that doesn't collapse if the founder steps aside. If your involvement is still the glue, the company isn't yet optimized for sale. Look closely at customer concentration, key-person risk, and operational dependencies. Address these weaknesses proactively, before a buyer uses them to negotiate down the price.

Also evaluate whether your company still has runway without dramatic reinvention. If the next phase requires radical shifts, major capital, or personal reinvestment of time and energy, that can be a signal. Sometimes the best time to sell is right before the next mountain, not after you've climbed it.

But here's the paradox. The best time to sell is when your company is strong, growing, and full of potential, but that's also the hardest time emotionally to let go. When your business is thriving—growing fast, margins expanding—buyers will pay the most. But that's precisely when you least want to walk away. You think to yourself, "One more year." That's how owners miss their windows.

Market Environment: The External Equation

Even if you're ready personally and your business is strong, the external environment still matters. In M&A, valuations move in cycles. When interest rates are low, credit is cheap, and private equity firms are flush with capital, deal multiples rise. But when rates climb or economic uncertainty increases, multiples compress. The same company might sell for eight times EBITDA one year and six times the next, through no fault of its own.

This is why keeping a finger on the market pulse is critical. Watch company sale trends and deal volumes. Are buyers paying premiums for companies like yours? Is your industry consolidating? When competitors are being rolled up by larger players, it means buyers are paying for scale. But that window doesn't stay open forever.

One of my clients, Chris, had built an incredible business, a $400 million company he'd run for more than forty years. When a large multinational firm approached him about buying his largest division, he hesitated. He believed he could grow it another year or two and maybe sell for an extra $25 million. He wasn't wrong, the fundamentals were strong and the market was still climbing.

But after several long conversations, he decided to move forward with the sale. Several months later, the deal closed and $300 million hit his account. Six months after that, the Great Financial Crisis hit. Markets collapsed, liquidity evaporated, and valuations across the board were cut in half. The division he sold would have been worth far less—maybe 50 percent less—if he'd waited.

Chris's story is a powerful reminder that no matter how talented or disciplined you are as an operator, some factors are beyond your control. You can outwork competitors, outthink the market, and build something extraordinary, but you can't outsmart macroeconomics.

I'm starting to have these same conversations again today—not about the housing crash or a credit crisis, but about AI. The parallels are striking. Many business owners I work with are sitting on highly successful companies, but the landscape around them is shifting faster than ever. Some clients tell me, "We're fine; our clients trust us," or "AI can't replace what we do." And perhaps that's true, for now. But I remind them of Chris. The biggest risks to valuation are often the ones you don't see coming.

The point here is to be aware. The best owners I know treat market awareness as a standing discipline. Even if they're not ready to sell, they know the metrics. They build relationships with potential acquirers early. They gather intelligence long before they need it. When the day comes, they're not reacting—they're ready.

When All Three Align

You don't need to sell at the exact top, but it helps if you sell before the world changes. There is no perfect formula for timing an exit, but when personal readiness, business strength, and favorable market conditions converge, that's when magic happens. Long-term business excellence and short-term market timing create exponential outcomes when they coincide.

The time to prepare is when you still love what you've built. That's when you'll negotiate from strength instead of fatigue.

The Timing Paradox

The best time to sell your business is when it's thriving, growing, and full of potential. That's when buyers pay the most. Strong financials, expanding margins, and clear momentum are the conditions that drive valuations up and create competition among buyers.

But that's also the hardest time emotionally to let go. When your business is crushing it, the future looks bright. You think, "I can stick around for one more year." The optimism that drives your growth also clouds your judgment about timing. You convince yourself that next year will be even better, and that you're leaving money on the table if you sell now.

Meanwhile, markets shift. Competition emerges. Economic conditions change. The window that looked wide open starts to narrow. Sellers who wait too long often end up selling in weaker conditions for less money.

The best time to sell isn't when you're desperate—it's when you're strong enough to walk away.

You're most attractive to buyers exactly when you're least motivated to sell—and that's precisely why you should consider it.

Why Owners Choose to Sell

Every sale has a story, but most fall into two broad categories: strategic and financial reasons or emotional and lifestyle reasons. The best exits happen when both converge, when the numbers make sense and your gut says it's time. Understanding your "why" is essential because when the process gets hard—and it will—it's what keeps you anchored and decisive.

Strategic and Financial Reasons

Owners often start thinking about selling when the math looks too good to ignore. Revenues are at a record high, margins are strong, and buyers are circling. Maybe the industry is consolidating, or maybe scaling further would require capital you don't want to spend or risk you no longer want to take.

Selling while the story is still great can feel counterintuitive, but it's often the smartest move. Think Mark Cuban selling Broadcast.com before the dot-com crash—he timed it perfectly. When most of your wealth is tied to your company, you're one lawsuit or downturn away from disaster. A sale turns concentrated wealth into security and freedom.

Market timing matters more than most owners realize. Industry cycles, valuations, and capital availability change fast. Selling at the right moment can add millions in value without changing a single number on your income statement. Strategic buyers often pay for what they can do with your business—distribution, cross-selling, global reach—not just what you've done. And smart owners sell before regulation, technology, or competitors disrupt their edge.

Sometimes it's about legacy. If there's no clear next generation or leadership bench, selling can preserve both the company and your employees' futures.

Emotional and Lifestyle Reasons

Sometimes the numbers add up, but your energy doesn't. You sell because you're ready for something different.

After decades of sixty-hour weeks, you want your life back. Selling buys you time—the one resource you can't earn more of. You've missed enough dinners, milestones, and vacations, and the people who matter most want you back. And, when stress or health issues start calling the shots, a sale isn't only practical, it's necessary.

Many founders sell not to retire, but to start again with a new vision, new energy, or a new industry. Big life moments like a milestone birthday, an illness, or the loss of a peer can shift priorities from accumulation to meaning.

In the end, the best time to sell isn't when your business is at its peak—it's when your life is ready for what comes next.

Running From or Running Toward

At an even deeper level, owners sell for one of two reasons: They're either moving away from something they no longer want, or they're moving toward something they deeply desire. On the surface, the motivations might look the same, but the emotional engine behind the decision is quite different. Selling out of fear is a retreat. Selling for freedom is an expansion.

Fear-based exits are driven by pressure, fatigue, declining passion, uncertainty, or rising personal and financial risk. When discomfort builds, selling becomes a form of escape, and relief becomes the finish line. There's nothing wrong with making a prudent risk-reduction decision. But when the primary driver is exhaustion or anxiety, owners often cross the finish line only to realize they never defined where they wanted to land. As the relief fades, restlessness appears, and without a vision pulling them forward, they drift.

Freedom-based exits, on the other hand, are built on intention, clarity, and anticipation. The sale isn't about what's ending, but what's beginning. These owners aren't running from pressure; they're stepping into possibility. They have a vision for the life ahead, such as time with family, new challenges, new ventures, creativity, travel, purpose, and reinvention. Freedom sellers don't just exit something—they enter something else. They don't finish a chapter—they launch the next one with momentum and identity intact.

The happiest sellers aren't defined by whether they were feeling fear or freedom, because almost everyone experiences both. The difference is direction. If you're moving away from something, pause long enough to also define what you're moving toward. That's the shift from exit to evolution, and the path that leads not only to liquidity, but also liberation.

The Real Reason Behind the Reasons

Every owner has two reasons for selling. A story reason and a soul reason. The story reason is what you say out loud: *"Market conditions are strong." "It's smart to diversify now." "Industry consolidation is accelerating."*

The soul reason is what you feel quietly: *"I want my life back." "I'm tired of carrying the weight." "I'm ready for something more than this."*

The story reason sounds strategic. The soul reason is human.

You need to know both, because both will surface during the sale. The story reason will help you negotiate clearly and confidently. The soul reason will help you stay centered when doubt, grief, or identity friction shows up. Selling your company isn't just a transaction. It's a transition. And like all meaningful transitions, logic and emotion will walk side-by-side.

Selling for the right reason doesn't mean selling because you're "finished." It means selling because you're ready to let go of one chapter and step into a new identity. Ready to exchange pressure for possibility and to build a life by design, not by default.

The owners who struggle are the ones who deny the emotional side and pretend this is only a liquidity event. The ones who succeed honor both truths. They let strategy guide the deal and honesty guide their feelings.

Once you see your motivations clearly and without judgment, you make better decisions. You negotiate from strength instead of fear. You don't cling to the business because you're scared of the unknown, or sprint toward the exit because you're exhausted. You move deliberately, intentionally, and powerfully.

When the deal closes, you walk away wealthier and lighter, because you didn't just sell a business, you opened a door to the next version of yourself. That's what surprises many owners. It begins as a financial decision, but ends as one of the most human decisions you will ever make.

Mistiming: When Waiting Too Long Costs Everything

The stories of sellers who waited too long aren't simply cautionary tales, they're reminders that timing a sale is unforgiving. Markets shift, buyers move on, and the window that looked permanent can slam shut faster than you imagine.

"My son started a company and he said it's growing. He would like some advice."

That single phone call kicked off one of the most incredible business journeys I've ever been part of—and one of the most painful to watch unravel. Two friends had started a company in a garage. They weren't improving an existing idea; they were creating a product that had never existed before. They filled a gap no one even realized was there, and customers couldn't get enough.

From the beginning, everything clicked and sales exploded. They couldn't manufacture product fast enough. Within a few years, their company was a household name in its niche. Their margins were insane—close to 90 percent. They were on fire.

As the growth continued, I suggested they at least consider selling while everything looked so good. The timing was ideal and we engaged an investment bank to quietly shop the deal. Within weeks, we had serious interest. Then came the big offer: nearly $100 million.

One partner wanted to sign and move forward. The other froze. He couldn't let go. He told himself the company was still only getting started, and that they could be worth twice that if they waited another year or two. His confidence—the same confidence that had helped him build a breakout success—now became the obstacle.

At first, it was subtle. Delays in providing information, pushing meetings and questioning why the buyer needed certain data. Every delay chipped away at the buyer's enthusiasm. The truth was, one founder had already emotionally sold the company, but the other couldn't bear to imagine life without it. His identity was tied to it. Ego, pride, and fear all mixed into a dangerous cocktail that quietly poisoned the deal.

Eventually, the buyer walked away. The founders were left holding the company they once could have sold for nearly nine figures. And then the market changed. Competitors flooded in and imitators built similar products that were much cheaper and often better marketed. What was once unique became commonplace. The company's growth slowed and margins shrank. They went from being the disruptor to being disrupted. A few years later, they finally sold the business for pennies on the dollar.

It was brutal.

This is the Skill Shift Paradox in action. The same confidence that built their breakthrough became the blind spot that destroyed it. Ego convinced one partner that waiting would make them richer. It made them poorer instead.

If there's a lesson in this story, it's that selling too late isn't just about losing money, it's about losing momentum, opportunity, and peace of mind. Every founder needs to ask themselves not only what their company is worth today, but also what it will cost them if they wait too long.

When Leverage Evaporates

I once worked with a seller who waited too long to take their company to market. In the beginning, during the pre-LOI stage, it all looked fine. The business was solid, the conversations were friendly, and there were multiple interested buyers. The owner felt in control—confident, even. They were the prize being pursued, the one deciding which buyer would earn the chance to move forward. But beneath the surface, time was working against them. Their personal circumstances were shifting, and their company's growth had started to plateau. Still, they hesitated, believing they could wait for "one more good year."

When they finally signed an LOI, everything changed fast. Once the buyer had exclusivity, the tone of the deal flipped. (In a later chapter, you'll learn how to prepare for the change of energy and power after the LOI is signed.) The buyer's team, now deep in due diligence, realized something the seller had hoped to conceal: The business wasn't improving and the seller needed to sell. That's when the leverage evaporated. The buyer started revising terms, chipping away at value, adjusting payment structure, and stretching out timelines because they could. They knew the seller no longer had alternatives. What began as a position of strength turned into a defensive scramble. It was a painful reminder that in a business sale, timing is everything. The longer you wait, the less options you have. Once you *need* to sell, the buyer no longer needs to please you.

Timing, readiness, leverage—everything I've laid out assumes you're the only one calling the shots. But what if you're not?

When There's More Than One of You

Throughout this book, I'll mostly write as if you're a solo owner. It keeps things simple. But I know many of you have partners, co-founders, or other shareholders sitting at the table with you. If that's your situation, everything I've said about getting yourself ready applies to them too.

Before you ever talk to a banker or meet with a buyer, every owner needs to answer the same questions. Why are we selling? What do we each want from this deal? What does life look like afterward? And here's the hard part: those answers need to be compatible, or at least reconcilable. Misaligned owners kill more deals than bad financials. Let me say that again. Misaligned owners kill more deals than bad financials.

I saw this play out with two partners who had built a successful professional services firm together over twenty years. They came to me thinking they were ready to sell. Both wanted to maximize value. Both were ready for "the next chapter."

But before we engaged a banker or talked to a single buyer, I sat them down separately and asked each of them a simple question: "What does your life look like two years after this deal closes?"

The answers couldn't have been more different.

One partner, let's call him David, was in his early fifties. He loved the industry and still had fire in his belly. He wanted to sell, yes, but he also wanted to keep working. His vision was to stay on for another ten or fifteen years, help grow the company under new ownership, and build more wealth along the way. The sale wasn't an exit for David. It was a new beginning.

His partner, Richard, was sixty-three and exhausted. He'd given the business everything he had, and he was done. He wanted to cash out, spend time with his grandchildren, and never sit through another operations meeting. For Richard, the sale was the finish line.

Same company. Same deal. Completely different goals.

If we had gone to market without surfacing this, it could have blown up the deal. Buyers would have sensed the tension. One partner pushing for a long-term role while the other is halfway out the door sends a confusing signal. Worse, they might have discovered their misalignment in the middle of a negotiation, with millions of dollars on the line and emotions running hot.

Instead, we addressed it before we ever talked to a buyer. Once David and Richard understood what the other actually wanted, they stopped assuming they were on the same page and started building a structure that could work for both of them. We went to market with a clear message: one partner wants to stay and grow, one wants a clean exit, and the right buyer will see value in both.

The strategic acquirer who emerged as the lead bidder appreciated the honesty. They wanted David's energy and industry knowledge for the long haul. They valued Richard's relationships and his deep knowledge of the business for a shorter transition. Because we'd already done the work internally, we were able to propose a structure that made sense for everyone.

David received a larger equity rollover, a longer employment agreement, and a meaningful role in the combined company going forward. His upside was tied to future growth, which is exactly what he wanted. Richard received more cash at closing, a minimal rollover, and a twelve-month transition agreement. He got liquidity, certainty, and a clear end date.

Same deal, different structures. Both partners walked away satisfied because we took the time to understand what each of them truly wanted before the process started.

The lesson here is simple. If you have partners, don't assume you're aligned just because you all agree it's time to sell. Sit down together, without advisors, without distractions, and have the honest conversation. What does each of you want from this deal? What does life look like afterward for each of you? Where are your goals compatible, and where do they diverge?

Have this conversation early, before you engage a banker, before you sign an NDA, before you're in the heat of a negotiation. Because if you wait until a buyer is at the table to discover that your partners want completely different things, you won't just lose leverage. You might lose the deal entirely.

Getting yourself ready means getting all of yourselves ready. The strongest sellers walk into the process united, clear on their collective goals, and ready to fight for a deal that works for everyone at the table.

Chapter Exit

The first step in selling your company isn't about spreadsheets, valuations, or buyers. It's about you. Getting yourself ready means recognizing that the sale of your business is more than a financial transaction; it's a personal transformation. It's about preparing your mindset, emotions, and expectations for one of the most significant transitions of your life. The Business Sale Mindset is all about being prepared. It's about anticipating the emotional turbulence before it comes, so when it does, you're ready. Emotional readiness isn't soft; it's strategic. It's what separates the sellers who thrive after a deal from those who second-guess it for years.

By now, you may have written your Why Letter and crafted your mantra. You've surrounded yourself with the right emotional support and assessed your timing—internal, external, and operational. You understand why you're selling and what you're moving toward, not just what you're leaving behind. You've confronted the identity loss that's coming, and you've developed your mental and physical conditioning to endure the marathon ahead.

In short, you've done the internal work that most sellers skip, and that's your competitive advantage.

But mindset alone won't close a deal. Once you've built that foundation and prepared yourself, it's time to prepare your business. The next chapter moves from the internal to the external, from mindset to mechanics. You'll learn how to get your company "sale ready" using the four levers that move valuation: strategic alignment, financial strength, transferable value, and risk reduction. This is where clarity turns into action. Getting yourself ready gives you the right headspace; getting your company ready gives you leverage. Together, they create the foundation for a deal that doesn't just close, but closes on your terms.

CHAPTER 2:

GET YOUR COMPANY READY

*Turn Your Business into
a Sellable Asset*

W hen one of my clients, a second-generation manufacturing owner, first called me about selling his company, he opened with a line I'd heard from many others. "We are crushing it over here. We've never been more profitable. I think I'm ready to sell."

He was right about the numbers: Revenue was up, margins were strong, and backlog was healthy. But as we started digging in, it became clear that while the business was performing well, it wasn't necessarily ready to be sold. His financials weren't clean enough for a buyer to trust without question. Half the company's key relationships ran through him personally. Plus, his number two was on a sabbatical in Central America, and there was a question of if she would even return.

He had built a fantastic *business*, but not yet a *sellable asset*. There's a difference. A great business generates income for you; a great asset creates confidence for a buyer. The former depends on you; the latter runs without you. That's the shift this chapter is about.

Most owners underestimate how much work it takes to turn a company that's thriving operationally into one that's irresistible to buyers. This chapter will walk you through the four key areas that make that transformation possible: getting aligned, optimizing financial readiness, building transferable value, and de-risking the deal. When you get these right, you don't just make your company attractive—you make the sale inevitable.

If Chapter 1 was about getting your mind ready to sell, this chapter is about getting your house ready. The sale of a business is a sequence of events. There's a rhythm to it, a choreography that, when done right, moves you from curiosity to commitment, and ultimately to closing.

The Four Pillars of Sale Readiness

Before you dive into the mechanics of preparing your company for sale—the numbers, the systems, and the presentation—you need a roadmap. After decades of working with business owners, I've found that every successful exit shares four essential pillars: strategic alignment, financial strength, transferable value, and risk reduction. These are the areas that determine whether your sale will be smooth, strategic, and profitable, or stressful, chaotic, and disappointing. They cover both the tangible and intangible elements of readiness: what your business looks like on paper and how it feels to a buyer.

Strategic alignment ensures that everyone—owners, partners, and key leaders—are heading in the same direction. Financial strength gives buyers confidence in your numbers and clarity in your performance story. Transferable value transforms your company from one that depends on you to one that runs without you, which is the single biggest driver of valuation. And risk reduction removes the landmines that can derail a transaction late in the process.

You don't have to perfect each area before going to market, but you do need to understand how they work together. Think of these four pillars as your pre-sale architecture that supports all the steps that come next. The stronger the foundation, the more leverage you'll have when it matters most.

Pillar 1: Strategic Alignment

Before you go to market, everyone who matters needs to be aligned. This may sound simple, but it's one of the biggest friction points in any sale. Alignment not only prevents conflict, but it also builds clarity and speed. Misalignment can quietly destroy deals before they even start.

In the years I've helped business owners sell their companies, I've watched plenty of deals derail not because of bad buyers or bad markets, but because of disagreement inside the sellers' camps. Sometimes it's between partners with different goals. Other times, it's between a spouse who's ready for a new chapter and an owner who isn't sure who they'll be without the business. Whatever form it takes, misalignment creates hesitation, hesitation creates delays, and delays kill deals.

Get on the Same Page with Co-Owners and Partners

If you have partners or co-owners, this is your first alignment test. You need to talk openly about why each of you wants to sell, what you hope to achieve, and what you're not willing to compromise on. Some may want to cash out completely and disappear to a beach. Others may want to roll equity and stay involved. These differences don't have to be deal-breakers, but they do have to be surfaced before you engage with buyers.

Every owner has a different definition of "enough." For one, financial security may be the goal. For another, it might be legacy, wanting to see the company continue to grow under new ownership. If you skip this conversation, you'll be forced to have it under pressure when the LOI hits your inbox. That's not the time to find out your partner doesn't want to sell after all.

Remember the story from Chapter 1 about the guys who started their company in a garage? One was ready to sell for nearly $100 million, while the other thought the company could double in value. He delayed, stalled, and made the process so difficult that the buyer walked. A year later, competitors flooded the market, margins collapsed, and they sold for pennies on the dollar. The lesson here is that alignment isn't just about agreeing on a price; it's about agreeing on timing, priorities, and reality.

Involve Your Inner Circle

Even if you're the sole owner, you're not making this decision in a vacuum. Spouses, family members, and key employees all play a role emotionally, financially, or operationally. I've seen more than one owner blindsided when their spouse expressed doubt about selling after an LOI was signed. Their hesitation came not from greed or fear, but from uncertainty. "What happens to us after the sale? What will you do next?" These are questions that need answers before you go to market.

Your spouse doesn't need to understand EBITDA multiples or working capital adjustments, but they do need to understand what this sale means for your shared life. What will you do with the proceeds? Where will you live? What will your days look like when you're no longer running the business? Having that clarity now prevents resentment later.

If you have adult children involved in the company, alignment becomes even more critical. They may assume they'll inherit or eventually run the business, and learning about a potential sale through the grapevine can be devastating. Be transparent early. If they're staying post-sale, talk to them about what that will look like. If they're not, discuss how they can prepare for their next chapter, too.

Be Careful What You Promise

A few years back, I worked with a client who was both generous and incredibly smart. He owned a small but wildly profitable firm, the kind of business that was practically printing money. As he got older, he knew a sale was on the horizon. But he also knew something else:

A handful of key employees had been instrumental to the company's success. Without them, there would be no firm to sell. So, a few years before putting the business on the market, he promised them a payout if he ever sold. It was a thoughtful move, and one that reflected his character, but when the time came to sell, that generosity created a problem. Buyers saw those promised payouts and grew nervous. They wondered if these employees would still be motivated and want to grind if they received a windfall at closing. From the buyer's perspective, it was a legitimate concern. They weren't just buying systems or cash flow—they were buying continuity, and that depended on the people.

So, we got creative. Instead of paying those key employees in cash, we used part of the equity rollover (the portion of the deal the seller would typically reinvest in the new company) to give those team members a stake in the future. That changed everything. Now, instead of being "paid off," they were "bought in." They had skin in the game and a personal incentive to help the new owners succeed. On top of that, my client still gave them a modest cash bonus—a few hundred thousand dollars each—as a gesture of appreciation. The buyers loved it. They saw a leadership team that was not only loyal, but also financially aligned with the success of the new company. The seller got to reward the people who helped him build the business, and the buyer got a team that was motivated for the long haul. Everyone won, because generosity, when structured wisely, became a deal enhancer, not a liability.

Reality Check with an Investment Banker

The details behind a successful exit aren't always obvious from the inside. We tend to assume we know what matters most because we've built and lived the business, and understand each lever inside the business.

But value in a sale isn't determined by the founder's view. It's determined by the market's view, and different buyers value different things. Private equity firms, strategics, roll-ups, family offices, and international acquirers each have their own scoring system. Some reward explosive growth, while others reward margin discipline, recurring revenue, depth of leadership, systems maturity, or market position. Guessing what buyers care about is a gamble. Knowing is an edge.

Once you're aligned internally, test your expectations externally. One of the smartest things you can do early on is have a short, informal conversation with an investment banker who specializes in your industry. This doesn't commit you to selling. It's a temperature check—quiet, strategic reconnaissance. A good banker will tell you what kinds of multiples companies like yours are getting, what deal structures are common, which buyers are active, and what metrics are moving valuation today. I've seen owners save months and tens of thousands of dollars just by getting a reality check early. Sometimes they learn the market is red-hot and timing is perfect. Other times, they discover the value they want is still eighteen to thirty-six months away. Either way, this knowledge saves you from chasing a deal prematurely or missing the ideal window. With real market intelligence, you stop optimizing blindly and start preparing intentionally.

And the cost of skipping that step can be enormous. One of my clients spent two full years preparing for what he believed would be his ideal sale. Then it all went sideways. He was at his industry's big annual conference and catching up with another founder he knew well. As it always does at these events, the conversation drifted toward valuations, deal chatter, and who was selling to whom.

That's when his buddy shared his take on the market. He told him that "buyers in our space couldn't care less about growth rates.

They only care about net earnings." My client, hearing what felt like wisdom from a peer, internalized it as truth—and that probably cost him $10 million.

He built his plan around that advice. He cut initiatives that wouldn't create immediate profit, paused hiring, and pulled back on expansion. He chose efficiency over innovation and spent two years tuning the business for maximum earnings, believing he was sprinting toward the finish line that buyers rewarded. And to his credit, he nailed it. Net income shot up. The business looked incredibly profitable and the numbers sparkled. On paper, it was a beautiful exit story in the making.

The problem was the rumor was wrong, and when he went to market, he learned the truth. Buyers in his sector weren't rewarding fully optimized profit profiles; they were paying premiums for growth acceleration! They wanted runway, momentum, and expansion curves, not a perfectly polished bottom line. His business suddenly looked less like a rocket and more like a fortress—strong, but not scalable. He had trained for the wrong race, not because he lacked discipline, but because he had followed rumor instead of research. A twenty-minute conversation with an investment banker, someone living in real deal flow, would have given him the right scoreboard before he started playing.

One of the most valuable steps owners can take, long before running a formal process, is to ask someone who sees deals every day what the current market is rewarding. Intelligence beats assumption, data beats rumor, and preparing for the sale you think buyers want is never as valuable as preparing for the one they're actually paying for.

When and How to Tell Your Team

One of the most common and emotionally charged questions I get from business owners is, "When should I tell my employees that I'm selling the company?" It's a question that reveals both their concern for their team and their fear of disruption. Tell them too early, and you risk sparking worry, gossip, or even departures from people who start looking for "safer" jobs. Deals take months (sometimes longer), and if the sale doesn't move forward, you've worried everyone for nothing. But wait too long, and you risk blindsiding the same people who helped build your success, and whose cooperation you'll need to get through due diligence smoothly.

The best time to start those conversations is usually after you've hired an investment bank but before the process fully ramps up. At that stage, the decision to sell has moved from abstract to real. You've got a partner helping you shape the story, prepare the financials, and organize the pitch deck—the confidential information memorandum (CIM). You'll soon need accurate, detailed data, and you'll likely rely on key employees to provide it. This is when you can bring a few trusted team members into the fold. Their early involvement helps ensure accuracy, builds buy-in, and allows them to give input on timing, messaging, and transition planning. They can become your allies in maintaining morale while protecting confidentiality.

For most owners, the best approach is a tiered communication plan. A small circle of top executives or department heads should be informed first, typically once you've committed to moving forward with the bank. These individuals will need to help gather information, refine financial projections, and occasionally participate in management presentations down the road. The rank-and-file employees, however, don't need to know until there's real momentum—ideally after you've signed an LOI and the likelihood of closing is high. That way, you can communicate with confidence, answer questions clearly, and minimize unnecessary stress or speculation.

Prepping Your Team for the Buyer Meeting

At some point in the process, either before the LOI or, more commonly, once you're deep into due diligence, the buyer will ask to meet your leadership team. On the surface, this might feel like a formality, a quick meet-and-greet to "put faces to names." But make no mistake: This meeting is one of the most pivotal moments in the entire deal. Buyers know you, the founder, will likely exit after the earnout period. Their real question is whether the business will still thrive without you. They're not only evaluating résumés, but also assessing culture, motivation, and continuity. They want to know if the team you leave behind has the energy, competence, and commitment to carry the company forward.

So how did we deal with the key employee gallivanting in Central America I mentioned at the top of this chapter? The timing could not have been worse. The buyers were excited about the deal, but made it quite clear they were investing not only in the founder, but in the leadership bench that would carry the business forward. They wanted the owner to stay for a couple years, but they also needed someone already inside the company who could ultimately step in and run it. If they sensed weakness (or worse, disengagement), they would walk. The owner and I had to move quickly. We got her back to the States and sat down for an honest conversation. No spreadsheets, no forecasts—just reality. "If you don't look fully engaged, this deal doesn't happen."

What came out in that conversation had nothing to do with competence, it was about emotion and identity. For years, she had been the driver behind the scenes—loyal and capable, building value, but always in the founder's shadow. When the sale discussions began, she felt blindsided and unconsulted, like a passenger instead of a partner. She worried the sale meant she wasn't valued, that her future was uncertain, and that she would be sidelined or replaced after the transition. That insecurity had turned into distance. But when she understood that she was central to the deal, that the buyers wanted her, and that she was not only included, but needed, everything shifted and her confidence snapped back. Days later, at the big meet-and-greet with the buyer group, she didn't just show up, she shined. She exceeded every expectation, demonstrated leadership presence and vision, and charmed the prospective acquirers. Her energy and clarity didn't only save the deal, it strengthened it.

Sometimes, the biggest risk in a sale is making sure your key people feel seen, respected, and part of the future you're building.

You can't walk into this meeting casually. You need to prepare for it like you're preparing for an investor pitch or a client presentation. Spend time with your team beforehand to align on messaging, tone, and confidence. I've held mock buyer meetings with clients where we role-play the kinds of questions the team might face. I'm not suggesting you script answers or encourage dishonesty, as authenticity matters more than polish, but helping your team anticipate what buyers care about is essential. Buyers might ask, "How do you feel about the transition?" or "What excites you about the company's next chapter?" These questions aren't small talk; they're tests. The wrong tone, hesitation, or uncertainty can plant doubt in a buyer's mind that the company's energy leaves when the owner does.

If, during this prep work, you discover that one of your key executives isn't on board with the sale or is anxious about the transition, it's far better to uncover that early. The last place you want to find this out is in front of the buyer. Once you know, you can take action. Address their concerns, clarify their role post-sale, or, in some cases, decide whether they should even attend the meeting. The goal is not to manipulate, but to ensure that your team's enthusiasm, professionalism, and commitment shine through authentically. Remember, buyers are looking not only for a strong company, but also a strong second layer of leadership. That reassurance can make the difference between a deal that closes smoothly and one that unravels in the final stretch.

Ultimately, this meeting is your chance to prove that your business isn't dependent on you, and that it's a well-run machine powered by capable, motivated people who believe in the company's future. It's the human validation of everything you've said on paper. If the buyer walks away feeling confident that the business has depth, stability, and momentum beyond your tenure, you've just reinforced the value of your deal. But if they sense uncertainty, disengagement, or internal resistance, even the best financials won't save the sale. Prepare your team, frame the moment, and treat that meeting with the respect it deserves, because sometimes that's the real closing argument.

Pillar 2: Financial Strength

You can have the perfect timing, strong buyer interest, and a brilliant story, but if your financials aren't clean, your valuation will suffer. Financial readiness is one of the most overlooked yet crucial steps in preparing for a sale. It's what separates a "good company" from a sellable company.

Every buyer, whether it's a private equity firm or a strategic acquirer, will eventually peel back the layers of your financials. When that happens, you want them nodding with confidence, not frowning in confusion. Clean, accurate, and well-organized financials do more than justify your valuation—they build trust. And when selling a company, trust converts directly to dollars.

Get Your House in Order

Start by making sure your books are clean, consistent, and current. If your accounting practices have been more "entrepreneurial" than GAAP, now is the time to tighten up. You don't need a full audit (though having one helps), but, at a minimum, ensure your financials are reviewed by a reputable CPA and comply with standard accounting principles.

Buyers want visibility. They'll look at your P&L, balance sheet, and cash flow statements for trends, consistency, and anomalies. Any irregularities, such as spikes in expenses, unexplained adjustments, or inconsistent categorizations, can raise questions, and questions reduce value.

Each unexplained item on your financials is a speed bump in your sale. The more speed bumps, the slower the deal and the lower the confidence. The best-run sales are the ones where buyers find exactly what they expect.

It's also important to prepare a data room early. This is a centralized, organized repository where all key financial, legal, and operational documents are stored. This includes tax returns, historical financials, contracts, leases, customer agreements, and insurance policies. Building it early forces discipline and allows your team to respond faster once due diligence begins.

EBITDA is the Language of Buyers

Most business owners run their companies based on top-line revenue or net profit. Buyers, however, speak in EBITDA—earnings before interest, taxes, depreciation, and amortization. That's the metric they use to value your company. While it may not perfectly reflect how you see your business, it's the lingua franca of business sales.

Buyers look at EBITDA because it measures the company's core profitability before financing and accounting decisions. It strips away variables and gives them a clearer view of operational performance. If you haven't already, start tracking and managing your business through this lens. Each dollar of sustainable EBITDA growth can translate into five, six, or even ten dollars in valuation, depending on your industry's multiple.

You'll also want to identify "add-backs", which are legitimate adjustments that increase EBITDA by removing one-time or non-recurring expenses such as personal expenses, owner compensation above market, or one-off legal costs. Done correctly, these can make a major difference in valuation. Done poorly, they can look like financial engineering. Your CPA or investment banker can help you determine what's appropriate and defensible.

Align Compensation and Discretionary Expenses

If you've been running personal or discretionary expenses through the company, now is the time to clean them up. Buyers expect some normalization, but excessive add-backs or "lifestyle accounting" can raise doubts about your professionalism and financial transparency.

Start by reviewing your compensation. If you've been paying yourself or family members above-market salaries, consider bringing them closer to industry norms. Buyers will adjust for this anyway, but showing consistency helps your credibility.

Eliminate unnecessary perks that inflate expenses, such as personal travel, vehicles, club memberships, or "consulting" agreements that no longer serve the business. The goal isn't to strip your company bare; it's to present a clean, credible financial profile that reflects sustainable, transferable profitability.

Also review your vendor relationships. Are there sweetheart deals, barter arrangements, or one-off expenses that won't continue under new ownership? Disclose them early. Surprises during due diligence erode trust and can lead to painful price renegotiations.

Finally, make sure your financial reporting cadence is tight. Monthly financial statements, accurate forecasts, and key performance indicators (KPIs) show buyers you're disciplined and well-managed. If you've been operating on intuition, now is the time to formalize systems and processes.

Pre-Sale Tax Strategy – The Earlier You Start, the More You Keep

When founders think about creating value, they instinctively think about the front end of their business: building, scaling, hiring, delivering, and innovating. Very few instinctively think about the final chapter in the same way. Yet the act of converting business value into personal wealth is not a passive transaction. It is its own discipline. It demands the same level of insight and intentionality as raising capital or expanding into new markets.

A liquidity event is not merely the conclusion of business ownership. It is the transition of value from one system to another: from the operating environment into the personal financial environment. The tax system governs that conversion.

Those who understand this treat tax planning as a fundamental pillar of exit design. Those who do not leave wealth behind unnecessarily. They discover too late that the sales price was never the number that mattered, the after-tax number was.

Meaningful tax optimization requires distance from the transaction itself—time to think, time to structure, and time to position. Tax planning done within the momentum of the deal is primarily defensive; tax planning done before a deal exists is strategic, creative, and expansive. For founders, the most important tax insight is not about which forms to file or which line items matter. Instead, it is the simple rule that the earlier you begin, the more options you have to save.

Three Critical Areas Demand Early Attention

While comprehensive tax planning involves many layers, three areas consistently create the most value for business owners preparing to sell: estate planning and gifting strategies, qualified small business stock (QSBS) treatment, and state residency planning. Each requires significant lead time (often years, rather than only months). Miss the window, and you've lost opportunities that could have saved millions.

Estate Planning: Move the Tree When It's Still a Seed

Once a business is sold, its value becomes fixed for estate purposes, a fact that can transform a generational wealth opportunity into an estate tax problem. For founders whose estates will exceed exemption thresholds, the core idea of pre-sale gifting is simple. Transfer ownership when the valuation is still modest, not once it becomes liquid wealth. A savvy tax attorney explained it to a client like this. "Move the tree when it's still a seed." That single timing decision often determines whether the next generation inherits future appreciation, or the IRS does.

Common structures include Grantor Retained Annuity Trusts (GRATs), Intentionally Defective Grantor Trusts (IDGTs), and Family Limited Partnerships or LLCs. These tools allow founders to maintain control while removing future appreciation from the taxable estate. Suppose a founder transfers equity when the business is valued at $8 million. If the business later sells for $20 million, the appreciation ($12 million) accrues outside the estate, not inside it. Without this planning step, that future appreciation could be subject to estate taxation at rates approaching 40 percent or more.

QSBS: A Rare Legislative Gift to Founders

The QSBS exclusion can allow founders to exclude up to $10 million (and with planning, sometimes far more) from federal capital gains tax. Yet the QSBS exclusion benefits those who confirm eligibility early and structure accordingly. To qualify, a company must be a C-corporation engaged in an active business, with gross assets below $50 million at stock issuance. In addition, the shareholder must hold the stock for at least five years. Changing the entity's form late in the game may reset the clock, mergers may disqualify eligibility, and improper planning can dilute or eliminate the exemption. Proper QSBS planning yields outcomes equivalent to negotiating an additional multiple of EBITDA, without the stress of negotiating.

Residency: Where You Live When You Sell Matters

State residency is one of the most overlooked yet financially meaningful components of exit planning. When you sell, your domicile determines which state has the right to tax your gains. In high-tax states, that can mean losing more than 10 percent of your sale price. On an eight-figure exit, the difference between remaining in

California or New York versus establishing residency in a no-income-tax state can easily exceed several million dollars.

But residency is not proven by a driver's license alone. It's demonstrated through the full arc of your life: where you live, vote, receive mail, seek medical care, join communities, and spend your time. Tax authorities scrutinize big exits closely, looking at cell phone records, flight logs, calendar history, and where your family actually lives. You cannot "weekend your way" into residency. The test is not "did you fill out the forms?" The test is "did your life move?"

Timing matters, too. Moving right before a sale raises red flags. But when the relocation is authentic, well-documented, and established well before the transaction begins, the transition may hold up. Residency strategy isn't about escaping obligation. It's about aligning your next chapter intentionally.

That's the essence of financial readiness. You are not only maximizing your company's value, but also maximizing your control over your future.

The Tax Paradox

Sellers spend months negotiating over price, fighting for every dollar of valuation. A $50 million offer feels meaningfully better than a $48 million offer, and they'll often walk away from deals over 4 percent differences in headline price.

But they spend almost no time thinking about taxes, even though taxes can easily swing 20 to 30 percent of what they keep. A $50 million sale might net you $35 million after federal and state taxes.

But with smart planning—residency changes, timing strategies, and structure optimization—that same sale might net you $42 million.

That's a $7 million difference—more than the price difference you spent months fighting over. Yet most sellers don't engage tax advisors until the deal is nearly done, when it's too late to implement strategies that require advance planning.

The best tax planning happens twelve to twenty-four months before you sell. Residency changes need time to establish. Structure decisions need to be negotiated early. Timing strategies require flexibility.

Price is what you sell for. After-tax cash is what you keep. One matters far more than the other.

It's not how much you sell your business for—it's how much you get to keep after taxes.

Pillar 3: Transferable Value

One of the biggest mindset shifts when preparing your company for sale is you're no longer just running your business, you're building a business that someone else can run.

That's the essence of *transferable value*. It's what turns your company from a personal success story into an attractive, stand-alone asset. Buyers don't pay top dollar for what *you* can do, they pay for what the *business* can do without you.

It's a paradox. The more dependent the company is on you, the less valuable it becomes. Yet most founders built their success on being indispensable. They are the visionary, the problem-solver, the one who can fix anything. That same strength now becomes a weakness when it's time to sell.

Your job now is to make yourself irrelevant—in the best way possible.

It feels unnatural, almost like betrayal. After all, your fingerprints are on everything: the product, the people, the culture, and the strategy. You've invested years building a business that relies on your vision, decisions, and drive. Your name, your story, and your reputation add value to your company. You're the face of the brand, the voice of the mission, and the energy that inspires the team. But the more buyers see the company as you, the less confident they are in what happens without you.

Buyers don't want a company that collapses when you take a vacation; they want one that keeps humming without you. They're not just buying your business, they're buying its independence from you. To maximize value, you have to start building systems, empowering your team, and delegating responsibilities so the company proves it can thrive without your constant involvement.

Letting go of control early feels counterintuitive. It may even feel like lowering your standards. But what you're really doing is increasing your company's transferability, and that transferability is the true hallmark of value. The bottom line is that personal charisma can boost valuation at first, but it eventually triggers questions about risk. Can the team deliver without you? Will clients stay? Will the culture hold? Buyers don't want to purchase your personality, they want to purchase a self-sustaining business.

If you want to maximize value, start shifting the spotlight before you sell. Put your leadership team forward. Let others make decisions, run meetings, and sign client contracts. The goal isn't to disappear, but to make yourself optional. That's when buyers start to see not just a great founder, but also a great company.

Systemize Everything

Transferable value starts with systems. The stronger your processes, the less risk a buyer sees. That means clear, documented procedures for every critical area of the business, from sales, operations, and finance, to HR, and customer service.

If someone on your team left tomorrow, could a new hire step in and perform their role from a written playbook? If the answer is no, start building one. Create standard operating procedures, checklists, and process maps. Buyers love documentation. It signals discipline and scalability.

Automation plays a role, too. If your business depends heavily on manual processes or tribal knowledge, buyers will discount it. But if they see software systems, dashboards, and repeatable workflows, that's value. It means less reliance on key people, fewer unknowns, and smoother integration post-acquisition.

Even simple steps, like centralizing passwords, creating shared drives, and using CRM and project management systems, make your company more "plug-and-play" for a buyer.

Reduce Key Person Risk

Key person risk is when your name is on all the major contracts, when clients call you directly and exclusively, or when nothing big happens without your approval. Buyers hate this.

Your mission is to make sure the business runs beautifully without you. This isn't about checking out; it's about setting up structures that ensure continuity. Start by identifying who your "mini-yous" are—the people who can handle major decisions and maintain client relationships. Then empower them.

One of the best ways to reduce key person risk is to make clients loyal to the *company*, not only to you. Bring other team members into meetings. Have them deliver results directly. The less the business relies on your personal involvement, the more buyers will believe it can thrive after the sale.

You stepping back will not make the business less successful. It often does the opposite. A business that doesn't need its founder tends to grow faster and more sustainably, because it's built on systems, not heroics.

The Growth Trap Paradox

To make your company sellable, you must make yourself less essential to its success. The better you've run it, the less you should be running it. Buyers don't want to buy your expertise—they want to buy a business that operates without you.

This feels wrong. You built the company by being indispensable. Your judgment, your relationships, and your instincts were competitive advantages. Removing yourself feels like weakening what you've built.

But the opposite is true. A business that depends on you is worth less than a business that doesn't. Key person risk depresses valuations. Buyers want systems, teams, and processes that continue after you're gone. They're buying a machine that works, not a machine that requires you to operate it.

The path to maximum value is building yourself out of the center of operations. Hire strong leaders. Document processes. Transfer relationships. Create a business that proves it can thrive without you.

The more essential you are to your business, the less valuable it becomes—because buyers pay for independence, not dependence.

Strengthen Your Leadership Team

Buyers don't just buy businesses; they buy teams. A strong second layer of leadership gives buyers confidence that performance will continue after closing.

If your managers are overworked, underpaid, or unprepared for a transition, address it now. Consider retention bonuses or phantom equity to keep key employees motivated through and after the sale. These arrangements show buyers that the team has both the incentive and the structure to stay engaged.

I've watched buyers walk away from good companies because they couldn't see who would run them once the owners left. I've also seen valuations jump by millions when sellers could demonstrate capable leadership teams ready to carry the torch.

Consider this. If you disappeared for three months, what would happen to the business? The more seamless the answer, the higher your company's value.

Diversify Customers and Revenue Streams

Customer concentration is one of the fastest ways to scare off buyers or trigger a price reduction. If 40 percent of your revenue comes from one client, the risk is enormous. Lose that client, and the whole deal's economics change.

Start spreading your revenue across a broader customer base. If that's not realistic before the sale, at least prepare a strategy and show buyers you recognize and are addressing it. Document how you're building pipeline, expanding into new markets, or cross-selling to existing clients.

Equally important is revenue *quality*. Predictable, recurring revenue is king. Buyers love anything contractual—subscriptions, service agreements, retainers, etc. If your business model allows, shift toward recurring income. It not only improves valuation multiples, but also smooths out the ups and downs that make buyers nervous.

Protect Intellectual Property and Brand Assets

Your intellectual property (IP), such as trademarks, patents, copyrights, customer data, and proprietary methods, is a core part of your company's value. Yet many business owners fail to protect it properly.

Review your IP portfolio and make sure everything is owned by the *company*, not by you personally or contractors. It's common for deals to be delayed and discounts demanded because a key piece of software is owned by a former developer or a logo was never trademarked.

Buyers will look for proof that all your IP is secure and transferable. Have all your documentation ready, including registrations, contracts, and license agreements. Protecting your brand and data isn't just legal housekeeping; it's part of the story you tell buyers about your company's professionalism, foresight, and stability.

Focus on the Metrics That Matter

While founders often emphasize growth or revenue, buyers look deeper at metrics such as efficiency, predictability, and margins. They analyze customer retention, gross margins, EBITDA trends, and working capital efficiency.

If your numbers are improving over time (even modestly), it tells buyers the business is healthy and scalable. If they're flat or declining, that's a red flag. Spend time now identifying the metrics that drive valuation in your industry, and work to improve them.

For example:

- In SaaS, retention rate and lifetime value matter more than top-line growth.

- In services, margins and client diversification drive valuation.

- In manufacturing, capacity utilization and supply chain efficiency are key.

Knowing what buyers prioritize allows you to focus your energy on the levers that truly move valuation.

Pillar 4: Risk Reduction

Buyers don't pay for potential, they pay for *certainty*. The more predictable, stable, and low-risk your business looks, the more valuable it becomes. And the fewer surprises that surface during due diligence, the smoother your deal will go.

One of the most important steps in preparing for a sale is learning to see your company the way a buyer will: through the lens of *risk*.

Every buyer is running the same mental checklist:

- What could go wrong?

- What's hidden beneath the surface?

- What might make this business harder to run once we own it?

Your job is to identify and fix those vulnerabilities before they discover them.

Operational Risk

Operational risk is what keeps buyers up at night. It's anything that threatens day-to-day continuity, from supply chain dependencies and key vendor relationships to overreliance on a single system or process.

Start by stress-testing your operations. Ask:

- What happens if a major customer delays payment?
- What if your top employee leaves?
- What if your core software goes down for a week?

Buyers will ask those same questions, and your answers determine how confident they will feel. The more contingency planning you've done, the stronger your negotiating position becomes.

Build redundancies. Document procedures. Create cross-training programs so that no one employee—and yes, especially you—becomes a single point of failure. Even small actions like dual-signing authority on accounts or secondary vendor relationships show buyers that the business is resilient.

Financial Risk

Financial risk is the quickest way to lose trust and valuation. Buyers always assume there are some issues hiding in the numbers, but what they can't tolerate is ambiguity.

Before going to market, review your books as if you were on the other side of the table. Reconcile everything. Clean up inter-company transfers. Remove personal expenses disguised as business costs. Buyers will find them anyway, so better for them to see you've already cleaned house.

Have your CPA prepare trailing twelve-month (TTM) statements. Buyers prefer this over calendar-year summaries because it gives them a rolling, up-to-date snapshot of performance. If there are seasonal fluctuations, explain them. Context reduces perceived risk.

It's also smart to do a quality of earnings (QoE) report before the buyer does theirs. Think of it as a proactive x-ray of your financials. A QoE validates EBITDA, identifies adjustments, and confirms that revenue and expenses are properly categorized. When you hand a buyer your own QoE, you send a message. "We're organized. We know our numbers. There are no surprises here."

Legal and Compliance Risk

Legal risks rarely kill deals outright, but they can slow them down, and slow deals cost money.

Before going to market, work with your attorney to identify potential landmines, such as outdated contracts, missing signatures, unresolved disputes, intellectual property issues, or employment agreements that aren't assignable.

Buyers will comb through each contract to confirm they can assume them after the sale. If you have contracts that require client consent before transfer, fix those now. Nothing halts momentum faster than discovering half your customers have to re-sign paperwork at closing.

The same applies to licenses, permits, and insurance coverage. Make sure all are current and transferable. If you operate in a regulated industry, confirm that compliance documentation is in order. These may seem like small details, but small details kill deals.

People Risk

Your employees are both your biggest asset and one of the biggest risks in a sale. Buyers want to know who's staying, who's critical, and how morale will hold up once the announcement is made.

You can't eliminate people risk, but you can manage it.

- **Retention plans:** Offer key employees bonuses tied to the successful completion of the deal or a post-close period.

- **Transparent communication.** Once the time is right, share enough information to build trust without disrupting day-to-day operations.

- **Defined roles:** Show that responsibilities are clearly distributed and the company won't lose momentum if you step away.

A stable, motivated team gives buyers confidence. A fearful, uncertain team does the opposite.

Uh Oh – How to Disclose Bad Information

Every business has imperfections. Sometimes they're small, like an outdated process or a messy contract. Other times, they're more serious: slowing growth, an aging client base, profit compression, customer concentration, or pending litigation. No company is perfect, and every buyer knows that. The question isn't whether issues exist, but how you deal with them. If you have the time and resources, your best move is to fix the problem before you go to market. Buyers pay a premium for clean stories and predictable outcomes. When they sense risk, they either lower the price or walk away entirely. Taking a few extra months to stabilize a key client, settle a dispute, or improve margins can pay off exponentially when it comes time to negotiate.

But sometimes you don't have that luxury. Maybe the issue is too big to fix quickly, or the clock is ticking on a personal deadline, health concern, or shift in the market. In those cases, don't hide the problem; frame it. You have to decide how to present it to potential buyers in a way that builds confidence instead of fear. This requires transparency and timing. Tell your Core Four, who you'll learn about in the next chapter, as early as possible.

What you must never do is try to conceal or downplay a material issue. It will be discovered during due diligence—and if, by some miracle, it isn't, it will come back to haunt you in the representations and warranties section of the purchase agreement. When you sign that document, you are legally affirming that all significant information about the business has been disclosed. If the buyer later finds out you hid something, the consequences can be severe. The cover-up is always worse than the flaw itself. Buyers will forgive problems; they won't forgive dishonesty.

Handled well, disclosure can build credibility. When you acknowledge a challenge directly and provide context ("Here's the issue, here's what we've done about it, and here's how it's trending"), you come across as professional and trustworthy. Buyers understand that risk exists in every business. The most successful sellers are the ones with the courage to be transparent about their imperfections and the wisdom to manage them strategically.

Always Have a Plan B

Every seller needs a Plan B.

In the same way you would never run your business without backup systems, you shouldn't approach a sale without one either.

Even great deals fall through. The best way to handle it is to plan for it early.

I always tell clients: Run your business like the deal won't close, because sometimes it won't. Keep pushing growth, keep your team motivated, and keep your operations sharp.

One of my clients was so confident his deal was going through that he started making decisions as if it had already closed. He had an offer in hand, due diligence was underway, and everyone seemed aligned. The problem was, he began operating from assumption, not reality. He knew he needed to hire a new CFO (his current one wasn't working out), but he decided to wait. "Why bring someone new in," he said, "if we'll be sold in a few months?"

Months later, the buyer hit pause. Then negotiations stalled. The deal that felt "done" evaporated. He found himself with no deal, no CFO, and a business that had started to slip because critical decisions were deferred. It was a painful reminder that until the deal closes, you still own the company and you have to keep running it like you will forever.

Deals fall apart for all kinds of reasons: buyer fatigue, financing, due diligence surprises, market shifts. Until the wire clears, you're still the CEO. Keep running your business. Hope for the sale, prepare for the close, but always keep your Plan B alive, because it may give you another $48 million.

When "Plan B" Becomes a $48 Million Difference

A failed deal doesn't mean failure. It often just means timing wasn't right. I've seen founders walk through an entire sale process, receive real offers, sit across from real buyers, and then intentionally step away, not because something was wrong, but because something wasn't right yet.

One of my clients received an offer for $19.5 million. It was a legitimate offer from a credible buyer. But the conversations stalled. The fit wasn't perfect, the valuation felt light, and momentum slowed to a crawl. Instead of forcing it, we made the harder choice. We walked.

That decision changed everything.

He didn't retreat. He went back to work with conviction. His industry was experiencing rapid expansion, and his company was growing at a pace that wasn't yet reflected in the trailing financials buyers were using. The growth was real; it just hadn't hit the books in a way private equity could model yet.

Over the next six months, he doubled down. He landed new contracts and expanded his backlog. He strengthened his financial reporting. Month after month, the trailing twelve-month earnings climbed, and the projections, backed by signed contracts and a full pipeline, accelerated sharply. The story didn't change, the timing did, and so did the value.

When we went back to market, we didn't show investors hope or potential. We showed them trajectory, evidence, and momentum. Buyers didn't have to imagine the future; they could see it in black-and-white financials.

The result? A $68 million offer.

Same company. Same founder. Same potential. Just better timing, better proof, and better leverage.

In exits, patience isn't passive, it's strategic. Sometimes the most powerful move isn't selling when you can, but waiting until you should. Walking away wasn't the end of the deal. It was the beginning of the right one.

You've worked to reduce risk in the transaction. You've identified what could go wrong in due diligence, in negotiations, in the handoff. But there's a category of risk most owners never address. It's not deal risk. It's family risk.

When the Sale Comes Home (Prepare Your Family, Not Just Your Business)

The business sale doesn't just change your life. It changes your family's life, often in ways nobody anticipated. Deals that succeed financially can create serious strain at home. Spouses get blindsided by a retirement they didn't ask for. Adult children feel wounded by sales they expected to prevent. Family gatherings turn tense when sudden wealth exposes long-buried resentments.

The financial planning is the easy part. The family dynamics are where the real complexity lives.

The Spouse Who Didn't Sign Up for This

For decades, your spouse built a life around your absence. They developed routines, friendships, and space of their own. They managed the household, raised the children, and created a rhythm that worked. Then, overnight, you're home. All day. Every day. Following them to the grocery store. Asking what's for lunch. Suggesting improvements to how they organize their day.

You thought retirement would bring you closer. Instead, it can reveal how separately you've been living for years.

This pattern is remarkably common. The owner sells the business expecting gratitude and companionship. The spouse experiences an invasion. Two people who love each other discover they don't actually know how to spend unstructured time together. They were partners in a system, not partners in daily life.

The solution isn't for you to disappear or for your spouse to simply accommodate. It's for both of you to acknowledge that the sale changes the marriage, not just the bank account. Conversations need to happen before the deal closes. What will your days look like? How much togetherness is too much? What space does each person need? These aren't romantic questions, but they're essential ones. The couples who navigate this well treat the transition like a joint project. The ones who don't often end up in therapy or worse.

When Equal Isn't Fair

Few family conflicts cut deeper than disputes over fairness when a business sells. Who deserves what? Who contributed more? Who sacrificed? These questions can tear families apart if left unspoken.

The pattern typically looks like this. An adult child spent years in the company. They started at the bottom, worked their way up, and eventually took on real responsibility. They assumed the business would be theirs someday. It was never explicitly promised, but it was understood. Or so they thought.

When the parent decides to sell, the child feels betrayed, dismissed, and foolish for investing their career in something that was never really theirs. The parent feels justified. The child wasn't ready to own it, the market timing was right, and the family needed liquidity. Both are telling the truth. Neither can hear the other.

These ruptures can last years. Sometimes they never heal.

But it doesn't have to go that way.

I worked with a client who had taken over his business from his father and ran it successfully for thirty years. He had two daughters. One worked in the business and was vital to its success. She had no interest in taking over, but her contributions were significant. The company likely would not have sold for nearly as much without her.

My client decided to sell to a strategic buyer. That's when the hard conversations started.

How do you fairly compensate the daughter who helped build the value? And what about the daughter who chose a different path? My client loved both of his children equally. But the situation wasn't equal, and pretending otherwise would have created resentment on both sides.

We held a family meeting and hit the awkwardness directly. No dancing around it. The daughter who wasn't in the business understood she had chosen not to work there. She didn't expect the same payout. But she also shared that she was still carrying student loan debt and would appreciate help if it was possible.

We structured a solution that honored everyone's reality. The daughter in the business received fair compensation for her contributions to the sale. The other daughter received a down payment on a house and had her student loans paid off so she could benefit now rather than waiting for an inheritance. And to balance things over time, my client updated his estate plan so that those gifts would be subtracted from that daughter's eventual share before the estate is divided. When he and his wife eventually pass, the estate will be divided equitably.

No one felt cheated. No one felt favored. The conversation was uncomfortable, but it prevented years of silent resentment.

This outcome was possible because my client was willing to surface the awkwardness instead of avoiding it. He didn't hope the situation would resolve itself. He didn't assume his daughters would "figure it out" after he was gone. He led the conversation while he was still alive to explain his reasoning and listen to theirs.

If you have children with different relationships to your business, the conversation about your intentions needs to happen before you sell. Not hints. Not assumptions. Direct conversation. What are your plans? What role do they see for themselves? What feels fair to them, and why? These discussions are uncomfortable, but they're far less damaging than the alternative.

The Money That Divided Them

Sudden wealth has a way of exposing fault lines that families worked years to plaster over.

Consider what happens when an owner sells and decides to gift each adult child a significant sum. The owner expects gratitude. What often follows is conflict. One child thinks the amounts should reflect their involvement in the business. Another wants the money held in trust, worried about a sibling's spending habits. A third resents being treated identically to siblings who have vastly different financial needs.

Within months, a family can fracture into factions. Holiday dinners become negotiations. Phone calls become accusations. The money that was supposed to bring freedom brings division instead.

Wealth doesn't create family dysfunction, but it accelerates it. Issues that simmered quietly for decades suddenly have stakes attached. Who gets what, when, and how becomes a referendum on love, fairness, and favoritism. Adult children regress into childhood rivalries. Parents feel trapped between competing demands.

The families who handle this well share a few traits. They communicate early and often about their intentions. They explain their reasoning, even when the reasoning is simply "this is what we've decided." They treat estate planning as an ongoing conversation, not a document to be revealed after death. And they accept that not everyone will be satisfied, but everyone deserves to be heard.

Preparing Your Family, Not Just Your Finances

Most owners spend months preparing their business for sale. They clean up financials, document processes, and rehearse presentations for buyers. They prepare almost nothing for their families.

That's a mistake. The family transition deserves the same intentionality as the business transition.

Before you sell, have direct conversations with your spouse about what daily life will look like. Talk about space, routine, and expectations. If you have children in the business, clarify their future before the LOI is signed. If you plan to distribute wealth, explain your philosophy before the checks are written.

Consider bringing in outside help. A family therapist, a family business consultant, or even a financial advisor experienced in these dynamics can facilitate conversations that feel impossible to have alone. These professionals create space for honesty without explosion. They help families separate the emotional from the financial, which is essential when both are in play.

And recognize that your family's adjustment will take time. Just as you need space to grieve the business and find your new identity, they need space to process what this change means for them. Your spouse is losing the structure they built around your absence. Your children may be losing assumptions they held about their future. Siblings, parents, and extended family may all have feelings about money that you never knew existed.

The sale changes everything. Not just for you.

The Opportunity Inside the Tension

Here's what I've also observed. Families who navigate this transition intentionally often emerge stronger than before. The forced conversations reveal truths that needed to surface. The sudden togetherness, once negotiated, can deepen intimacy. The wealth, when handled thoughtfully, can become a shared project rather than a source of division.

Some couples use the sale as an opportunity to redesign their marriage. They travel, not to escape, but to discover what they actually enjoy doing together. They return with new shared interests and a schedule that gives each of them both autonomy and connection.

Some families hold facilitated meetings after the sale, airing grievances that festered for years. The process is painful. It's also necessary. These families often end up closer than they've ever been.

The business sale doesn't have to fracture your family. But ignoring the family dimension guarantees tension. The owners who invest as much energy in preparing their families as they do in preparing their balance sheets are the ones who find that the best returns from the sale aren't measured in dollars.

That's the full picture of preparation. Let's review where you stand.

Chapter Exit

Preparing your business for sale is like tuning an engine before a race. Everything must be running smoothly before you hit the starting line. You've cleaned up your financials, strengthened your team, protected your intellectual property, and built a company that can run without you. At this stage, you've transformed from an operator into a strategist. You're no longer only leading the business, you're also positioning it for transfer. This groundwork isn't glamorous, but it's what separates a smooth, high-value sale from one that stalls halfway through.

The work you've done in these first two chapters forms the foundation of what follows. You've prepared yourself mentally and emotionally. You've prepared your company operationally and financially. But foundation alone doesn't close deals. Execution does. And execution requires expertise you don't have, experience you haven't accumulated, and perspective you can't gain from the inside.

This is what mastering the before looks like. While others rush to market with mediocre preparation, you've built a foundation that maximizes value. You've avoided the 98 percent trap by doing the work most sellers skip—and buyers will notice the difference.

The next phase, during the deal, is where strategy meets execution. Once you go to market, the process becomes faster, more intense, and exponentially more complex. You'll be dealing with investment bankers, attorneys, accountants, and buyers who live and breathe deals. They do this every day. You don't. That's the rub—the biggest financial transaction of your life will likely be your first. The only way to level the playing field is to surround yourself with people who have been here before—professionals who know the terrain and whose sole job is to protect you, your value, and your sanity.

That's where your Core Four deal team comes in. These are the trusted experts who will guide you through every twist and turn of the sale process: your investment banker, your attorney, your CPA, and your wealth advisor. Each plays a distinct role, but together they form your shield, your strategy, and your sounding board. The next chapter dives into how to assemble this team, what to look for, how to align their incentives, and how to make sure they're working together toward one goal—getting you the best deal possible. Because once the deal process starts, you won't have time to build your team. You'll need them to already be in the fight with you.

STAGE TWO:
DURING

Take a breath. You've just completed the hardest preparation work most sellers never do—building the mental foundation and transforming your company into something someone else can buy. This wasn't glamorous, but it will determine whether you negotiate from strength or desperation. That's about to shift. Up until now, you've been in control. Once you enter the during stage and start talking to buyers, the deal takes on a life of its own. The calendar becomes relentless. Due diligence will feel invasive. You'll move from architect to athlete, and the momentum shifts from you driving the process to managing it under pressure. This is where deals are won or lost and where small mistakes cost millions. But you're ready. You've done the prep work. Now you just have to trust it.

CHAPTER 3:

BUILD YOUR DEAL TEAM

Discover the Core Four Who Determine Your Success

One of my clients built a highly successful business where his entire job was negotiating deals. He was smart, strategic, and tough—a master at getting others to agree to his terms. So when it came time to sell his own company, he figured it would be easy. After all, he'd spent decades sitting across the table from lawyers, executives, and dealmakers. But what he quickly learned was that negotiating for yourself was an entirely different experience. When it's your business, your people, and your legacy on the line, emotions blur logic. Every point feels personal. Every concession feels like defeat. Even the most seasoned negotiators can lose perspective when the deal involves their life's work.

The most accomplished dealmakers still need help when selling their own companies. It's not about skill, it's about objectivity. You can't be the CEO, the seller, and the negotiator all at once. You're too close. You need a buffer—an investment banker, an attorney, an advisor—someone who can see the big picture and protect you from reacting emotionally in high-stakes moments. Selling your company is unlike any other deal you've done. The irony is that the more experienced you are at negotiating for others, the more likely you are to underestimate how hard it will be to negotiate for yourself.

You spent years building your company, but when it comes time to sell, you're entering a completely different business—the business of selling a business.

It's a process filled with complexity, emotion, and more zeroes than most people will ever see in their lifetime. You may be a seasoned entrepreneur, but this is a one-shot deal. You'll probably only sell one company in your life, but the people across the table do this for a living.

Choosing your Core Four is one of the most important decisions you'll ever make.

You built your company by surrounding yourself with great people. Selling it requires the same strategy—but the stakes are even higher. The right advisors can help you increase your sale price, protect your wealth, and preserve your sanity. That last part about preserving your sanity is not an overstatement. As we will discuss later, you will likely go a bit crazy at some point in the process. Over the past thirty years, I've seen the most level-headed sellers lose it. It's all part of the process. But it is still critical that you have the right team, because the wrong one can drag out the process, create unnecessary conflict, and cost you millions.

Your Core Four

Your deal dream team will usually include four key players:

1. **Investment banker** – Your quarterback and lead negotiator. Your banker helps you maximize the value of what you have built.

2. **M&A attorney** – Your legal strategist and shield. Your attorney protects what you've earned.

3. **CPA / tax advisor** – Your tax engineer and truth-teller. Your tax expert preserves what you keep.

4. **Wealth manager** – Your personal CFO and long-term strategist. Your wealth advisor helps you convert assets into a stream of income to fund your new life.

Together, they can transform your life's work into lasting freedom. Each has a distinct role, and together they form the backbone of your sale process. Let's go deeper into how to find them, how to manage them, and how to make sure they work for you.

When to Bring Each Advisor into the Process

One of the most common questions I get is, "When do I actually hire these people?" The answer matters, because timing can mean the difference between a tax-efficient, well-structured deal and one that leaves millions on the table.

You don't want to hire all four at once, but you also don't want to wait until you have an offer to assemble your team. The Core Four enter at different stages, each playing a specific role at the right moment in the process.

Twelve to Eighteen Months Before the Sale: Wealth Manager and CPA

Long before you contact a single buyer or investment banker, you need to bring in your wealth manager and CPA. This is the strategic planning phase. Your wealth manager helps you model different deal structures, understand tax implications, and design a post-sale financial plan. While your CPA ensures your financials are clean, identifies tax optimization strategies, and helps structure the sale in the most tax-efficient way possible. These two set the foundation. They're thinking years ahead, not months.

Six to Twelve Months Before the Sale: Investment Banker (If Using One)

Once you've decided to sell and your financials are in order, it is time to bring in your investment banker. They need time to understand your business, build the marketing materials (teaser, CIM), identify potential buyers, and create competition. Rushing this process weakens your negotiating position. A good banker needs runway to do their job well. I'll be honest, though—it's rare for a company to bring in a banker this early. If you're on top of it (and since you are reading this book, you likely are), that timeframe is ideal but not essential.

At the LOI Stage: M&A Attorney

Your M&A attorney enters if you want them to review your banker agreement, or when you have an LOI in hand. Before that, there's not much for them to do. But once you're negotiating terms and preparing for due diligence, they become essential. They'll review the LOI, negotiate the definitive purchase agreement, protect you during due diligence, and make sure you're not agreeing to anything that will hurt you later. Don't wait until you're deep into due diligence to hire them—by then, you've already agreed to terms that might be difficult to change.

Throughout the Entire Process: Your Wealth Manager

Here's what most owners miss. Your wealth manager should be coordinating the entire process from start to finish. They're the one advisor who sees the full picture—before, during, and after. They work with your CPA on tax strategy, consult with your banker on deal structure, and collaborate with your attorney to ensure the terms align with your financial goals. Your wealth manager makes sure everyone is working together toward the same outcome: maximizing your financial result and protecting your future.

The mistake most owners make is hiring reactively, and waiting until they're in crisis mode, or until someone tells them they need help. By then, opportunities have been missed. Assemble your team strategically, bring each advisor in at the right time, and let them build the framework for a deal that works not just on paper, but in your life.

The Investment Banker – Your Quarterback

If there's one advisor who will have the greatest influence on the sale, it's your investment banker. They are the quarterback of your deal—coordinating the process, managing potential buyers, and setting the tempo from start to finish.

A great investment banker doesn't just find buyers. They masterfully pitch your company and create enthusiasm. They tell your story and sell the future, creating competition among buyers. They fight for you.

When multiple buyers are at the table, you have leverage. That's the key!

How Investment Banks Operate

To sell well, you need to understand how the players around you are incentivized—especially your investment bank. Investment bankers are invaluable partners in a sale. They craft the narrative, position the deal, run a competitive process, screen buyers, negotiate terms, and guide you from interest to LOI to closing. But like every professional in a transaction ecosystem, they are motivated by the structure of their fee. Understanding that structure helps you negotiate intelligently and avoid misalignment.

Most investment banking engagements follow a standard model with a monthly or one-time retainer and a success fee.

- **Monthly retainer:** The retainer is a flat monthly payment. This is typically between $0 and $100,000 per month, although most fall between $10,000 and $25,000. What you may also see is a one-time upfront fee. Either way, this fee is designed to compensate the bank for front-end work: research, positioning, building marketing materials, identifying buyer lists, and preparing you for the market. This fee is highly negotiable, so don't feel bad grinding them to lower it or waive it completely.

- **Success fee:** The success fee is where the investment bank makes most of their income. This is a percentage of the transaction value paid at closing. Each industry is different, but for a rough idea on what you might pay, 4 to 6 percent is common for deals under $30 million. As deal size increases, that percentage typically declines. Many banks will charge 2 to 4 percent on mid-market deals and 1 to 2 percent for nine-figure transactions. Different banks have different philosophies, but the principle is consistent: The more complex and time-intensive the deal is relative to its size, the higher the fee.

Where things get interesting, and where many founders get caught off guard, is in the fine print around earnouts and contingent payments. Some banks attempt to charge their full success fees on the total theoretical deal value, including future payments you haven't earned yet. That means if your deal includes an earnout tied to performance after closing, they may expect full commission immediately, even though you may never receive that portion of the sale price. In other words, you could end up paying real dollars today on hypothetical dollars tomorrow.

A fair banker won't insist on this, because fair bankers know it violates economic logic and trust. But some will try. And owners who are exhausted, excited, or new to the process sometimes sign without questioning it. Don't get stuck in this trap. Structure matters. If an earnout is part of your deal, protect yourself by ensuring the bank's commission on that component is paid only if you receive those funds. It keeps incentives aligned and prevents you from financing someone else's upside without certainty of your own.

The right banker will respect this. If they push back, consider it a red flag. Your sale partner should win when you win, and not just when the paperwork is signed. Alignment doesn't just make the deal fair; it makes it smoother, cleaner, and far more collaborative. And in a process where hundreds of little decisions compound into millions of dollars of outcome, alignment is not a luxury. It's a requirement.

What Makes a Great Banker

A great investment banker is part strategist, part storyteller, and part therapist. They don't just analyze spreadsheets. They understand people. They grasp the psychology of both sides of the table. They know what motivates buyers, what scares them, and what drives their decision-making. They also understand you—your emotions, your attachment to your business, and your goals beyond the sale. Their role is to translate your story into a compelling investment narrative that resonates with the right kind of buyer, whether that's a strategic acquirer, a private equity firm, or a family office looking for its next platform.

Great bankers orchestrate the entire process like conductors. They know how to create deal momentum and, just as importantly, how to sustain it. They manage deadlines, coordinate buyers, and keep everyone focused and energized. When a deal drags on, and interest fades, great bankers know how to keep multiple buyers moving in sync so that competitive tension builds instead of dissipates. They also know when to apply pressure and when to let things breathe. Timing, tone, and tempo are everything.

Average bankers are reactive. They gather your financials, assemble a boilerplate CIM, send out a few teasers, and then wait for the phone to ring. They're process administrators, not dealmakers. Great bankers, by contrast, drive the deal. They're on the phone constantly, nudging buyers, countering objections, and managing egos. They know how to control the narrative and keep your company positioned as a scarce, desirable asset. They sell your story, and they never let the process lose energy.

Perhaps most importantly, a great banker protects you from yourself. Selling a business is emotionally exhausting. Fatigue breeds mistakes, such as agreeing to bad terms, taking your eye off the business, or losing enthusiasm at the finish line. The best bankers keep you steady through the highs and lows, reminding you why you started the process, helping you stay focused on the outcome, and carrying the burden when the weight of the deal starts to feel heavy.

The best investment banker isn't the one who flatters you, it's the one who asks the hard questions and isn't afraid to push back.

How to Identify and Select the Right Investment Banker

Choosing the right investment bank is one of the most consequential decisions you'll make in your exit. This isn't a vendor relationship; it's a partnership with people who will shape buyer perception, set process cadence, influence valuation, and negotiate terms on your behalf. Treat selection as a disciplined search, not a casual referral. Start broad, filter fast, and then go deep, building a list of firms that regularly close transactions in your revenue band and in your vertical (or an adjacent one). Specialization matters, and a banker who has seen dozens of deals in your space understands what buyers actually underwrite, where they push on diligence, and which levers move value. That pattern recognition is an advantage you can't recreate mid-process.

Email is your first filter. Share a concise overview of your business and ask pointed questions about size range, sector coverage, recent comps, process design, team composition, and fees. Their speed and specificity in responding will tell you as much as their pitch book. Then move to live conversations. Video calls let you test how they think in real time. Are they clear, grounded, and fluent in your industry, or are they generalists speaking in abstractions? A strong banker won't inflate valuation to win the mandate; they'll give you a defensible range and explain the assumptions behind it.

After a few conversations, narrow your shortlist and meet in person (they usually come to you so they can see your operations). Presence reveals things video calls can't, such as how they hold a room, how they probe, how quickly they absorb nuance, and whether you trust them to represent you with buyers who negotiate for a living. You want a tactician and a diplomat, not a cheerleader.

What to look for:

- **Industry expertise.** Experience in your specific space matters more than firm size. A mid-sized boutique that specializes in your sector will often outperform a global firm that doesn't. Look at the other companies they have represented in sales, specifically as the sell-side advisor.

- **Transaction volume.** How many deals have they closed in your industry? Ask for details. How many teasers went out? How many signed NDAs? How many management meetings? How many LOIs? What was their internal valuation range? What did the company ultimately sell for? How long did it take? Was it a strategic buyer or private equity? Dig into the process and outcomes.

- **Team structure.** Will you work directly with senior partners or be handed off to junior associates? Who is your point person? Can you see yourself working closely with this person for the next year or more?

- **Chemistry.** You'll be in constant communication for months. Choose someone you like, trust, and feel energized around.

The Power of Meeting in Person

One of my clients had her mind made up: She was going with a large, brand-name firm. She even protested about meeting another bank in person because she believed the decision was done. But after some encouragement, she took the meeting—and changed course completely. The team that looked best on paper (and on video calls!) fell flat in person. Another firm, which was smaller, hungrier, and more connected to her story, won her over.

Selling a company can feel like going to war at times; you want people you trust and connect with in the trenches. Trust your instincts and choose the team you can be direct with—who will challenge your thinking when needed, who won't disappear after the engagement letter, and who will still be calm, prepared, and persuasive on day 147 of a hard process. The right banker doesn't just promise a result—they build the process and the buyer set that makes that result likely.

Watch for Conflicts

Many founders overlook a subtle but important dynamic: how bankers enter the picture and who influences that introduction. If you work with a financial advisor at a major brokerage, there's a high probability they'll recommend their internal investment banking team or a banker they "happen to know well." Large financial institutions often have compensation systems that reward internal referrals. Advisors are encouraged, and sometimes financially incentivized, to steer clients toward affiliated bankers.

I once worked with a client who met a financial advisor at an industry conference. The advisor was charismatic and introduced my client to an investment bank he strongly recommended. My client trusted the recommendation and hired the bank. After I joined his advisory team, I asked a few questions about how the banker came into the picture. After a little digging, it became clear the financial advisor who made the referral was receiving a portion of the banker's fees. The client had never been told. By the time we discovered it, we were already deep into the process, and my client felt betrayed. Neither of us fully believed that banker was the best choice in the first place.

This is why, when a banker is introduced to you by any advisor, I recommend asking a simple, direct question before you take a single step forward:

"Do you, or does your firm, receive any compensation or benefit from this introduction?"

Ask it plainly. Ask it early. Ask it every time. A trustworthy advisor will answer clearly and without hesitation. An honest banker will never object to transparency. The sale of your company is a once-in-a-lifetime moment. Make sure the people sitting at your table are there for the right reasons.

Expect Disciplined Communication

You should receive a structured weekly update summarizing activity, buyer discussions, feedback from the market, next steps, and any issues requiring your input. These updates typically include a pipeline report, status against the timeline, and any obstacles or opportunities that have emerged. The goal is to keep you strategically engaged without being consumed by details.

A few years back, I worked with a founder who had been receiving clear weekly updates from his investment bank throughout the early stages of his sale process. Then, without warning, the weekly emails stopped. He still spoke to the bankers occasionally, but that regular cadence disappeared. When we discussed it, I encouraged him to address it directly. I drafted a firm but respectful message reminding the banker how valuable that weekly summary had been and making it clear that we expected it to resume immediately. The banker apologized, explaining that the holiday season had slowed activity—but that was precisely the point. Even when deal activity is light, communication should not be. Silence creates uncertainty and erodes momentum.

It always amazes me how even highly compensated bankers, who stand to earn millions in fees, can become complacent or lose discipline. Don't blindly trust that just because they're working for you, they are actually working for you. During a sale, discipline matters and a weekly update is not optional. It's a commitment you should insist on and protect.

Investment Bank or Business Broker?

Before we dive deeper into the Core Four, I want to address a common question about who should be on your team. Many business owners wonder whether they need an investment bank or if a business broker might be a better fit. The distinction matters because choosing the wrong advisor can cost you millions during an already complex process.

Business brokers typically work with smaller transactions, usually businesses valued under a million dollars. They operate more like real estate agents for businesses, often working on their own or in small teams. They list your business on marketplaces, handle initial buyer outreach, and facilitate the basics of the transaction. For Main Street businesses like restaurants, retail stores, or small service companies, a business broker can be an efficient and cost-effective choice.

Investment banks specialize in middle market and larger transactions, typically starting around fifteen to twenty million dollars in enterprise value. They bring institutional rigor, deeper market knowledge, and sophisticated deal structuring capabilities. An investment bank will create a detailed marketing memorandum, run a competitive process, and leverage relationships with private equity firms, strategic buyers, and family offices. They understand complex deal structures and have the resources to manage multiple workstreams simultaneously while you continue running your business.

If you are unsure which route makes sense for your situation, start by reaching out to a few investment banks. You will learn quickly whether your company is the right size and complexity for their services. Investment banks are typically candid about fit, and if your business falls outside their target range, they will often point you toward reputable business brokers. Since this book focuses on complex transactions where the Core Four truly makes a difference, we will assume you are working with an investment bank moving forward. The principles still apply if you choose to work with a broker, but the sophistication of your advisory team becomes even more critical as deal complexity increases.

The Trust Paradox

Building a business rewards self-reliance. You made hard calls, trusted your gut, and succeeded without anyone's permission. That independence is a founder's superpower.

But selling requires the opposite. The process demands trust in advisors to navigate unfamiliar territory. An investment banker negotiating terms you don't fully understand. An attorney protecting against risks you can't see. A tax advisor structuring the deal to minimize what you owe.

This feels uncomfortable. These people weren't there in the beginning. They didn't build what you built. Yet now your financial future depends on their expertise.

The truth is advisors who've done this hundreds of times know things you don't. They see patterns that aren't obvious. They anticipate problems that won't surface until it's too late. The best founders recognize when to lead and when to follow.

You built your business by trusting yourself—but selling it requires trusting others with what you've built.

The M&A Attorney – Protection Without Paralysis

If your investment banker is the quarterback driving the field of play, then your M&A attorney is your left tackle, protecting your blind side, absorbing hits you never see, and making sure you cross the goal line intact. A great banker gets you the offer, while a great attorney gets you safely to closing. And in a deal environment where complexity increases with each turn, the attorney's role is not just mechanical—it's strategic.

Don't assume that a business transaction attorney just "reviews documents." They are a gatekeeper to the legal, structural, and financial integrity of your outcome. They comb through hundreds of pages of agreements: asset purchase agreements, stock purchase agreements, disclosure schedules, representations and warranties, indemnification clauses, earnout formulas, escrow mechanics, working capital adjustments, non-competes, transition agreements, and more. They scrutinize language you would never think to question because hidden in one sentence could be a risk worth millions.

They are the ones who spot the vague indemnity clause that shifts unlimited liability onto you. They are the ones who tighten earnout triggers so the buyer can't manipulate targets. They are the ones who fight for caps on post-closing claims, push for reasonable survival periods, and protect you from "gotcha" language buried in definitions. They save you from future disputes by anticipating them in drafting. When they do their job well, the deal closes smoothly, and you sleep at night. When they fail, you learn painful lessons in hindsight, and often do so alone.

The paradox is that the trait that makes great attorneys invaluable, their ability to see risk everywhere, is the same trait that can derail a deal if unchecked. Lawyers are trained to identify problems, not to weigh them. Each sentence becomes a potential liability. Each clause becomes a battlefield. And in service to protecting you, some attorneys unconsciously begin practicing perfection instead of practicing strategy.

Deals typically don't die from one big blow. They die from friction. They die from over-lawyering, from rewriting entire sections out of preference, from turning commercial points into legal crusades, and from losing momentum as weeks stretch into months. I've observed attorneys insist on revisiting agreed-upon business terms simply because they believed they could word them "better." They could, but in doing so they almost killed the deal!

A good attorney protects you. A great attorney protects you and the deal.

They know which risks matter, and which are theoretical. They understand the game isn't to win every clause, but to avoid losing the war. They push on the right terms and concede on the ones without real consequence. They don't make the negotiation adversarial in all directions. They are measured, strategic, and grounded in commercial reality.

And they know their role is not to lead the negotiation. That's your banker's role. The banker drives valuation, structure, and deal terms. The attorney ensures the legal language reflects the economics and protects your interests. Trouble begins the moment those lanes get blurred.

How to Choose a Great M&A Attorney

A foundational mistake sellers make is hiring the attorney who handled their estate plan, corporate formation, or real estate closings. Talent is contextual. The best heart surgeon isn't the person to repair your knee. M&A is its own specialty. The stakes are too high and the nuances too deep to wing it.

When choosing counsel:

- **Look for specialization.** You want an attorney who does business sale transactions full time. "Corporate lawyer" is not specific enough.

- **Ask about deal volume and deal size.** Someone who mostly handles $3 million family business sales may not be the right fit for a $40 million exit and vice-versa.

- **Ask about industry familiarity.** They don't necessarily need to be an expert in your sector, but they need to know the norms.

- **Evaluate communication style.** Do they explain clearly, or make you feel small? The latter will translate directly into friction during closing.

- **Look for commercial judgment.** Ask how they decide when to push and when to let go. Their answer will reveal everything.

Also notice whether they ask about your priorities, personality, and appetite for risk. A great attorney tailors their style to the founder. Some clients want aggressive defense, while others want speed and finality. A mediocre attorney treats every deal the same.

You know you've hired the right counsel when:

- They start by asking about your goals and deal priorities, not showing off legal jargon.

- They explain concepts in plain English, without condescension.

- They tell you not only what the risk is, but how likely it is and whether it's worth fighting over.

- They pick up the phone instead of sending long adversarial memos.

- They collaborate with the banker and other advisors instead of treating them as competition.

- They preserve relationships instead of leaving scorched earth.

Remember, after the sale, you may be working with the buyer for years. You don't want a lawyer who "wins" arguments and loses goodwill. You want someone who keeps momentum and credibility. Closing is not the end. It's the beginning of a transition period, earnout performance period, and integration chapter.

Even great attorneys occasionally get too deep in the weeds. If you see negotiations slowing unnecessarily or arguments erupting over secondary points, it's your job to recalibrate the room. A gentle but firm reminder works wonders. "Let's stay focused on the big picture. We don't need to win every point. We just want to close the deal we want." The attorney's job is to protect you. Your job is to ensure they don't protect you out of a great outcome.

Managing Legal Fees

A great attorney can protect your interests, preserve economic value, and keep a deal alive when negotiations become tense. They are essential. But they also operate in a profession built on billable hours, where each revision, call, and clause has a price attached to it. Most attorneys are honest, skilled advocates, but incentives matter. Without clear expectations, legal bills can balloon shockingly fast.

The key is not to micromanage your attorney, but to manage the process. Start by setting expectations early. Before they begin drafting or reviewing anything, ask for estimated fee ranges by phase— from LOI review and due diligence support to definitive agreement negotiation. You are not demanding fixed pricing; you are establishing transparency. Attorneys operate more efficiently when they know their clients are paying attention.

Next, use your lawyer where they add the most value. Pull them in for negotiation strategy sessions and reviewing key documents, not for every minor call or email. You should be the primary point of communication with the banker and buyer unless a legal issue is being discussed. Buyers appreciate hearing directly from the founder, and it signals confidence, accessibility, and leadership—not to mention keeping your legal meter from spinning unnecessarily.

Finally, recognize and reward pragmatism. The best attorneys know the goal is to close a good deal. That often means winning some points and losing others. That's okay. They focus on risks that matter, not theoretical problems that will never materialize. When your lawyer prioritizes clarity and progress over ego and perfection, acknowledge it. Reinforcing effectiveness encourages more of it.

Legal counsel should not be feared; they should be directed. You are not trying to minimize hours at all costs. You are trying to ensure those hours truly drive outcomes. When attorneys and founders operate as strategic partners instead of adversaries over invoices, legal fees transform from a source of frustration to an investment in a clean, durable, and profitable exit.

Your Tax Advisor – It's Not What You Get, It's What You Keep

When you sell your company, taxes are not a line item at the end of the process—they are a dominating force shaping the outcome. They quietly sit in the background, unseen until the numbers hit paper, and then they can shock you. Depending on how your deal is structured, the IRS and your state can end up taking nearly half of your proceeds. In larger deals, that number can run into the tens of millions of dollars.

Before you get too far into the negotiations, you need to know this: The taxes owed on a business sale are not fixed, they are engineered.

A sale is not like a W-2 paycheck. The way your deal is structured, documented, and timed has an enormous impact on your tax bill. Every decision, from the allocation of purchase price, earnout mechanics, escrow structure, to election type, and even your state of residence, affects the amount owed—sometimes by millions.

The bad news is that taxes can quietly erode a stunning amount of your net proceeds. The good news is that, with the right tax strategist, you can often legally and strategically push that number down dramatically.

However, this is not the right time for your accountant who files your year-end returns or processes payroll. They may be excellent at what they do, but this is a different arena. What you need now is someone who lives and breathes business-exit tax strategy. Someone who speaks in structures, elections, allocation schedules, trust mechanics, charitable vehicles, QSBS exceptions, and after-tax modeling, and who has seen enough transactions to know what to anticipate and how to avoid problems before they exist.

Think of it this way:

- Your investment banker creates value.

- Your attorney protects value.

- Your tax strategist preserves value.

You need all three.

What a Great Tax Strategist Does

A seasoned M&A tax advisor performs four essential functions.

1. They model after-tax outcomes.

A high-caliber advisor will not just quote tax rates. They will model multiple scenarios and show you, in black and white, how different deal structures affect what you ultimately take home. They'll break down:

- Stock sale vs. asset sale outcomes

- All-cash vs. earnout vs. rollover equity comparisons

- Impact of different allocation methods

- Federal vs. state vs. local tax exposure

- Timing differences across tax years

- How charitable structures alter the math

It is one thing to see a $25 million headline number. It is another thing entirely to see $13.7 million hitting your account after taxes, fees, and allocation mechanics. Great tax planning can turn that same $13.7 million into $17.2 million instead, all without changing the buyer's offer. The only thing that changed was the structure.

2. They engineer the transaction for tax efficiency.

In a sale, paperwork is power. Tax language buried inside the purchase agreement (sometimes in what seems like throwaway definitions) determines whether you're taxed at ordinary income rates, capital gains rates, or in some cases not taxed at all (QSBS, CRT structures, etc.). A deal tax expert understands:

- Section 1202 QSBS exclusions

- Installment sale mechanics

- Purchase price allocation between assets, goodwill, and consulting agreements

- State residency rules

- Trust and foundation tools

- Rollover equity tax treatment

- Earnout-specific tax timing

- Passive vs. active classification issues

Your banker negotiates price. Your attorney negotiates legal structure. Your tax strategist negotiates with the tax code.

3. They coordinate timing.

Timing alone can meaningfully change your outcome. For example, selling in December versus January may alter the effective tax year, depending on proceeds, elections, or other liquidity events. Estimated payment schedules shift, depreciation recapture timing matters, and fiscal year vs. calendar year considerations come into play.

A sophisticated advisor will look at:

- Whether you have capital losses to offset gains
- Estimated payment schedules
- Tax-bracket timing
- Pre- and post-sale liquidity planning
- Whether gifting strategies must occur before the binding agreement
- Coordination with trust structures already in place

Tax planning is a calendar strategy as much as a numbers strategy.

4. They prepare you for life after the wire hits.

Once your company sells, you transition from business owner to family CFO—a completely different financial identity. You are no longer building liquidity through operations. You are protecting and deploying liquidity you've already earned.

Your tax strategist guides you through:

- New filing requirements

- Investment structures

- Multi-state considerations

- Tax-efficient withdrawal plans

- Charitable giving plans

- Family wealth structures

- Future gifting and legacy design

They help you shift from offensive owner to defensive wealth steward without losing momentum or accidentally triggering penalties, inefficiencies, or unnecessary audits.

Finding the Right Tax Advisor

You do not need to become an expert in tax law, but you do need an expert next to you. Someone who sits at the table, watches the documents, and speaks up early. Someone who collaborates with your banker and attorney during the term sheet and drafting process, when the leverage is highest and the options are widest.

I have seen owners spend tens of thousands on specialized tax counsel to save millions. That is not an expense. It is one of the highest-ROI investments in the entire exit process. For founders who spent decades grinding to create equity, spending a fraction of a percent to protect a significant portion of the outcome is not a cost. It is stewardship.

The Wealth Advisor – Your Personal CFO

Before the sale, your business was your plan. It was your wealth engine, your safety net, your retirement account, your identity, and your mission, all tied into one entity. You built your financial future inside it. Each reinvested dollar, sleepless night, key hire, and strategic decision was in service of growing the value of the business.

Then the sale happens and overnight, everything changes.

You shift from company-builder to wealth-owner; from having your net worth locked inside an operating business to having it liquid—visible, measurable, and suddenly exposed to market forces, tax decisions, and personal choices.

The business that once structured your life and dictated your financial direction is gone. And now its growth, protection, and purpose becomes the new enterprise. Your money becomes the business, and you become the CEO of that capital.

A great wealth advisor steps in as your personal CFO, as someone who can help you design, manage, and protect the life you worked so hard to create. They help translate liquidity into long-term freedom, security, and meaning. They help you make smart decisions with your capital in the same way you made smart decisions with your company.

This role is too important to be treated casually. It is not about "finding someone to manage investments." It is about choosing the person who will guide you through the sale process and help you steward your life's work. And the best time to bring them into the conversation is when you first start thinking about selling. I've found that this is when I can provide the most value.

Why a Wealth Advisor Matters Before the Exit

Most owners don't realize how much pre-sale planning affects outcome. They think wealth planning begins after the deal closes, but many of the most valuable decisions happen months and sometimes years earlier. A sophisticated advisor collaborates with your tax attorney, CPA, and estate counsel to help optimize the transaction long before closing day.

Here's what a great wealth advisor does before the exit:

1. Helps You Define Your "Freedom Number"

Many business owners don't know how much they truly need, or want, after they sell. They guess. They default to vague phrases like "as much as possible" or "I want to be comfortable." But "as much as possible" isn't a financial plan. It's a hope. It's a feeling. And feelings change. A wealth advisor's job is to turn that uncertainty into clarity by modeling how different lives look and feel, and what each version requires financially.

This is my favorite part of the planning process because it's where the work stops being about spreadsheets and becomes about vision. It's where the founder finally gets to take off the operator hat and start dreaming again, not in terms of business goals, but in terms of life goals. We begin exploring questions like, "What does your ideal life look like when time and money are no longer constraints?" "What would you build, explore, protect, or experience if you didn't have to think about quarterly results ever again?"

From there, we model scenarios. Real, tangible, human scenarios and not just abstract projections. For example, one client dreamed of owning a quiet mountain home where he could hike with his dog, and a modern condo in the city where he and his spouse could enjoy theater, restaurants, and culture. We modeled the costs, taxes, and lifestyle implications of maintaining two homes, plus travel between them. Suddenly, it wasn't only a dream. It was a line item, a timeline, and a plan.

Another client wanted to spend six months sailing around the world with his family. We modeled the boat purchase, maintenance, crew, travel costs, and, most importantly, the opportunity cost of stepping away from active investing during that time. When he saw the numbers clearly, he realized something surprising: He could do it, but not right away. He decided to sail for three months first, as a trial run, and build from there. The dream didn't disappear; it became structured, approachable, and real.

Sometimes, the scenarios are simpler, but just as meaningful. A client wanted to help fund their grandchildren's college tuition, support aging parents, and fly first-class instead of commercial coach. Another wanted to take a sabbatical year and do nothing but participate in cooking courses and language immersion abroad. We modeled each of those lifestyles, stress-tested withdrawal rates, layered in charitable giving goals, and accounted for taxes. In each case, the client walked away with clarity—not because we told them what to want, but because we helped them see what was possible.

A great wealth advisor doesn't start with money, they start with meaning. The capital becomes the tool to build the life you want. Once you see the numbers behind your vision, you stop guessing and start designing.

2. Guides Tax-Efficient Structuring

A wealth advisor doesn't replace your CPA or your tax attorney—they sit beside them. Their job isn't to do the tax work or draft the trust documents, but to ensure everything fits together cohesively. When you sell your business, financial decisions suddenly connect in ways they never had to before. Charitable planning isn't just philanthropy, it becomes a tax strategy. Roth conversions aren't just retirement planning, they become part of how you manage income in the first few post-sale years. Even the simple question of where different investments should live (taxable accounts, retirement accounts) can dramatically change your long-term outcome.

A great advisor helps you think through how money flows after the sale. Where does income come from? How do you structure distributions? When does converting to a Roth IRA make sense? How do you sequence withdrawals to minimize lifetime taxation? They sit with your estate attorney before the deal closes to make sure gifting strategies, family trusts, or legacy vehicles are established while valuations are still favorable. They look ahead, not backward.

Most business owners focus on maximizing the sale price, believing that the biggest headline number equals the biggest win. Sophisticated sellers know better. They know the only number that matters is the one that reaches their account after taxes, fees, and structure. I've watched owners celebrate a $30 million offer, but then discover they would keep less after taxes than if they had taken a well-structured $25 million offer. A great wealth advisor understands this instinctively. They help you focus on getting the deal done, and ensuring it funds your life.

3. Coordinates the Advisory Team

During a business sale, you suddenly find yourself surrounded by specialists: attorneys, CPAs, deal-tax experts, bankers, estate planners, insurance professionals, etc. Each one has mastery in a narrow field. Their expertise is invaluable, but when everyone is focused exclusively on their part of the process, it becomes easy for the big picture to get lost. That's where a great wealth advisor steps in.

A skilled advisor acts as your integrator and orchestrator. They coordinate between your CPA and estate attorney to ensure the tax strategy aligns with trust planning. They make sure your M&A attorney and deal-tax strategist are aligned on structure and language. They stay in contact with your banker, anticipate liquidity timing and cash-flow needs, and check in with your asset-protection and insurance professionals to ensure your coverage evolves as your wealth does. They are the connective tissue between experts who otherwise might never speak directly.

Another benefit is that your wealth advisor can play bad cop when needed. Deals are emotional as people get protective, tense, and frustrated. You're trying to preserve relationships, reputation, and momentum, but sometimes you need someone who can apply pressure without jeopardizing your standing. Remember the earlier story about the financial advisor who referred a banker because he was quietly getting a cut of the deal? Well, that banker ended up phoning it in with slow updates, weak effort, and no urgency. My client was furious, but didn't want to be the one to blow things up. That's where I stepped in. I had the tough conversations, and I demanded accountability. I lit a fire under their team. Fortunately, it worked without my client having to be the "bad guy".

While your banker is focused on closing the transaction, your wealth advisor is building the world you will step into afterward. They help you shift from running a business to managing wealth, which are two completely different disciplines. They design cash-flow systems, help prioritize estate and tax planning, and build investment structures around your new life, not your old obligations.

4. Acts as an Emotional Anchor

Deal processes are emotional in ways spreadsheets can't measure. Selling a business is not just a financial transaction; it is a psychological transition. For years, and sometimes decades, your identity, purpose, and confidence have been tied to building and leading your company. Entering a sale process means confronting the reality that you are letting go of something that has defined you. Excitement and pride show up, but so do uncertainty, worry, and moments of doubt.

During a sale, emotions rarely stay quiet. One day, the deal feels unstoppable. Then something shifts. A diligence request adds stress, legal language becomes a battle, and a buyer questions projections or tries to re-trade the deal. A week of silence can send your imagination into overdrive. As fatigue sets in, even confident owners can find themselves thinking, "Why am I putting myself through this?" or "Maybe I should walk away." A seasoned advisor helps keep things steady and bring perspective when the process becomes overwhelming, and they help you respond thoughtfully instead of reacting emotionally.

Although I list this role last, I genuinely believe it may be the most important contribution I make during a sale. I have a master's degree in psychology and was trained as a therapist, so perhaps I lean into this more than most wealth advisors. But I have seen how often a deal is won or lost not because of numbers, but because of mindset. Selling a company stretches one's identity, confidence, patience, energy, and sense of control. Strategies and structures matter, but emotional clarity matters almost as much. My job is not only to help clients negotiate and structure the exit, but also to help them stay grounded, avoid emotional decision-making, and maintain a sense of strength and purpose throughout the process.

Why a Wealth Advisor Matters After the Exit

The day after closing is euphoric, and then surprisingly quiet. One moment, your life is filled with meetings, responsibilities, urgency, and purpose. The next, the calls slow, the inbox quiets, and the familiar rhythm you lived in for years disappears. Celebration is followed by a pause that many owners are not prepared for. Relief arrives, but so do uncertainty, boredom, and the question, "Now what?"

This is where a wealth advisor becomes essential. A major liquidity event is not just a financial transition, but also a psychological one. How you navigate the first twelve to twenty-four months after a sale can shape the rest of your life.

Protect First, Grow Second

In my book, *The Sudden Wealth Solution*, I wrote that the goal after a windfall is not to get rich—it is to stay rich. After a sale, many founders feel an itch to deploy capital quickly. There is excitement, curiosity, and opportunity everywhere. A great advisor slows the world down enough for you to make wise decisions. The priority is not aggressive growth, but secure footing, and that begins with liquidity, diversification, and a thoughtful pace. It means structuring income so your new life is supported, not strained. It means protecting assets so a single mistake doesn't undo decades of effort. You've already built the wealth, now you need to preserve it while you adapt to your new reality.

Plan for Your Life, not Just Your Money

Winning financially and living well are not the same thing. Many wealthy people struggle not because they invest poorly, but because they lack structure and clarity. A wealth advisor helps build a framework for spending, cash flow, and financial discipline so you don't drift. They help create buckets of money with purpose: liquid reserves, long-term growth capital, income generators, and opportunity funds. Money is only empowering when it is organized and intentional. Without a plan, wealth can become confusing and overwhelming. With one, it becomes fuel.

Turn Liquidity into Purpose

A sale gives you money, but it also gives you space, and space without purpose can feel empty. A wealth advisor helps you explore what fulfillment looks like now, without rushing you into decisions. They ask deeper questions. "What kind of life do you want to build now that you are no longer running a company?" "How do you want to spend your days?" "What relationships, pursuits, and contributions matter most?" The goal is not to fill your time, but to direct it with intention so wealth supports meaning, not restlessness.

Manage Risk with Intelligence

Sudden wealth attracts opportunity—and noise. You will hear from enthusiastic investors, founders, friends, and acquaintances with deals. A wealth advisor plays the role of filter and sparring partner—not to shut down ideas, but to evaluate them rationally. They bring discipline, frameworks, and perspective when excitement runs high. Protecting your capital is about knowing when to say yes and when to say no.

Build Legacy Intentionally

Legacy is not simply what you leave behind. It is also what continues because of you. A thoughtful advisor helps translate wealth into structure: estate plans, trusts, charitable vehicles, and multi-generational strategies. They help you teach values alongside wealth, so the next generation is equipped rather than overwhelmed. Wealth can be a gift or a burden. With guidance, it becomes a foundation your family can build on.

Choosing the Right Wealth Advisor

Not all wealth advisors are created equal, and the industry does a poor job of helping you tell them apart. Titles are confusing. Compensation structures are opaque. Conflicts of interest are common. Without knowing what to look for, you are likely to choose based on personality or a referral from a friend rather than on the factors that actually matter.

This is a high-stakes decision. The difference between the best advisors and the rest can mean millions of dollars over your lifetime. A great advisor will help you minimize taxes, avoid costly mistakes, and build a portfolio that supports the life you want. A mediocre one will collect fees while delivering generic advice. A bad one can do real damage through negligence, conflicts of interest, or outright fraud.

The Fiduciary Question

The single most important question to ask any prospective wealth advisor is whether they are a fiduciary. A fiduciary is legally and ethically bound to act in your best interest at all times. This sounds obvious, but many financial professionals operate under a different standard called "suitability," which only requires them to recommend products that are appropriate for your situation. Appropriate is not the same as optimal. An advisor operating under the suitability standard can legally recommend an investment that pays them a higher commission even if a lower-cost alternative would serve you better.

When you ask about fiduciary status, listen carefully to the answer. It should be a simple yes or no. If the advisor hedges or explains that they are "sometimes" a fiduciary, that is a red flag. You want someone who is always a fiduciary, in every interaction, with no exceptions.

Understanding How They Get Paid

Advisor compensation directly affects the advice you receive. There are several ways advisors earn their money, and each creates different incentives.

Fee-only advisors charge you directly for their services, either as a percentage of assets under management, a flat annual fee, or an hourly rate. They do not receive commissions from product companies. This structure tends to create the fewest conflicts of interest because the advisor's income is not tied to selling you specific products.

Fee-based advisors charge fees but also earn commissions on certain products like insurance, annuities, or mutual funds. This dual compensation creates potential conflicts. The advisor might recommend a product partly because it pays them a commission rather than because it is the best choice for you.

Commission-only advisors earn their entire income from selling products. Every recommendation they make generates revenue for them. This model creates the most significant conflicts of interest and is generally not recommended for someone managing substantial post-sale wealth.

Ask for complete transparency about all forms of compensation, including any underlying investment fees. A trustworthy advisor will have no problem providing this information clearly and completely.

Verifying Credentials and Experience

The financial industry is littered with impressive-sounding titles and designations. Some carry real weight. Others require little more than a weekend seminar and a check. The Certified Financial Planner® designation requires extensive coursework, thousands of hours of experience, a comprehensive examination, and ongoing continuing education. It represents broad competence in financial planning, tax planning, estate planning, and investment management.

Experience matters tremendously, but the right kind of experience matters even more. An advisor who has spent their career working with business owners and sudden wealth recipients will understand your situation in ways that a generalist never could. Ask how many clients they have helped through business sales. Ask what percentage of their practice involves clients like you. The answers will tell you whether you are a good fit or just another account.

Checking Their Record

Before hiring any advisor, check their regulatory history. Every registered investment advisor must file a document called Form ADV with the Securities and Exchange Commission. This form discloses how the advisor is compensated, what services they offer, and whether they have faced any disciplinary actions, customer complaints, or regulatory sanctions. You can access this information for free through the SEC's Investment Adviser Public Disclosure website. If the advisor also holds a brokerage license, check FINRA's BrokerCheck database for additional background information. A clean record is the minimum requirement. Multiple complaints or disciplinary actions should disqualify an advisor immediately, no matter how impressive their credentials.

The Custodian Question

Your advisor should never hold your money directly. Instead, your assets should be held by a third-party custodian, typically a major brokerage firm like Schwab, Fidelity, or Vanguard. This separation of duties is a fundamental protection against fraud.

When Bernie Madoff ran his Ponzi scheme, he served as both the investment manager and the custodian of client assets. This allowed him to fabricate statements and hide his crimes for decades. With a proper third-party custodian, you receive independent account statements directly from the brokerage firm. You can log in and verify your holdings at any time. The advisor can manage your investments, but they cannot simply withdraw funds or manufacture fictitious returns.

Ask every prospective advisor who holds your assets. If the answer is anything other than a well-known, independent custodian, walk away.

Beyond the Technical

Credentials and compensation structures matter, but they do not tell the whole story. After you have confirmed that an advisor is a fiduciary with transparent fees and proper custodial arrangements, you still need to assess the relationship itself.

Did they ask about your goals before discussing their services? Did they seem genuinely curious about what you want from life after the sale, or were they primarily interested in the size of your liquidity event? Did they speak in plain language or hide behind jargon? Did you feel heard and respected, or did you feel like a transaction?

The relationship with your wealth advisor may last decades. You will share sensitive information about your family, your fears, your hopes, and your finances. You need someone you trust completely, someone who will tell you hard truths when necessary, someone who genuinely cares about your wellbeing beyond the fees they earn.

Your company may have taken decades to build. The wealth it generates deserves protection from people who have spent their careers learning how to preserve and grow it. Take your time. Ask hard questions. Trust your instincts. The right advisor is out there, and finding them is one of the most important decisions you will make after the sale.

Managing Your Team – When to Drive and When to Ride

Selling your business creates an interesting power dynamic. On one hand, it's your money, your life, and your future. You built this company, you're hiring the team, and, ultimately, you call the shots. You're the driver. On the other hand, most business owners haven't sold a company before. They may not be comfortable navigating complex tax law, deal structures, or post-sale financial strategies. In those moments, you have to rely on your team to guide you. You're the passenger.

Some owners swing too far to one side. They throw their hands up and hand over all control because they feel overwhelmed. Others try to stay in the driver's seat for everything, challenging recommendations and micromanaging details. Both approaches can be disastrous. The key is understanding when to drive and when to ride.

Be the driver when defining your goals, values, and vision. Well-meaning advisors may sometimes prioritize form over function, designing complex structures that are technically correct but ignore what really matters to you—simplicity, clarity, and peace of mind. Don't be dazzled by technical jargon. Be vocal about what you want your wealth to accomplish and what kind of life you want after the sale.

Also be the driver when setting expectations for your team. Your advisors work for you. It doesn't matter how many credentials they have, you are the client. You set the tone for communication. Establish how often you'll meet, how you want updates, and how clearly you expect things explained. And always ask questions. Every question you have is valid and deserves an answer. What's "obvious" to your advisors might be brand new to you.

But don't try to drive everywhere. You're paying your team for their expertise, so let them use it. Give them space to collaborate, debate, and strategize. Keep an open mind to their perspectives and let them do what they do best. The best outcomes happen when the owner paints the big picture about what they want their life to look like and lets their team design the roadmap to get there. Focus on the destination. Let your team handle the route.

Your Role in the Process

Even with a great banker, you can't just hand over the keys. This is your company, your story, and likely your one shot at getting it right. Your banker might manage dozens of deals in a year, but you only sell your company once. For them, it's a transaction. For you, it's the culmination of decades of work, risk, and sacrifice. No one can represent the heart of your business better than you.

You can't outsource your passion. You know what makes it special in a way no outsider ever will. Your banker can manage process, valuation, and buyers, but you must bring the soul. Review the CIM carefully. Make sure the story captures your company's culture, values, and vision. Add your perspective, your language, and your truth. A well-written CIM should read like both a financial document and a narrative of belief about what your company stands for and where it can go.

Most bankers are brilliant with numbers, but not with emotions. They'll describe your company logically—market position, EBITDA growth, margins—but logic doesn't sell, emotion does. Buyers are human. They want to feel what makes your business different. They want to understand not only how it operates, but also why it matters. You can't leave that to a spreadsheet or bullet points.

Stay involved. Stay visible. Your presence sends a message to buyers that you still care deeply about what you've built, and that energy is contagious. When you show up with conviction, buyers will feel it. They start to believe not just in the numbers, but in the future.

The Delegation Paradox

Hiring a deal team doesn't mean stepping back. It means stepping into a different role. You hire experts so you don't have to master M&A law, negotiate like a banker, or structure tax-efficient deals. But you can't abdicate your leadership entirely.

Some sellers hire their teams and then disappear, assuming the professionals will handle everything. They show up for signatures and expect results. But disconnected sellers make weak decisions. They don't understand the tradeoffs. They can't respond quickly when negotiations shift.

Other sellers hire experts, but then micromanage every detail, second-guessing advice and slowing progress. They hire a team, but won't let the team do its job.

The best approach is active partnership. You stay engaged on strategy and key decisions, trust your team on tactics and execution, and provide the context they need. They provide the expertise you don't have.

You can't sell your business alone—but you also can't let others sell it without you.

The "Best Money You'll Ever Spend" Principle

Founders understand return on investment instinctively. As a business owner, you've analyzed capital allocation, weighed risk against reward, and decided when to spend money to make more of it. The sale of your business should be treated the same way. Advisory fees are not just expenses. They are strategic investments in protecting and maximizing the value of the asset you spent a career building. The right team does not cost you money. The right team makes you money.

Think about the math. A strong investment banker who increases your sale price by 10 percent on a $30 million deal has effectively put $3 million in your pocket. A tax expert who reduces your total tax burden by just 5 percent has preserved $1.5 million for your family instead of sending it to the government. A skilled attorney who structures representations, warranties, and indemnifications correctly might prevent a post-closing dispute that saves you six figures in legal fees and months of mental strain. And a wealth advisor who designs a disciplined plan for safeguarding and growing your proceeds may protect your financial independence for the rest of your life. These are not small numbers—they are life-changing sums.

Once you start viewing expertise through the lens of leverage, it becomes obvious that trying to save money by hiring mediocre advisors is a false economy. When the stakes are high, you want precision, experience, judgment, and calm decision-making. The sale of your business has long-term consequences. And the difference between a clean outcome and a catastrophic one often comes down to the quality of the professionals guiding you.

The principle is simple. You did not build a valuable company by cutting corners, so don't dismantle your life's work by doing it now.

When you are dealing with the monetization of decades of effort, the goal is not to find the cheapest advisors, but to secure the smartest, most capable, and most aligned partners you can. In the context of a multi-million-dollar transaction, paying for excellence is not a luxury—it is the purest and most rational investment you will ever make.

Chapter Exit

Assembling your deal team isn't about filling seats around a conference table. It's about building the foundation for what comes next. These are the people who will protect you, guide you, and push you when you're too tired to keep fighting for another clause, another dollar, and another inch. They are your buffer and your leverage. The sale process can be long, emotional, and unpredictable, but with the right team beside you, you can move through it strategically instead of reactively. With the wrong team, you'll find yourself second-guessing decisions, feeling outmatched, and losing control of your own deal.

Now that you've built your Core Four, it's time to put them to work. The next phase is where things start moving fast: teasers, NDAs, CIMs, management meetings, LOIs, due diligence, and the definitive purchase agreement. Each stage has its own traps, timing, and tension points. This is where experience pays off and preparation meets reality.

In the next chapter, we'll break down the mechanics of the deal—the moving parts that determine your outcome. You'll learn what each step really looks like, how to keep control of the process without micromanaging it, and how to anticipate what's coming before it lands. Because once you're in motion, there's no slowing down. Understanding how the process flows is what separates calm, confident sellers from the ones who get swallowed by it.

CHAPTER 4:

MASTER THE TRANSACTION

Learn the Mechanics and Psychology of the Sale

I was once introduced to a woman who had built a thriving medical device company and was in the early stages of thinking about a sale. When we sat down for our first meeting, she told me she hadn't slept well in over a month. It wasn't because the business was struggling or she had doubts about selling. What kept her awake was that she had "No f-ing idea where to start!" (her words). She didn't know what the process looked like, how long it would take, or what pitfalls to avoid.

So she did what any driven entrepreneur would do—she listened to podcasts, watched YouTube videos, read deal books, and, for reasons she couldn't quite explain, even watched the movie *Wall Street*, hoping to glean some insight into how deals actually work. After all of that, she said she felt "even dumber" (again, her words).

What made her story so striking is that this wasn't someone who crumbled under pressure. By day, she was an ER doctor at an urban trauma center. She had no problem keeping her cool while removing bullets from shooting victims and treating knife wounds. She was smart, controlled, and fearless—a real-life badass in the ER! And yet when it came to selling her company, she felt completely lost and disoriented.

We spent an hour together that day. I walked her through the entire process—stage by stage, milestone by milestone. I explained what happens from the moment you decide to sell to the day the money reaches your account. I told her about teasers, management meetings, LOIs, due diligence, and what a typical deal looks like. I showed her where leverage lives, where it shifts, and how to protect it. By the end of the conversation, she wasn't anxious anymore and she'd regained her ER swagger. She successfully sold her company, and she is still a client. When I see it's her calling, I'll often answer, "Gordon Gekko."

Everything we talked about in that meeting is what you'll learn in this chapter. Once you understand it, you can master two critical parts of the transaction: the *mechanics* of the sale and the *psychology* of the sale.

PART A: THE MECHANICS OF THE SALE

Understanding how deals actually work—from the first teaser to the final wire—will give you the clarity and confidence to navigate each stage strategically.

The Business Sale Process – Understanding the Funnel

Think of the sale process like a funnel, wide at the top and narrow at the bottom. In the beginning, dozens or even hundreds of potential buyers may be contacted. Your banker's job is to cast a wide net, generate interest, and filter out those who aren't serious or financially capable. At this stage, it's about awareness and intrigue. Buyers get a teaser—a high-level snapshot of your company. Hopefully it's enough to spark curiosity but not reveal your identity. Those who want to learn more sign an NDA and move deeper into the funnel.

As the process moves forward, the pool narrows quickly. Most buyers do not pass because of problems with your business. They bow out due to fit, strategy, timing, capital constraints, or internal priorities. That is not rejection; it is normal deal flow.

Don't hold me to these numbers, because each industry and deal are different, but a typical buyer pipeline might look something like this:

Teaser sent: 200-1,000+ potential buyers receive an anonymous teaser.

NDAs signed / CIM access: 50-200+ review the full CIM.

Initial passes: ~100 decline after seeing details such as size, geography, or strategic fit.

Management calls: 5-20 request calls or virtual meetings.

In-person meetings: 3-15 invest time to visit and go deeper.

Letters of intent: 3-10 submit formal offers.

Final buyer: One signs the purchase agreement and closes.

The goal is to attract a handful of serious, well-capitalized buyers who understand your business, value what you have built, and can close. When you grasp this dynamic, you do not panic when buyers fall away. You stay focused on the right buyers, maintain momentum, and let the process do its work.

All deals are different, but here is the process most follow:

Teaser → Non-Disclosure Agreement → Confidential Information Memorandum → Management Meetings → Letter of Intent → Due Diligence → Definitive Purchase Agreement → Wire

Milestones vs. Faux Finish Lines

Selling your business is a long, complex journey. It can feel endless if you don't break it into manageable stages. The smartest sellers set milestones for each major step: hiring the investment bank, completing the CIM, signing the LOI, finishing due diligence, and finally closing. Each of these phases is a victory in its own right, and celebrating them helps you stay motivated and maintain perspective. Whether that's a nice dinner out, a weekend off, or pausing to acknowledge the progress you've made, these small moments of recognition are vital for your energy and sanity.

But here's where many sellers get tripped up—what I call faux finish lines. These are moments that feel like the end of the race, but they're really just checkpoints. You've spent weeks negotiating the LOI, and when it's signed, it feels like the deal is done. It's not. You've only reached the halfway mark, and due diligence (which is the most demanding and emotionally draining part) is about to begin. Faux finish lines lull you into thinking you can relax, which can lead to costly mistakes or burnout when the next phase kicks in. The key is to always know where you are in the overall process and to pace yourself like a marathoner, not a sprinter. Celebrate? Yes! But keep your eyes on the real finish line.

Phase 1: Generating Interest

The Teaser – Your Movie Trailer

A teaser is a short, anonymous summary of your company that highlights the opportunity without revealing your name. Think of it as the movie trailer for your business. Have you ever watched a movie trailer, and it is so long that when you finish it feels like you've seen the entire movie? This is what you want to avoid.

The goal with the teaser is to generate intrigue so potential buyers ask for more information. It's not to sell the company. I remember working on one teaser with a client, and their banker wanted to add more and more information. The teaser got so long that it lost its punch. Two words that will deflate the teaser are "What about...." If you printed it and can't staple it, it's too long. Trust me when I say less is more at this stage.

So what should be in your teaser? It depends on your industry, but it should provide a short overview of your company, present financial information such as revenue or net income, and paint an exciting future. Most teasers are a few pages. Don't be afraid to use graphics and visuals, but PLEASE do not use stock photography or clip art (I've seen bankers try!). Instead, get a good graphic designer if your banker is struggling. Don't spend $100 million making a movie and $100 on the trailer.

Non-Disclosure Agreement (NDA)

Interested buyers who want more information will sign an NDA, which is usually a simple document that basically prevents a buyer from sharing any information they learn about your company with others. Is an NDA foolproof? Not at all. This is why it is important for you to be aware of who is getting more detailed information on your company. I've had bankers ready to send confidential information on a client's company to a competitor. The bankers don't know your industry and competitors like you do. All they see is an interested buyer who wants more information, but you may recognize a scheming competitor who wants to peek under the hood to get an edge.

The Confidential Information Memorandum (CIM or the "Deck")

A CIM is the centerpiece of your company's sale process—it's the primary document potential buyers use to understand your business. You may hear it called the "pitch deck" or sometimes the "deck."

Created by your investment banker, the CIM tells the story of your company: what it does, how it makes money, why it's valuable, and what opportunities lie ahead. Like the teaser, the CIM is designed to generate interest and advance buyers to the next stage. It helps them decide whether to move forward with a video call or meeting or drop out of the process. The CIM blends sales pitch with due diligence, combining marketing, storytelling, and analysis.

A typical CIM includes an overview of the business, its history, products or services, market positioning, and competitive landscape. It also details the company's financial performance (usually three to five years of historical statements and several years of projections), along with key metrics like revenue growth, EBITDA margins, and customer concentration. Operational information, such as management bios, key contracts, intellectual property, and facilities, are also included. The best CIMs go beyond data. They weave a narrative around your company's strengths, culture, and future potential, outlining why a buyer should be excited to own it.

In practice, the CIM is one of the most important marketing tools in the entire business sale process. It gives potential buyers a comprehensive look at your company, saving time by answering many of their early questions. Buyers use it to decide if your business fits their investment criteria, how much it might be worth, and whether it's worth pursuing further. For serious buyers, it becomes the foundation for financial models, valuation analysis, and initial offers (LOIs). In short, the CIM sets the tone and expectations for every discussion that follows.

For you as a seller, this document is a reflection of your life's work and it needs to shine. Don't assume your banker will capture your company's essence perfectly on their own. You may have spent 30 years building your company, but your banker has only known it for 30 days. They are usually good at nailing industry trends and financials, but they often miss the mark on talking about opportunities and selling the future. You should review each section. Add your voice, making sure it feels authentic, not generic. The CIM is the market's first impression of you. Done right, it positions your business as an attractive, credible, and exciting opportunity. Done poorly, it can undersell your company's true potential.

Many sellers face a disconnect. When you sell, you naturally focus on what you've built—the history, the achievements, and the blood, sweat, and tears. You see the company's worth through the lens of what it was. Buyers, on the other hand, focus on what's ahead—growth, scalability, and future potential. Buyers value it for what it could be. To bridge that gap, you need to tell a future-focused story in your CIM, highlighting what's next, new markets, untapped opportunities, and potential synergies.

The best sellers treat the CIM like a marketing campaign for their legacy—because that's exactly what it is.

Management Meetings – Showtime

If the CIM did its job, it will have filtered the buyer pool down to the serious contenders with genuine interest, strategic fit, and financial capacity. The goal isn't to attract every buyer; it's to attract the right buyers. In a typical process, hundreds of buyers may sign an NDA and review your CIM, but only a fraction will take the next step and request a management meeting.

At this stage, you're no longer selling information. You're selling confidence, credibility, and culture. The management meeting is the first time buyers see the face and hear the voice behind the business. It's your chance to bring the numbers and narrative to life and to show not only what the company does, but why it's special. Buyers want to see your leadership in action. They're evaluating your energy, vision, command of the business, and attitude about the future. Think of it as a job interview where the position you're applying for is the person they're willing to write an eight-figure check to. Your investment banker will be on these calls, too. They'll brief you beforehand, manage introductions, and sometimes moderate. But remember this: Every call is showtime, and every meeting counts.

The biggest mistake sellers make is by treating these meetings as routine. After a handful of them, fatigue can set in. The same questions, the same slides, and the same story. Sellers start phoning it in, assuming they can tell who's serious and who isn't. Don't do it. I've seen buyers everyone dismissed as "tire kickers" end up closing the deal. You never know which conversation will turn into a signed LOI. Each interaction is an audition for your company's future.

The way you show up matters. Bring energy, clarity, and enthusiasm to each conversation. Tell your story like it's the first time you've ever told it. Buyers aren't only evaluating your numbers, they're evaluating you. They want to see belief, conviction, and purpose.

Approach each meeting like Bruce Springsteen approaches each concert. He famously said, "You know, tonight is tonight, and what you do tonight, you don't make up for tomorrow, and you don't ride on what you did last night. I always keep in mind that you only have one chance." Again, you never know who's going to fall in love with your company.

Preparation is key. Review the buyer's background before the call. Rehearse your talking points. Know your numbers cold. Have stories ready that demonstrate your company's resilience, growth potential, and culture. And above all, let your passion show. Buyers can read financials, but they can't read belief. They need to feel it from you. This is your moment to make them see what you see. When you combine authenticity with preparation, you turn a management meeting into momentum—and momentum closes deals.

Selling your company becomes a full-time job, but you still have a company to run! And here is the trap. The more available you are, the more your business suffers. The more you protect your time, the more you risk alienating buyers. The solution is disciplined screening. Think twice before meeting a prospective buyer in person without at least one or two calls first. A video call costs you an hour. An in-person visit costs you a day. Reserve your days for buyers who have earned them.

Phase 2: Letters of Intent (LOIs)

After weeks or months of conversations, management meetings, and data sharing, you'll finally reach the milestone all sellers anticipate: receiving one or more LOIs. These are offers for your company. This is where the proverbial rubber meets the road. All the late nights wondering what your company is worth and speculation about valuation with your investment banker meets reality.

It's an exciting milestone. An LOI is the buyer's way of saying, "We're serious." But it's also where things start to get real and complicated.

Many business owners think of the LOI as a formality, a placeholder before the "real" contract. But make no mistake: While the LOI may not be legally binding, it's psychologically binding. It sets the tone, the framework, and, in many ways, the moral precedent for everything that follows.

A good LOI acts like the architectural blueprint for your deal. It outlines the price, structure, timeline, and key terms that will eventually make their way into the definitive purchase agreement. Even though lawyers will later refine the details, those first brushstrokes matter. Once an expectation is set in writing, it's hard to erase.

I've had buyers reference LOI terms long after the final agreement was signed, sometimes even during post-close disputes. "It's right there in the LOI," they'll argue, as if it were carved in stone. So while the LOI isn't technically enforceable, it can carry surprising weight in how both parties interpret intent and fairness later on.

Your job is not just to get an LOI—it's to get the right LOI.

IOI vs. LOI: Choosing Your Sale Process Strategy

One quick note before we go further into the LOI stage. Depending on your investment bank's strategy and the nature of your deal, you might encounter an additional step before Letters of Intent ever hit your desk. Some banks request buyers proceed directly to a Letter of Intent while others implement a phased process beginning with Indications of Interest (IOI). Neither approach is inherently superior, as each offers distinct advantages depending on your transaction circumstances, business nature, and buyer pool composition.

The IOI strategy serves as a filtering mechanism in complex sale processes, particularly when dealing with a large pool of potential acquirers. When an investment bank markets a business to dozens or even hundreds of prospective buyers, requiring immediate LOIs would be impractical since LOIs are detailed transaction proposals that buyers refuse to submit without substantial diligence work, including management meetings and access to detailed operational data. The IOI phase solves this coordination problem by establishing a mid-stage checkpoint where buyers submit preliminary bids based on the CIM and initial bank discussions, allowing the investment bank and seller to identify which groups demonstrate genuine interest and offer valuation ranges that merit further conversation. This winnowing process enables everyone to focus on perhaps five to ten finalists rather than accommodating dozens of potential acquirers who may lack strategic fit, financial capacity, or genuine commitment. The alternative approach of accepting LOIs immediately after initial interest offers compelling benefits in certain situations, as going directly to LOI can accelerate the transaction timeline significantly and works particularly well when you have a small, pre-identified group of logical buyers or when speed is a priority. Your investment bank will evaluate factors such as the likely buyer universe, current market conditions, your business complexity, your timing preferences, and competitive dynamics to recommend the approach that will most effectively achieve your goals, and trusting their expertise on process strategy is essential.

A Typical Offer

Every LOI looks a little different. It is shaped by your industry, the type of buyer, and the unique story of your company. But while each deal has its nuances, it helps to have a general sense of what "normal" looks like before the first offer lands in your inbox. One of the most grounding things an owner can do is understand the basic anatomy of an offer. Not the fantasy version whispered about at industry conferences, but the real-world structure of how buyers actually frame value and payment.

Most owners I work with are extraordinary at what they do. They know their industries inside and out, but when it comes to selling their companies, they're often flying blind. That's not a knock; it's completely natural. You only sell a business once, maybe twice in a lifetime. You might know how to negotiate with suppliers, land clients, or structure partnerships, but selling a company is a different game with different rules. This is why having a baseline understanding of what a legitimate offer looks like can be so empowering. It shifts the conversation from mystery to strategy.

Typically, a buyer will value your company based on a multiple of its net earnings. Most commonly, that's EBITDA. While we've looked at this in detail previously, it's worth repeating: earnings before interest, taxes, depreciation, and amortization. Think of EBITDA as a proxy for your company's true operating performance. The cleaner and stronger it is, the more attractive your business looks. Some industries use revenue multiples or other performance metrics, especially for high-growth or recurring-revenue models, but EBITDA remains the most common benchmark.

What does that look like in practice? In many industries, valuation multiples range anywhere from three times to twenty times EBITDA—and sometimes higher if the company is large, growing fast, or has something special buyers are competing for. Let's say your business generates $10 million in EBITDA, and similar companies in your industry typically sell for eight to twelve times. Because you've done the work outlined in this book by preparing before the deal, strengthening both your company and you, you don't only attract average buyers. You create competition. And that competition translates to an offer on the high end of that range: twelve times EBITDA, or $120 million.

That number feels great, but it's only the starting point. How that $120 million is structured matters as much as the number itself. In most cases, a deal will be split among three main components: upfront cash, equity rollover, and an earnout. Each serves a different purpose. The cash is immediate liquidity—the tangible reward for years of risk and effort. The equity rollover represents your continued investment in the new, combined company and your "second bite at the apple." The earnout is the contingent piece, which is typically tied to performance over the next few years.

In our example, let's assume the buyer offers 60 percent upfront in cash, 20 percent in rollover equity, and 20 percent as an earnout spread over three years. On paper, that looks like $72 million wired at closing, $24 million rolled into the new company, and another potential $24 million if future targets are met. That sounds impressive—and it is—but as you'll learn in the coming sections, each component comes with its own risks, tax implications, and emotional challenges. The upfront cash is certain. The value of the rollover depends on someone else's leadership. The earnout depends on performance you may no longer control.

The LOI Paradox

After months of work, you finally receive an LOI. It feels like you've reached the finish line. You negotiated a price. The buyer committed. You "have a deal."

But signing the LOI isn't the end—it's the beginning of when the real deal-making starts. And the moment you sign, the power dynamic flips. Before the LOI, you controlled the process. You had multiple buyers competing. You could walk away. You had leverage.

After you sign, the buyer gains control. They have exclusivity. They begin due diligence. They start finding issues, asking for adjustments, and requesting concessions. You've already invested months. You've told key employees. You've mentally moved on. Walking away now feels impossible.

This is why what you negotiate before the LOI matters so much. The price, the structure, the earnout terms, and the reps and warranties are much easier to negotiate when you have leverage than after you've given it away.

The LOI feels like the deal is done—but it's just the moment when leverage shifts from you to the buyer.

Decoding the LOI

Think of the LOI as an "agreement to agree." It captures the main economic and structural elements of the deal, including the purchase price, timing, asset or stock sale, potential earnouts, equity rollovers, employment terms, and key contingencies.

But while most of the LOI's terms are nonbinding, the exclusivity clause is almost always binding. Once you sign, you agree not to negotiate with anyone else for a specified period (usually sixty to ninety days). During that time, you're effectively "off the market." You should use the LOI stage to test and compare offers before exclusivity begins. It's one of the last times in the entire process when you hold real influence.

I always recommend that sellers identify their top three or four must-have issues and push for those during the LOI phase. Maybe it's the total price, the earnout structure, your ongoing role, or how your employees will be treated. Whatever those priorities are, raise them early. (In Chapter 5, I'll give you a complete framework for mapping your priorities before you ever sit down at the table.)

Why? Because you can still negotiate multiple LOIs at once. You can see how different buyers respond to your requests, how flexible they are, and how they behave under pressure. This tells you more about the buyer than any spreadsheet ever could. Once you sign exclusivity, the dynamic flips and the buyer controls the process, and your negotiating leverage drops dramatically. So make the most of this moment.

The Two Types of LOIs

Not all LOIs are created equal. In fact, they tend to fall into two distinct categories.

Detailed LOIs. These are where the buyer invests serious time in specifying every term, condition, and assumption.

High-level LOIs. These summarize the broad strokes, and defer details until due diligence.

Each type has its place, and understanding which approach fits your situation is critical.

Detailed LOIs are great when you have multiple strong offers. If two or more buyers are close in price and structure, push for as much detail as possible before you commit. This gives you the ability to negotiate key points while you still have competition. A detailed LOI also helps prevent surprises later. The more you agree on now, the less friction you'll face when attorneys start drafting the definitive agreements.

However, there's a tradeoff. Detailed LOIs take time to negotiate, and they can stall momentum if over-engineered. Too many revisions, and the buyer may lose enthusiasm or start looking elsewhere.

On the other hand, high-level LOIs are better suited when you have only one serious offer on the table. In that case, it's okay to move quickly with a simpler LOI that outlines the headline terms such as price, structure, and timing, and leaves the rest for later. The key is to recognize your leverage. When competition is strong, go deep. When it's not, go fast.

Why Buyer Valuations Vary So Wildly

Throughout the sale process, from initial expressions of interest through formal letters of intent, prepare yourself for what often feels like whiplash when offers start arriving. You might receive ten proposals with valuations that range from $15 million to $30 million, and it's not uncommon to see some bids coming in at literally half of what others are proposing. This dramatic spread can feel personal, as if the low bidders are insulting what you've built or questioning your business acumen. But the reality is far more mundane and has nothing to do with your company's actual worth. I recently worked with a client who owned a specialized services company. The lowest offer came in at 5.9x EBITDA while the highest was 11.5x EBITDA. We're talking about a valuation difference between $25 million and $55 million. Every potential buyer has their own valuation methodology, their own thesis about what they can do with your business after they acquire it, and their own risk tolerance. Some groups are conservative by nature or policy, assigning lower multiples because they're skeptical about their ability to grow your business or integrate it smoothly into their operations. Others are more optimistic, perhaps because they see specific synergies with their existing portfolio companies or believe they have operational expertise that will unlock additional value. Some are strategic buyers who can realize cost savings you never could as a standalone business, while others are financial buyers focused purely on cash flow multiples. The wide range of valuations is actually healthy and provides valuable market intelligence about how different buyers perceive your company's potential.

These varying offers also serve an important filtering function throughout the process. A buyer who initially comes in significantly below market can receive clear feedback about where competitive bids are landing. They can reassess their assumptions, sharpen their pencil, and come back with a revised proposal that's competitive, or they can acknowledge they're not the right fit and bow out gracefully. Either outcome is fine. If a buyer isn't willing to move meaningfully closer to where the market is valuing your business, you don't want them consuming your time and energy. Let them go without guilt or second thoughts, and focus your attention on the buyers who are genuinely excited about your company and willing to pay accordingly. The goal isn't to get every buyer to the table. The goal is to identify the two or three serious contenders who see real value in what you've built and are prepared to compensate you appropriately for it. And as I've emphasized throughout this book, the headline valuation number is only one piece of the puzzle. You also need to carefully evaluate the structure of each deal, including earnout provisions, equity rollover requirements, employment agreements, and cultural fit with the acquiring organization. A $50 million offer with a massive earnout and mandatory three-year employment contract might actually be less attractive than a $45 million offer with all cash at closing and a smooth transition plan.

Two Types of Buyers: Understanding Your Options

Now that you understand how the process works and what LOIs look like, it's important to understand who's making those offers. I once had a client in the early stages of selling her company. We were reviewing the pros and cons of different types of buyers when she half-joked, "I don't care who buys me. I just need their check to clear!" It was funny, but it reflected a common belief that the highest bidder wins and everything else is secondary. But that mindset overlooks real operational and financial consequences. The buyer you choose determines deal complexity, payout timing, future operating structure, and whether you spend the next few years enjoying your exit and the people you work with or hating Monday mornings.

When it comes to external buyers, they generally fall into two main categories: private equity firms and strategic buyers. Both can be excellent partners, but they approach acquisitions with fundamentally different motivations, structures, and goals. Understanding these differences isn't about semantics, it's about aligning your decision with what kind of future you want after the sale.

Private Equity Buyers

There are far more private equity buyers in the US than strategic buyers, and for good reason. Private equity is an entire industry built around acquiring companies. These firms raise capital from investors such as pension funds, endowments, family offices, and high-net-worth individuals, and their mandate is to deploy that capital into businesses, grow them, and eventually sell them for a profit. A private equity fund has a defined lifespan, typically between five and ten years. That means they are on a clock from the moment they buy you. Their goal is clear: enhance value, scale operations, and sell again within that window. It's a professional, process-driven approach, and one that rewards efficiency and results.

For sellers, that can be both appealing and challenging. On one hand, private equity firms know deals inside and out. They can move quickly, bring financial sophistication, and often keep you involved after the sale through retained equity, a consulting role, or a continued leadership position. That "second bite of the apple" can be incredibly lucrative if the company grows under their ownership. On the other hand, private equity buyers are laser-focused on performance. They will expect measurable improvements in revenue, margins, or operational efficiency. Their success depends on turning your company into a stronger, more profitable version of itself, and they won't hesitate to make tough changes to get there.

Private equity deals often involve a mix of cash, rollover equity, and earnouts. That complexity can be intimidating, but it can also create upside. If you stay on and help grow the business, your retained equity could multiply in value when the firm sells again. It's a continuation of your journey, not an abrupt ending. The flip side is that earnouts tie part of your payout to future performance. If the business doesn't hit its targets, or if post-sale dynamics change, you might not realize all the headline value you thought you were getting.

Strategic Buyers

Strategic buyers operate from an entirely different playbook. They're not buying your company to sell it again. Instead, they're buying it to integrate. A strategic buyer is usually an operating business in your industry or a related one. They might be a competitor looking to expand market share, a supplier trying to move up the value chain, or a company in an adjacent space looking to enter your market. Their motivation is synergy—the belief that combining forces will make both businesses stronger. That might mean cross-selling opportunities, sharing resources, or eliminating redundant costs.

That difference in motivation often shows up in how deals are structured. Strategic buyers tend to offer a simpler transaction with more cash up front, fewer contingencies, and a cleaner exit. However, that simplicity comes with tradeoffs. Once the deal closes, you may lose control over how your company is run. Your brand could be absorbed and your culture might not survive integration. A strategic buyer's goal is to make your business fit seamlessly into theirs, which sometimes means the identity you built disappears in the process.

Choosing the Right Fit

Choosing between a private equity and strategic buyer often comes down to what you value most: certainty or control, simplicity or potential, a clean break or continued involvement. A strategic buyer may give you closure, while private equity may give you continuity. There's no universal right answer. It depends on your goals, your risk tolerance, and what you want your post-sale life to look like. Do you want to walk away with your check and start your next chapter? Or do you want to stay in the game and help build something even bigger?

The challenge is that both options can lead to success or disappointment, depending on alignment. The wrong fit, even at a higher valuation, can drain your energy and satisfaction long after the deal closes. The right fit, even at a slightly lower price, can give you purpose, partnership, and freedom. The smartest sellers don't ask, "How much will they pay me?" They ask, "What kind of life will this deal create?" Because when the ink dries, the deal isn't just about the buyer.

Phase 3: Due Diligence

One of my clients described it perfectly: "Due diligence is like competing in an Ironman triathlon, except it's longer, harder, and there are no snack stations."

That line always gets a laugh, but it's true. You'll feel like you're running an endurance event you didn't sign up for. You'll wake up to new document requests, late-night emails from attorneys, and conference calls that seem to multiply. You'll upload files to virtual data rooms until your eyes blur. And when you think you've finally answered every question, another one appears—this time from the buyer's lender, auditor, or risk officer.

Owners tend to underestimate how grueling this phase will be. It's long. It's intense. And it can test your patience, your confidence, and even your sanity.

It's easy to get frustrated and think, "Why are they questioning me? Don't they believe what I'm saying?" But that's exactly the wrong mindset, and if you can shift it early, you'll survive due diligence with your sanity intact.

What Due Diligence Looks Like

Here's what to expect. You'll receive a long list of requests from the buyer's due diligence team. These requests cover everything from financial statements, customer contracts, and leases to employment agreements, intellectual property, and insurance coverage. They'll want to know how revenue is recognized, how expenses are allocated, and how dependent your business is on certain clients or employees.

You'll be asked for your tax returns, your accounting policies, and even your cybersecurity protocols. You'll be asked about pending litigation, warranty claims, and product liabilities. And then they'll ask for backup documentation to prove each answer.

A quality of earnings (QoE) report is one of the most important parts of due diligence. It's a deep dive into your company's true, sustainable profitability. Buyers use it to verify that your reported earnings reflect reality, not accounting noise or one-time windfalls. A QoE dissects your revenue streams, normalizes expenses, adjusts for owner perks or nonrecurring items, and identifies trends that might affect future performance. In short, it answers the question the buyer is thinking, "How much money will this business actually make once we own it?"

A detailed QoE analyzes revenue quality, examining recurring versus one-time sales, customer concentration, and whether reported revenues are collectible. It reviews expense adjustments for items that won't continue after the sale. Things like above-market owner salaries or personal expenses. These "normalizations" reveal the company's true earning power in the hands of a buyer.

If you think it sounds like overkill, you're right. But that's the process. And while it can feel invasive, it's also the moment your business transforms from a private company into a verified, investable asset. Buyers, lenders, and investors rely on due diligence to confirm what they're buying, and if you've built a great company, this process will ultimately validate that greatness.

The key is to stay patient, stay organized, and don't take it personally.

Phase 4: The Finish Line

The Definitive Purchase Agreement (DPA)

After months of teasers, NDAs, CIMs, management meetings, LOIs, and endless rounds of due diligence, you finally arrive at the moment that makes it all real. You reach the definitive purchase agreement (DPA). This is where intent becomes obligation and aspirations turn into legally binding commitments. Everything you've discussed, negotiated, shaken hands on, and assumed must now appear on paper in precise legal form. If the LOI was the promise, the DPA is the proof.

The DPA is not a short summary or a friendly closing note. It is often a thick, dense contract that can run to hundreds of pages. It details the exact purchase price, how and when funds will be paid, whether any portion is contingent on future performance, and how that performance will be measured. It outlines representations and warranties that you stand behind, the circumstances where you may be required to return some of the purchase price, and what happens if there is a dispute. It specifies closing conditions and post-closing responsibilities. It anticipates problems, disagreements, financial surprises, and even acts of bad faith, and assigns consequences accordingly. In other words, it is the legal backbone of your exit.

Alongside the DPA, there are usually several supporting agreements, often called ancillary agreements, that deserve as much attention. These may include employment, consulting, or non-compete agreements for you or key members of your team. They define your role after the sale, how you will be compensated, and what expectations the buyer has for your transition period. They determine how long you must remain involved, how much control you retain or surrender, and what restrictions you may face if you want to start or invest in another company later. I sometimes joke that we call them ancillary only because we have not found a more dramatic word. They matter. Sometimes, these documents shape the next two to three years of your life more than the purchase price itself.

When you finally reach this stage, you will likely be tired. In fact, tired may not even adequately describe it. You will have been negotiating, revisiting financials, answering buyer requests, and making high-stakes decisions for months. You will feel a pull to finish quickly. You will want to sign, celebrate, and move on. That is exactly why this is the most dangerous part of the process for a seller who is not mentally ready. The DPA phase requires your best focus and clearest judgment. Small word choices can change economic outcomes, and a seemingly minor adjustment to a warranty or a working-capital clause can shift millions of dollars. I have watched worn out sellers surrender terms that would never have been accepted at the beginning. Do not let fatigue negotiate for you.

This is where your M&A attorney earns their fee. Their job is to translate legal terminology into real-world impact. But while your attorney will lead the technical work, you cannot disappear. Read the key sections, paying special attention to earnout language, indemnification clauses, working-capital adjustments, dispute mechanics, and post-closing obligations. If something is unclear or feels off, ask. This is not the time to assume someone else will catch it. You have lived this business. You know the risks, responsibilities, and nuances in a way outsiders do not. Your experience and intuition matter here.

The signing of the DPA is a profound moment, as it marks the end of your stewardship of the business you built and the beginning of a new chapter in your life. It is a time of pride and relief, yet also a time of emotion, reflection, and possibility. When you put your signature on that agreement, you are not merely finalizing a transaction. You are stepping into a new identity. The business becomes someone else's responsibility, and your future, for the first time in a long time, becomes entirely yours again.

The Wire

There is one more milestone after the signatures that we can't forget... the wire!

This is the moment every founder imagines, yet few are prepared for emotionally. One morning you wake up, open your bank app, and see a number that represents decades of sacrifice, faith, risk, and perseverance suddenly converted into liquidity. Sometimes the wire arrives with a quiet, almost anticlimactic ping. Other times there are tears, celebration, disbelief, or even a strange sense of emptiness. Money replaces identity in an instant, and that transition can feel both thrilling and disorienting. This book so far has focused on how to get here and how to do it well, but the wire is not the finish line. It is the doorway to a new phase of life. In Part Three, we will explore what happens after the money is deposited into your account, how to adapt, how to protect what you have built, and how to create a life that feels as meaningful and energizing as the one you lived as a business owner.

PART B: THE PSYCHOLOGY OF THE SALE

Understanding the mechanics gets you to the table. Mastering the psychology determines what you walk away with.

The Power of Leverage: Why You Want Multiple LOIs

One LOI is nice. Three is powerful.

Earlier I explained that you can negotiate multiple LOIs at once. Now let's talk about why that changes everything.

You only need one buyer to close a deal. But one buyer means one perspective, one set of terms, and one opinion of what your company is worth. That's not a negotiation. That's a take-it-or-leave-it.

Three LOIs change the game. One offer gives you data. Two give you context. Three give you truth. Industry multiples and professional valuations are estimates. They're educated guesses until someone is actually willing to write a check. When three buyers compete, you finally see what the market truly values and where your story resonates most.

Competition also changes psychology. Buyers act differently when they know they're not alone at the table. They move faster.

They sharpen their pencils. They stretch further. When buyers sense urgency, you gain control. When there's only one buyer, the dynamic reverses. They control the pace, the terms, and sometimes even the tone of the deal.

Your goal should be at least three LOIs. Not because you'll close with all three, but because comparing, negotiating, and analyzing them gives you clarity, leverage, and confidence. You don't really know what your company is worth until real buyers compete to own it.

Strategic Negotiation: LOI Leverage

The LOI stage is a window of opportunity. It provides a rare moment when you can shape the terms of your deal before you're locked into exclusivity.

I encourage clients to use it as both a negotiation tool and a stress test. Negotiating multiple LOIs gives you a feel for each buyer's personality, flexibility, and integrity. You'll quickly see which buyers are transparent and collaborative, and which ones are rigid, defensive, or vague. These early interactions are predictive. The way a buyer behaves during the LOI phase is almost always how they'll behave during due diligence and final negotiations.

If you find a buyer who's overly aggressive, dismissive of your concerns, or vague about deal mechanics, take note. That's a sign of how the relationship will feel post-sale. On the other hand, a buyer who listens, explains, and problem-solves collaboratively is likely to be a better long-term partner.

Remember that the LOI isn't just about numbers, it's also about alignment. Culture, trust, and communication matter. You're not selling to a spreadsheet; you're selling to a team of humans who will carry your legacy forward.

The Right Mindset for Due Diligence

The most important thing you can do during due diligence is avoid the "us versus them" mentality. It's not helpful, and it's also inaccurate. Yes, it can feel adversarial when the buyer's team is probing, dissecting, and double-checking everything you've said. But this isn't about distrust—it's about diligence. Their accountants, attorneys, and analysts aren't trying to attack you; they're doing their jobs. They get paid to make sure their client isn't getting screwed.

And that's exactly what you want.

You want the buyer to dig deep. You want them to ask tough questions. Because when you have clear, confident answers, you're building trust. The buyer wants to buy a good company. You want to sell a good company. You're both aiming for the same goal.

When you frame it this way (not as "us versus them," but as "we're on the same side of the table working toward a fair, successful deal"), everything changes. You stop reacting emotionally and defensively and start responding strategically, anticipating what they need to feel confident in buying your company. The right mindset will not make due diligence easy, but it will make it survivable.

The Diligence Distraction Paradox

During due diligence, buyers need your attention constantly. They request documents, ask detailed questions, and want meetings to clarify issues. Responding quickly and thoroughly keeps the deal moving and builds buyer confidence.

But the more time you spend feeding due diligence, the less time you spend running your business. You're pulled into conference rooms when you should be in customer meetings. You're answering questions about three-year-old contracts when you should be closing this quarter's pipeline.

And the cruel twist is if your metrics slip during diligence, buyers use it as justification to renegotiate. The distraction that kept the deal moving becomes the reason they want to cut the price.

The solution is delegation. Your CFO handles financial requests. Your COO manages operational questions. Your attorney coordinates legal items. You stay visible enough to show you're engaged, but you protect your time to keep the business performing.

Taking your eye off operations to feed due diligence can create the miss that justifies the price cut you feared.

Six Strategies to Survive Due Diligence

During due diligence, the tone of the process changes dramatically. Before the LOI, buyers were trying to win you over by flattering your leadership, praising your company, and promising a smooth partnership. After the LOI, that dynamic flips. Now the buyer is in verification mode, and the mood shifts from courtship to scrutiny. Their job isn't to charm you anymore; it's to confirm that everything you said about your business is accurate and sustainable. They'll test your assumptions, dig into your numbers, and question your systems. That's not personal; it's due diligence. But for many owners, it feels personal, and that's when frustration and tension can creep in.

Here's how to survive it.

1. Reframe: "I get to…"

The due diligence period can be one of the most draining phases of a sale. It's a relentless cycle of questions, document requests, and follow-ups that seem to have no end. You answer one inquiry, only to receive five more. It's easy to grow resentful, and even angry, as every request feels like an accusation, and every new spreadsheet feels like a test. It's no wonder so many founders describe diligence as the emotional low point of the entire process.

But here's the shift that changes everything: Instead of thinking "I have to do this," start thinking "I get to do this." You get to be here. You get to be the owner of a company so valuable, so desirable, that someone is willing to spend millions (maybe hundreds of millions!) to buy it. You get to be in the rare position where your hard work, risk, and vision are being validated by people who want to invest in it. When you look at diligence through that lens, the frustration doesn't disappear, but it transforms. It becomes part of the privilege of having built something truly worth buying.

Reframing diligence this way doesn't only protect your sanity; it strengthens your leverage. Buyers can feel your energy. If you approach diligence with defensiveness, they sense it and dig deeper. But if you engage with openness and professionalism, you build confidence and trust. Instead of looking like a seller under scrutiny, you look like a partner in discovery, which changes the tone and the outcome. The best founders stay grounded in gratitude. "I get to do this. I get to show them what I built." That mindset isn't naïve, it's strategic. It's how you stay composed, protect your value, and turn one of the hardest parts of the process into one of the most affirming.

2. Don't negotiate your own deal—delegate wisely.

I've had some of the best negotiators completely fall apart when they tried to handle their own sales. It's not because they didn't know how to negotiate, but because the deal was personal. The emotional attachment to the company they've built made it nearly impossible to stay objective when they care deeply about the outcome.

One of the smartest things you can do during this stage is to create some distance between yourself and the daily back-and-forth. Let your CPA handle the financial questions. Let your attorney respond to legal requests. Let your CFO coordinate data delivery. Your role is to remain the "good cop"—positive, cooperative, and available for high-level strategy conversations. You don't want to get pulled into the weeds or let emotions sour the relationship.

The only caveat is that your CFO or CPA must be competent, calm, and careful with their words. A careless comment or show of defensiveness can spook a buyer and set off unnecessary alarms. That's why, in many cases, it's safer to rely on external advisors such as your CPA or banker who knows the process, isn't emotionally attached, and can maintain professionalism under pressure. They become the buffer that keeps you out of the friction and preserves your relationship with the buyer, which is critical to getting the deal done.

This dynamic matters more than you might think. You'll likely be working with the buyer after the sale, especially if you have an earnout or rollover equity. You don't want to be the one who damaged the relationship during negotiations. Even if you're not using an investment bank, find someone to run point. Don't be your own hammer and nail.

3. Protect your time and energy.

One of the smartest things you can do during due diligence is intentionally step away from it. Deals have a way of consuming the last mental inch of your life, if you allow them to. It can easily become all you talk about, all you think about, and all you feel capable of doing. That is the path to burnout and bad decisions.

Build in enforced distance. Schedule one evening each week when you absolutely do not discuss the deal. No updates. No "quick thoughts." No venting or rehashing. Protect that space like you would an investor presentation. Go to dinner. Get outside. Do a workout. Have a glass of wine on the porch. See friends. Watch a movie. Go for a walk with your spouse and talk about literally anything else. Remind yourself there is a world outside the transaction.

This break is not laziness. It is discipline. When you step away, you create space for clarity. Your nervous system resets, your thinking sharpens and you return with more patience, better judgment, and a steadier emotional baseline. Distance protects your perspective.

At the same time, treat the sale as a second job, and give it dedicated time instead of allowing it to consume all time. Block specific hours on your calendar for the transaction. You might reserve 9:00 to 12:00 for deal tasks, or set aside two full days each week to focus solely on diligence and buyer communication. Whatever rhythm you choose, the point is containment. During those blocks, immerse yourself fully in the transaction. Outside of them, run the business.

This approach is not theoretical. Some of the most effective leaders in the world operate this way. Elon Musk has publicly discussed how he allocates specific days to each major company he runs. SpaceX gets one day, Tesla another, X another, and so on. He does this because he knows attention must be allocated consciously if you want multiple missions to succeed at once.

You may not be juggling rocket launches and electric vehicles, but the principle is the same. When you discipline your time, you preserve business momentum and deal momentum at the same time. Structure is not a restriction. It is power.

4. Stay ruthlessly focused on what matters.

When you choose to sell a company, your world compresses. There are only two priorities that matter: running the business and closing the deal. Everything else is noise. This is not the season to multitask or carry the same load you always have. It is the season to protect your time and attention like a scarce resource, because that is exactly what it becomes during a sale.

I once heard an M&A attorney tell a business owner a story about Elton John. He explained that at Elton's concerts, the star walks on stage, sits at the piano, and performs. That is it. He does not haul equipment. He does not check the lighting rig. He does not negotiate backstage catering or coordinate parking or tune the piano. He does one thing, and it is the most important thing. Everything around him exists to support the performance. The attorney paused and said, "During this process, you need to be Elton John." It was not a suggestion to be glamorous. It was a reminder to stay focused on the single highest priority and let others handle the rest.

When I shared that analogy with a client who was getting distracted by lower-value tasks during his sale process, he smiled and said, "I do not want to be Elton. I want to be Sting!" Whether you prefer Elton, Sting, Springsteen, or someone else entirely, the lesson remains. Your job is to show up and perform where it matters most. You delegate to your team. You let your spouse or partner handle personal details. You give yourself permission to hand off responsibilities that do not drive enterprise value or deal success.

And along those same lines, don't add more work to your plate! When the transaction feels promising and momentum is building, it is tempting to make upgrades, expand, or launch new projects. I once worked with a client who, right in the middle of diligence, decided it might be the perfect moment to buy a new office building and move the entire team. In reality, it would have been a massive distraction. We had no idea yet whether the buyer would want to consolidate operations with another portfolio company or even maintain the current location. Taking on a real estate purchase and a corporate relocation while answering diligence requests and negotiating terms would have stretched his time and attention to a breaking point. I encouraged him to wait, and he did. During diligence, additions like that are almost always a burden, not a boost. Protect your bandwidth. You will need it.

For a brief period, you need to commit to ruthless focus, because there is a narrow window where your attention is the difference between a deal that merely closes and a deal that changes your life.

5. Stay composed—don't take the bait.

During due diligence, you will encounter questions that feel aggressive, skeptical, or even insulting. Buyers' attorneys and diligence teams are trained to probe, challenge assumptions, and test responses under pressure. They want to see how you handle stress and scrutiny. They want to confirm that the story you presented holds water when examined closely. And sometimes, they want to see if you will lose your cool. It's not personal, it's part of their process.

Your natural instinct may be to defend yourself, argue, or push back hard. Resist that urge. The calmer you remain, the more confident you appear. Buyers are evaluating more than the business. They're evaluating the person leading it. Even if you plan to exit quickly, they want to know that you are rational, steady, and professional under pressure. If you react emotionally, buyers begin to wonder. Is this how they handle stress? Will they be difficult post-closing? Is there something they are hiding? You never want to give them a reason to doubt you or the operation you've built.

Emotional discipline is leverage. Each question is an opportunity to demonstrate maturity, competence, and control. You do not have to win every exchange or "prove" anything in a single conversation. What matters most is the impression you leave. When the buyer walks away feeling that you are confident, measured, and unshakable, the deal strengthens. An owner who can keep their cool during due diligence communicates power in the clearest way possible, and signals that they refuse to be rattled.

6. You are in the arena.

You're not reading about someone else's life-changing transaction on a website. You're not passively listening to a podcast where an entrepreneur recounts their deal war stories or watching a documentary about founders who sold their companies. You are living it right now, in real time, with real consequences and real stakes. You are in the arena.

Theodore Roosevelt captured this truth perfectly when he said, "The credit belongs to the man who is actually in the arena, whose face is marred by dust and sweat and blood; who strives valiantly; who errs, who comes short again and again, because there is no effort without error and shortcoming; but who does actually strive to do the deeds; who knows great enthusiasms, the great devotions; who spends himself in a worthy cause; who at the best knows in the end the triumph of high achievement, and who at the worst, if he fails, at least fails while daring greatly, so that his place shall never be with those cold and timid souls who neither know victory nor defeat."

You're feeling pressure and the weight of responsibility, and you have the sense that it all depends on you. That's because it does depend on you, and it always has. Now is not the time to wallow or give up. It's on you. It's always been on you. So embrace it. Revel in the fact that you're doing something difficult and consequential. Not everyone gets to be in the arena. Most people spend their entire lives watching from the cheap seats. You're actually in the fight, and that's something to be proud of, even when it hurts.

I have never worked with a business owner who sailed through due diligence without moments of frustration, doubt, or anger. Not one.

Chapter Exit

By now, you've seen that the mechanics of a deal are anything but mechanical. Each stage, from the first teaser to the final signature, is part art, part strategy, and part endurance. You've learned how the pieces fit together, how the momentum shifts from seller to buyer, and how the smallest details in an LOI or earnout formula can have million-dollar consequences. But more than anything, you've seen how this process tests your patience, preparation, and ability to stay focused under pressure.

Once you understand the mechanics, the next challenge is maximizing what you get out of them. The real money and the real opportunity come from how you navigate these steps. There's a world of difference between closing a deal and closing your best possible deal. That's where leverage, positioning, and negotiation come in.

In the next chapter, we'll shift from process to power, from how deals work to how you make them work for you. We'll talk about structure, timing, psychology, and the dozens of subtle decisions that determine whether you walk away satisfied or second-guessing what could have been. This is where good becomes great. The mechanics get you to the table. Now it's time to make sure you leave it with everything you've earned.

CHAPTER 5:

MAXIMIZE YOUR DEAL VALUE

*Earn the Highest Price
Through Skilled,
Strategic Negotiation*

A client of mine once received two offers for his company within the same week. On paper, the first offer looked like a clear winner: $10 million higher than the second. It was full of the kind of numbers that make your pulse quicken. The second offer seemed more conservative and less exciting. But when we dug deeper, the "better" deal wasn't better at all. The headline number was inflated with earnouts that were nearly impossible to achieve, equity in a company the buyer hadn't even formed yet, and tax treatment that would eat up almost half of his take-home. The second offer, though smaller at first glance, was cleaner, simpler, and far more certain. When the dust settled, he walked away with more money and far fewer headaches by taking the lower offer.

That's the thing about deal value: It's not always what it seems. The best deal isn't always the one with the biggest number. Instead, it's the one that delivers the most real value to you after taxes, contingencies, and time. The difference between a great exit and a disappointing one rarely comes down to luck; it comes down to understanding how value is created, negotiated, and protected.

In this chapter, we'll dive into the art and strategy of maximizing your deal value, not just by pushing for a higher price, but by structuring a smarter deal. You'll learn how to identify where the real money is hidden, how to use leverage without losing credibility, and how to negotiate from a position of clarity and control. Because at this stage, you're negotiating the financial outcome of a lifetime.

When the offers start coming in, it feels like the finish line is finally in sight. After months or maybe years of preparation, you're staring at the numbers you've dreamed about. But this is where most sellers make their biggest mistake. They see a big number and assume that means a big win.

Negotiating your sale isn't just about maximizing price. It's about maximizing outcome. And that requires a deeper understanding of structure, certainty, and what you take home.

The Three Pillars of Deal Structure

Let's return to an example from earlier. Imagine you receive a $120 million offer for your company. On paper, it looks impressive. But how it's structured determines how much you actually receive and how much risk you're taking on. In most cases, the deal will be split among three main components. The buyer might propose 60 percent in upfront cash ($72 million), 20 percent as an equity rollover ($24 million), and 20 percent as an earnout ($24 million) tied to future performance. That sounds straightforward, but to evaluate whether this is objectively a good deal, you need to understand what each component actually means.

Deals often have these three basic components: cash, equity rollovers, and earnouts. Understanding how each works—and how they work together—will help you maximize value. Let's examine each component of our $120 million example.

1. Cash

This is the cleanest and simplest form of payment. You get your money at closing, pay your taxes, and move on. Cash is king because it's certain, and not dependent on future performance, buyer promises, or macroeconomic conditions. It's done. If you walk away with a deal that's mostly cash, you've traded your illiquid asset for liquidity, and that's real value.

The downside? All-cash deals often come with lower valuations. Buyers paying entirely in cash are taking on all the risk up front. They'll pay less for certainty, but the tradeoff might be worth it, depending on your goals.

2. Equity Rollovers

A rollover means you keep a percentage of equity, usually 20 to 40 percent, in the new entity after the sale. You're reinvesting in your own company, but under new ownership. This can be lucrative, especially if the buyer grows the business and sells it again later. The downside is obvious. You're now a minority shareholder. You used to call the shots, but now you answer to someone else. If the new owners make decisions you disagree with or underperform, your equity can go to zero. Before agreeing to a rollover, ask yourself a hard question. Do I trust these people to run my business better than I did?

The Second Bite

Private equity firms love talking about the "second bite." When I first heard this phrase decades ago, I nodded along but didn't have any idea what they were talking about. Here's how it works. They buy a majority of your business—say 70 percent—and keep you on with the remaining 30 percent. They help grow the company, professionalize operations, and scale it. Then three to five years later they sell again at a potentially higher valuation.

If things go well, your retained equity can be worth more than your original payout. I've seen sellers make more on the second bite than the first. That's the upside. The second bite sounds amazing, but it only works if the buyer executes. If they miss targets, change direction, or run into market headwinds, that equity can be worth nothing. And psychologically, it's tough. You've already sold your company, paid taxes, and mentally moved on, but now part of your wealth is still tied up in a company you no longer control.

Before agreeing to roll over equity, do your own due diligence on the buyer—what I call "reverse due diligence." Have they delivered second bites for other founders? Have you spoken with any of them? How long do they hold their investments? It's likely the equity rollover will be a meaningful amount of money for you, so it's important to get comfortable with the new owners, their strategy to grow the company, and their track record.

If you want the upside, but not the anxiety, consider keeping your equity rollover smaller, maybe 10 percent or less. That's enough to benefit if things go well, but not enough to keep you awake at night.

3. Earnouts

Earnouts allow buyers to reduce their upfront risk by deferring part of the purchase price and making it contingent on future performance. From their perspective, earnouts are brilliant as they shift risk from buyer to seller while keeping you motivated to support the transition.

But what they won't say out loud is that earnouts also give buyers a tool to reduce the effective purchase price after the deal closes. Once they control the business, they control the levers that determine whether you hit your targets—budgets, staffing, pricing, marketing spend, and strategic priorities. If they decide your division isn't the focus anymore, your earnout evaporates, regardless of how hard you work.

Most buyers act in good faith, but incentives matter. Buyers are incentivized to pay as little as possible, and earnouts give them flexibility to do exactly that.

Your job is to structure the earnout so it's achievable even if the buyer's priorities shift. That requires clear metrics, tight language, and strong protections.

Metrics That Work vs. Metrics That Don't

Not all earnout metrics are created equal. Some are objective and hard to manipulate. Others are subjective, easily gamed, and outside your control.

Metrics That Work (Use These)

Revenue. Revenue is the cleanest earnout metric. It's objective, measurable, and harder for buyers to manipulate without obviously sabotaging the business. Buyers can still slow down sales cycles or change pricing, but, compared to profit-based metrics, revenue is far safer.

Customer retention or renewal rates. If your business depends on recurring revenue, retention or renewal rates make strong earnout metrics. These are hard to manipulate and directly measure the health of the business you're handing off.

Gross profit. Gross profit measures revenue minus the direct cost of delivering your product or service. It's less easy to manipulate than net profit, because it excludes overhead and corporate allocations the buyer controls.

Metrics That Don't Work (Avoid These)

EBITDA or net profit. This is the most common and dangerous earnout metric. Buyers have enormous flexibility to reduce reported profit through accounting decisions, cost allocations, and overhead charges. Even if revenue is growing, the buyer can kill your earnout by allocating corporate overhead, increasing management fees, reclassifying expenses, or cutting marketing spend. Unless the earnout agreement has ironclad definitions and restricts cost allocations, avoid this structure.

Subjective performance metrics. Earnouts tied to vague goals like "successful integration" or "customer satisfaction" are disasters waiting to happen. Subjective metrics give the buyer total discretion over whether you've "performed."

Metrics outside your control. Avoid earnouts tied to things you can't directly influence, such as total company profitability, stock price, or strategic outcomes that depend on the buyer's decisions. If you have no control, you're gambling, not earning.

The Price Paradox

A higher headline price can sometimes be worse than a lower one. Most sellers fixate on the number at the top of the offer. After all, $50 million sounds better than $45 million. It's simple math.

But deals are never that simple. The $50 million offer might have 40 percent in earnouts that require hitting aggressive targets under new management. It might have broad reps and warranties that expose you to clawbacks. It might have working capital adjustments that reduce what you get at close.

Meanwhile, the $45 million offer might be 90 percent cash at closing, with minimal earnout, tight reps, and clean terms. After taxes and risk adjustments, the "lower" offer delivers more certain value.

Buyers know this. They use high headline numbers to win deals, then structure terms that protect their downside and shift risk to you.

Sellers who only look at price leave millions on the table by accepting terms they don't understand.

The best deals aren't the ones with the biggest numbers. They're the ones with the most cash at close, the clearest terms, and the least risk.

A higher price with terrible terms is worth less than a lower price with clean structure—but most sellers don't realize it until it is too late.

Structuring Earnouts for Achievability

Even with good metrics, earnouts can fail if the structure sets you up for disappointment. Consider these proven strategies:

1. **Keep earnout periods short.** Push for twelve to eighteen months. If the buyer insists on longer periods, structure annual payouts rather than one lump sum at the end.

2. **Set conservative, achievable targets.** A smaller earnout you actually collect is worth more than a big one you never see. Model the earnout assuming things will go slightly worse than expected.

3. **Define metrics with legal precision.** Vague language kills earnouts. Work with your attorney to define every term precisely. What counts as revenue? When is it recognized? What costs are deductible?

4. **Maintain operational control (if possible).** The more control you have during the earnout period, the better your chances of hitting targets. Negotiate to retain authority over budgets, hiring, pricing, and strategy.

Protection Mechanisms That Save Earnouts

Even with good metrics and structure, you need legal protections to ensure payment. Every deal is different, so please seek the counsel of your attorney.

1. **"Operate in the Ordinary Course" Clauses** – Requires the buyer to run your business consistently with past practices without sabotaging your earnout.

   Sample language: "Buyer agrees to operate the business consistent with past practice and will not take actions intended to reduce Seller's earnout without legitimate business justification."

2. **Earnout Adjustment Provisions** – Allows earnout targets to be adjusted if the buyer makes significant changes that impact your ability to achieve targets.

   Sample language: "If Buyer materially changes budgets, staffing, pricing, or strategy impacting earnout targets, targets shall be adjusted proportionally."

3. **Dispute Resolution and Audit Rights** – Negotiate binding arbitration with an independent accounting firm to resolve disputes quickly. Ensure you can audit earnout calculations.

   Sample language: "Seller retains the right to audit earnout calculations annually. Disputes shall be resolved through binding arbitration with a mutually agreed upon accounting firm."

4. **Escrows and Guarantees** – Your earnout should be guaranteed, not contingent on the buyer's overall success. If you have leverage and/or are worried that even if you hit the numbers for your earnout they won't be able to pay you, a portion of the earnout can be secured via escrow or letter of

credit to reduce counterparty risk. While this is not standard, these protections are sometimes achievable.

Sample language: "Earnout payments shall be funded through escrow or backed by irrevocable letter of credit to ensure payment upon achievement of targets."

Earnouts aren't inherently bad, but they are inherently risky. You give up control while remaining financially dependent on outcomes you can no longer fully influence.

If you agree to an earnout, go into it with your eyes open. Understand that you're betting on the buyer's intentions, the business's trajectory, and your ability to perform in an environment you no longer control. Structure that bet carefully, protect yourself legally, and never assume the buyer's interests will align with yours once the deal closes.

The GAAP Accounting Trap in Earnout Formulas

Most private companies run their books using cash basis or tax basis accounting because it's simpler, cheaper, and frankly more useful for managing a privately held business. You track what comes in, what goes out, and you structure things to minimize your tax bill. But here's a critical detail that catches many sellers off guard during earnout negotiations. The earnout formula in your purchase agreement will almost certainly require that post-closing earnings be calculated using Generally Accepted Accounting Principles, or GAAP. This matters enormously because GAAP accounting can produce dramatically different financial results than the method you've been using to run your business. Revenue recognition timing differs. Expense categorization changes. Depreciation schedules shift.

If you've been running your company for years showing strong profitability on a cash basis, you might be shocked to discover that under GAAP those same operations look significantly less profitable, which directly reduces your earnout payment. Before you agree to a GAAP-based earnout formula, have your accountant prepare pro forma financials showing what your recent results would look like under GAAP accounting standards. If there's a meaningful difference, you need to either negotiate for the earnout to use your existing accounting method, adjust the earnout targets to account for the GAAP conversion, or at minimum understand exactly how much money this technical accounting change might cost you. The buyer's finance team already knows what your numbers will look like under their accounting standards. You should know too before you sign.

In the end, the only earnout that matters is the one that actually pays out, and that requires more than good faith. It requires good structure, good metrics, and good protections written into the agreement before you sign.

The Earnout Paradox

You sell your business to get out. To be done. To move on with your life. That's the whole point of selling.

But earnouts often require you to stay longer than you ever planned. You need to hit targets to get paid. You need to remain employed, involved, and accountable—often for two or three years post-close. And you're no longer in control. New ownership makes decisions. They change strategy, restructure teams, and adjust priorities.

Now you're stuck. If you leave, you forfeit the earnout. If you stay, you're working for someone else under terms you didn't set. The very thing you sold to escape becomes an extended prison.

Earnouts aren't inherently bad. They can bridge valuation gaps and align incentives. But they're only worth what you'll actually receive. Aggressive targets, subjective metrics, and buyer-controlled outcomes make earnouts risky.

The best approach? Negotiate earnouts with reasonable targets, clear metrics, and provisions that protect you if the buyer makes decisions that undermine your ability to hit goals.

You sell to get out—but earnouts often mean staying longer than you want.

Looking Beyond the Headline Price

It's easy to focus on the biggest number on the page. After all, $50 million sounds better than $40 million. But you don't spend gross proceeds. You spend after-tax, after-structure proceeds. That's the number that actually changes your life.

Ask three questions when comparing offers:

1. How much cash am I getting up front?

2. How certain are the contingent payments (earnouts, rollovers, notes)?

3. What are the after-tax proceeds?

I always tell clients to start with one simple question. "How much cash am I getting up front?"

Cash is the only piece of the deal that's guaranteed. The earnouts, equity rollovers, and seller notes might be worth something later, but they also might not. I tell clients to assume the earnout and rollover are worth zero and ask, "Would I still do this deal?"

If the answer is yes, you're in a good position. If the answer is no, you're probably rationalizing because you want the deal to work. If 70 percent of your sale price is tied to future performance or illiquid equity, that's not a win. That's a wager.

The Break-Even Analysis

With every owner I advise, I run a quick but eye-opening break-even analysis. The goal is simple. Figure out how many years you'd have to keep operating your business to earn, after taxes, what you'd receive from only the guaranteed portion of your sale.

Here's how to run the calculation. Start with your company's after-tax annual income. That's what you actually take home each year after taxes—not top-line revenue or pre-tax profit. Then compare it to the guaranteed portion of your sale proceeds. That means only the cash you'll receive at closing after taxes. Exclude earnouts or rollover equity. Finally, divide the guaranteed, after-tax sale proceeds by your after-tax annual income.

Here's an example. Your business generates $750,000 per year in after-tax income. A sale would net you $10 million after taxes. To earn that same $10 million by continuing to run the business, you'd need 13.3 years. That's your break-even point.

To make the analysis even more realistic, factor in what your sale proceeds could earn if invested conservatively. If your after-tax proceeds are $10 million and you invest them at 5%, that generates

$500,000 per year without employees, overhead, or operating risk—while preserving your $10 million in principal.

Now the comparison changes. By continuing to operate, you earn $750,000 per year, but only $250,000 more than the passive income generated by selling. At that rate, it would take 40 years of incremental operating income to generate an additional $10 million beyond what selling delivers immediately—assuming the business could even be sold later for the same after-tax value.

This simple math reframes the entire decision. Consider two scenarios. If your deal offers enough upfront cash to equal more than a decade of after-tax earnings, it might be time to move on. You'd eliminate all the risk, stress, and operational drag of running the business. But if the guaranteed proceeds only equal a couple of years' profit, you might want to push for better terms or wait for stronger performance. Numbers have a way of cutting through emotion, giving you the clarity to make a decision based on fact, not fear or fatigue.

At the end of the day, deal components fall into one of two categories: guaranteed or speculative. This doesn't mean you shouldn't take deals with rollovers or earnouts. Many can be great opportunities. It means you should understand exactly what's guaranteed and what's speculative. You've already taken enormous risk building your company. The sale is your chance to de-risk your life, not double down.

The Deal Clarity Framework – Build Your Exit Playbook Before You Negotiate

One of the greatest advantages you can give yourself going into a sale is clarity: clear priorities, clear boundaries, and clear goals. When owners don't define these in advance, they end up negotiating from fatigue, emotion, or ego. When they do define them, they negotiate from strength, calm, and conviction.

Before you talk to buyers, build your internal deal map.

1. Musts: Your Non-Negotiables

These are the conditions that must be true for you to sell. They are not preferences. They are requirements. Musts are where you plant the flag.

Examples:

- A minimum after-tax number

- Guaranteed employment or meaningful roles for key employees

- Specific terms about brand continuity or location

- A set timeline for your transition/exit involvement

- No aggressive retrade on price or structure after diligence

- Cultural alignment in how staff and customers will be treated

If a deal breaks a must, you walk, no matter how shiny the headline number looks. Musts are the backbone of your deal.

2. Maybes: Your Flex Points

These are areas where you prefer one outcome, but have flexibility. They are negotiable variables.

Examples:

- Earn-out structure and duration

- Amount of rollover equity

- Employment contract length or advisory period

- Leadership title or formal role post-deal

- Certain benefits or non-financial terms

Maybes are where creative deal-making happens. They give you range without exposing your core priorities. When your banker trades on your behalf, these are the tools that keep momentum moving.

3. Magnifiers: Your Value Enhancers

These are the bonus wins—the elements that take a good deal and make it exceptional. They're not make-or-break, but they elevate the outcome dramatically. Think of them as your wish list items.

Examples:

- Higher rollover equity into a promising buyer (to participate again in upside)

- Performance-based kicker opportunities you believe you can hit

- Personal brand or thought-leadership involvement

- A philanthropic carve-out or funding of a donor-advised fund at closing

- Special consulting structure that gives you long-term optionality

- Favorable tax structuring or payout sequencing

Magnifiers are optional, but incredibly powerful. A win or two in this category can radically improve the deal and post-sale happiness.

4. Mirages: Your Strategic Giveaways

Now the advanced layer. Mirages are the terms buyers think you value, and that you deliberately allow them to believe matter. They appear important, but they aren't essential to you. Mirages become your high-leverage bargaining chips.

Examples:

- A title or office you don't care about

- A slightly longer advisory role than you'd prefer, if it gets you better terms elsewhere

- Minor comp details that don't affect your post-sale life

- Certain integration timelines or reporting mechanics

- Symbolic operational involvement

You don't mislead in a way that is unethical. You just don't reveal your indifference too early. Experienced sellers know that sometimes the fastest way to gain is to give strategically. Mirages are the "currency" you spend to protect your musts and secure your magnifiers.

Strategic Negotiation – Understanding the Buyer

The Buyer Mindset

Want to know what can help you sell your company? Put yourself in the shoes of a buyer. If you are like me, you do a ton of research before you buy a new car. I watch far too many videos, spend countless hours digging into review sites, and scour message boards before I buy a car that is worth less than $100,000. Think about what you are asking a buyer of your company to do. They review a document, run some projections, have a few calls and meetings with you, and then you want them to wire you tens or hundreds of millions of dollars.

From their perspective, they're stepping into the unknown. Remember the transferable value work from Chapter 2? This is where it pays off. Buyers crave confidence, not perfection. They'll accept flaws (every company has them) as long as they believe they understand the risks, and that you've been transparent.

You're Selling the Future, not the Past

Many founders make a critical mistake: They believe they're selling history. They talk endlessly about what they've achieved, the growth they've driven, and the loyal customer base they've built. While that matters, it's not what keeps a buyer up at night. Buyers don't lose sleep over your past. They lose sleep over your future.

Your financials show what has happened, but buyers are buying what will happen. They're betting that your company will continue to thrive and expand under new ownership. Your job is to help them see and believe in that future. You need to sell possibility as much as performance.

When I coach clients through this stage, I tell them to focus on the big three questions every serious buyer asks, consciously or not:

1. How big is the market?

2. How fast is it growing?

3. How much market share can this company realistically capture?

If your materials and management meetings clearly answer those three questions, you've done half your job. Buyers want to see evidence of potential, and that means framing your story around where the business is going. Paint the vision of what's next: the opportunities you haven't yet tapped, the products in development, and the partnerships on the horizon. Buyers don't fall in love with spreadsheets; they fall in love with stories.

Passion and Energy Sell

Here's something sellers underestimate almost every time: Your enthusiasm matters. Buyers want to feel that you still believe in what you've built, and that you're excited about its future. Passion is contagious, and in a business sale, it's persuasive.

I've seen founders walk into management meetings drained from the process, cautious not to seem "too eager," and deliver flat, mechanical presentations. They think professionalism means restraint. It doesn't. What buyers see instead is fatigue, ambivalence, or even hidden problems. Remember, these people are deciding whether to write a gigantic check (or not). They want to believe they're buying something alive, something that still has room to grow.

When you speak about your business, light up. Let them feel your pride. Show them the spark that got you here. Buyers will notice. Their logic might close the deal, but their emotion, and their excitement about what's possible, is what opens the wallet.

Good Reasons to Sell vs. Bad Reasons to Sell

Buyers are also evaluating *why* you're selling. They're trying to read your motivation, because that tells them what kind of partner you'll be post-closing and how confident you are in the company's future.

Good reasons sound like this:

- "I've built something incredible and want to find a partner who can help it scale faster than I can on my own."

- "We've reached a stage where the company needs more resources to grow internationally."

- "Personally, I'm ready for the next chapter, but I care deeply about the future of the business and my team."

These reasons communicate intentionality and care. They tell buyers that you're not desperate, disengaged, or trying to offload problems.

Bad reasons, on the other hand, are red flags:

- "I'm tired."

- "I want out."

- "I don't like dealing with employees anymore."

- "I'm worried about where the economy's headed."

Statements like that make buyers nervous. They signal burnout, instability, or hidden weaknesses. Buyers worry that if the founder's passion is gone, maybe the company's momentum is, too.

Don't Bury the Lead

When you finally sit across from serious buyers, you step into the most valuable real estate in the entire deal process: face-to-face time. This is the moment when your business stops being numbers on a spreadsheet and becomes a living, breathing opportunity. The challenge is that these meetings move fast. There are questions, sidebar discussions, buyer introductions, and slide decks to get through. Almost every founder walks out saying some version of "We did not even get halfway through what we wanted to cover."

That is not a failure of preparation. It is a failure of prioritization. In these meetings, time is your scarcest resource, and your job is to lead with what matters most.

The instinct for many owners is to save the big reveal for the end, kind of like a movie trailer that builds suspense. That is a mistake. If you run out of time, buyers may never hear the most compelling part of your growth story. In person, you do not want polite interest. You want active imagination. You want buyers leaning in, asking follow-up questions, and picturing themselves owning and scaling your company.

The question you should ask yourself before you walk into that room is simple. If I only have twenty minutes, what must they walk away knowing? Put that content at the front, not the back. Open strong by showing what is working, how fast it is growing, and where the momentum is heading.

Once you have grounded buyers in performance, shift quickly to potential. Growth rates, retention metrics, customer adoption, and product margins are critical, and you should absolutely highlight them. But numbers alone put a ceiling on imagination. Eventually, buyers reverse-engineer what they see. They model, discount, and rationalize, which means you cannot let the entire conversation live in what exists today.

When to Reveal Your Secret Weapon

The most compelling founders balance proof with possibility. They say, "Here is what we have built, and here is where it can go." This dual narrative triggers logic and aspiration at the same time. It is the difference between a business that looks successful and one that feels boundless.

That is where your "Columbo" moment comes in. In the old television show, Detective Columbo solved cases by pretending the discussion was over, only to turn back with "just one more thing" that changed everything. You want to do the same thing. Toward the end of the conversation, once trust and credibility are established, pause, lean in slightly, and casually introduce something new.

In this context, your moment is not a gimmick. It is a strategic reveal. It is something you have not shown in the data room, not offered in earlier calls, and not fully built yet. A new product concept. A new market category. A new distribution channel. Something big enough to spark curiosity, but early enough to feel like unlocked upside. Buyers love discovery, and you are giving them a glimpse into a future they can help create.

This approach mirrors an interesting truth in capital markets. Early-stage companies often raise money more easily than mature ones. Before revenue, hope is limitless. As soon as a product launches, reality steps in. Buyers can evaluate margins, velocity, adoption curves, and churn. Potential narrows to a spreadsheet.

In a business sale, the same dynamic applies. Established results build confidence, but undiscovered opportunity creates desire. I once worked with a founder who had a fast-growing product line. The traction was undeniable, and the numbers supported a premium valuation. But we both knew that as strong as the growth was, it was measurable and knowable. Every buyer could project it. There was no mystery left in the model.

Together, we developed a brand-new product concept that extended the core technology into a completely different market. It wasn't a fantasy, but a real idea with compelling logic. No prototype existed yet, but we could speak credibly about the market size, customer pain point, channel strategy, and why we believed it could be transformational. When buyers heard that, their posture changed. They stopped thinking like accountants and started thinking like visionaries. The deal ultimately commanded a higher multiple not because of what the company had *done*, but because of what it could *become*.

That is the power of framing. In the limited, high-stakes moments when you sit across from potential buyers, you are not only selling the business you built, but also selling the future they want to own.

The Shifting Power Dynamics

There are three distinct emotional and power shifts that unfold as a deal progresses, three invisible but predictable chapters in the psychology of transactions. Most owners are prepared for the financial and legal mechanics of a sale, but few are ready for these shifts in tone, leverage, and energy. They sneak up on you, altering the emotional temperature of the deal before you even realize what's happening.

When you understand these transitions, you'll navigate the process with greater composure, and it will help you get the most for your company. If you don't, you'll find yourself wondering how a conversation that once felt exciting suddenly feels adversarial.

1. Pre-LOI: The Courtship Phase

Before you sign an LOI, everything feels light and full of possibility. You're being courted. Buyers are upbeat, enthusiastic, and generous with praise. They tell you your company is exactly what they've been looking for, your culture is impressive, and your margins are strong. Every conversation feels positive. Every question you ask is met with reassurance. You're in the "rainbows and cotton candy" stage of the business sale process—the pre-LOI honeymoon.

At this point, you, the owner, hold all the power. There may be several interested parties, and the buyer knows it. Their job is to convince you that they are the best fit financially, strategically, and personally. They want you to like them. Their tone is deferential, accommodating, and charming. They'll tell you they're flexible on structure, that integration will be painless, and that they'll take care of your team. This is by design. Their goal is to win exclusivity and be the one you choose when you finally sign the LOI.

Many owners mistake this enthusiasm for a preview of what's to come. They think, "These people get me. This is going to be smooth." But that's the first emotional trap. What you're experiencing isn't the reality of the relationship. It's the sales pitch. Buyers at this stage are in marketing mode. They're not evaluating you; they're auditioning for you. And you, as the seller, are in control. You set the pace, decide who gets access, and choose who stays in the race. You're the prize everyone's chasing.

2. LOI to Purchase Agreement – The Reality Check

Then, almost overnight, it all changes. The ink dries on the LOI, and the tone shifts from enthusiasm to evaluation. It's not that the buyer suddenly turns unfriendly or distrustful, it's just that the relationship enters a new phase. They've already won you. Now they need to decide if they actually want to buy you.

Once the LOI is signed, you've entered into an exclusive agreement. That exclusivity changes the power dynamic. Before, you had multiple suitors; now, you've committed to one. The buyer no longer has to compete. Their focus shifts from selling to verifying and their questions multiply. The document requests grow longer, and the calls get more detailed. You'll be asked to explain line items, justify assumptions, and defend adjustments. This is when founders start to feel the emotional fatigue of the process.

It's easy to take this personally. After all, it can feel like the same people who were praising your leadership and culture last month are now dissecting each expense and questioning your decisions. You might feel defensive, or even insulted. But this is not betrayal. It's diligence. Their lawyers, accountants, and analysts are now running the show. The buyer's tone shifts because their goal has shifted from winning the deal to de-risking it. They're no longer asking, "How do we get this done?" They're asking, "Should we still do this?"

During this stage, the power firmly tilts toward the buyer. They hold the pen on timing, on diligence, and often on final terms. You're no longer the one choosing; you're being chosen. Your job becomes proving that your business is everything they hoped it would be. The biggest mistake a seller can make at this stage is to panic or take offense. The best thing you can do is stay calm, professional, and proactive. This is where preparation, both emotional and operational, separates strong sellers from frustrated ones.

3. Purchase Agreement to Closing – The Reversal

Once the purchase agreement is finalized and the deal nears closing, the dynamic tilts yet again. Buyers, now deep in diligence and integration planning, are heavily invested financially, strategically, and emotionally. They want the deal to close. And the surprise is that the leverage you thought you lost begins to return.

Time pressure flips the script. The buyer's team is burning hours, fees, and reputation. They've told their board and investors this deal is happening. The closer you get to closing, the more your steadiness and professionalism can strengthen your position again. Sellers who understand this rhythm can use it to maintain confidence through the middle chaos, knowing the power pendulum will eventually swing back.

Deals moves through three acts: courtship, scrutiny, and commitment. The wise seller knows not to get swept up in the highs or rattled by the lows. The buyer's tone will change, their posture will shift, and their power will rise and fall, but your steadiness is the constant. Understanding these emotional transitions enables you to lead them. When you recognize the pattern, you stop reacting and start responding, and that's where the real mastery of deal-making begins.

When you expect the shifts in tone, from charm to pressure to calm, you can stay grounded. You'll know when to press, when to pause, and when to let the process breathe. And you'll see the bigger picture: that the deal isn't a financial negotiation alone. It's a psychological one. The best founders don't manage numbers and sell their companies; they manage the emotional rhythm of the transaction and lead their exits.

Choosing the Right Buyer

On the surface, selling a company appears to be about the numbers, with buyers competing with term sheets, valuation multiples, earnout percentages, and closing dates. Those are measurable and easy to compare side by side. They feel objective and rational, and because owners live in a world of metrics and performance, it is natural to gravitate toward the cleanest spreadsheet verdict.

But here is the truth that every founder learns sooner or later: The offer price is only one part of the outcome, and it may not even be the most important part. The harder work—the much harder work—is choosing the right buyer. This is not just a transaction; it's a transition. It's a partnership, and in many cases a multi-year relationship after the close.

You are not just selling what you built. You are choosing who will inherit it, shape it, and lead it forward. You are choosing the people you will be tied to throughout your earnout period or during your advisory phase. You are choosing the people who will influence your brand, your employees, and possibly your legacy in the community.

If you get the buyer wrong, no valuation multiple will save you from frustration or regret. If you get the buyer right, even the deal that did not squeeze out every last dollar can feel like a win for decades.

But choosing the right deal and the right buyer isn't always easy.

One of the most common things owners tell me at this stage is "I thought this would feel clearer. I have three offers, but I'm more confused than when I didn't have any." This confusion is not a sign you're bad at decisions. It's a sign you're looking at genuinely complex trade-offs where there is no objectively "right" answer. Every founder faces this paralysis.

Talk to Founders Who Have Sold to Them

No one can give you better insight into a buyer than the people who have already sold to them. This is founder due diligence, and it might be the single most valuable step in your entire process.

When a buyer wants your company, they will share a polished track record. They will describe their culture, their post-acquisition support, and their long-term strategy. They will point to successful integrations and other satisfied sellers who stayed on, thrived, and celebrated their exits. Your job is to look behind the talk.

Reach out to other founders who have sold to the same buyer. Ask about their real experiences once the champagne corks hit the floor and life moved from celebration to execution. Ask them what surprised them, what they would do differently, what mistakes they made, and what expectations were met or missed. Ask them if they would do another deal with the same buyer. That last question tells you almost everything.

These conversations often reveal the truth in ways that slick slides never will. You might hear about shared strategic alignment, transparency, and real investment in growth. Or you may learn about cost-cutting that gutted teams, aggressive oversight that stifled the culture, or earnout structures that became battles rather than celebrations.

In my experience, most founders are willing to have these conversations. They remember how uncertain they felt. They remember the emotions, the vulnerability, and the stakes. They remember sitting in your shoes. And because owners have a sense of loyalty to one another, many will be candid and direct about their experiences.

Do not rely solely on introductions that come from the buyer or from your banker. Those referrals will be carefully curated. Find your own. Network quietly, reaching out through industry contacts, and connect on LinkedIn. You are not trying to dig dirt. You are engaging in responsible stewardship of what you built. Those conversations may save you from the wrong buyer, or give you the confidence that you found the right one.

Reverse Due Diligence – The Second Negotiation Most Owners Miss

When you go through due diligence, the buyer will examine each aspect of your business. That is their responsibility. But what many founders forget is that they also have a similar responsibility. You should be doing due diligence on the buyer—what I call "reverse" due diligence.

Rollover equity is often presented as the "upside opportunity," but sophisticated sellers treat it as a new capital commitment, not a reward. In most transactions, the buyer is asking you to reinvest part of your own proceeds back into the business you sold. That means you must evaluate the rollover with the same rigor you would apply if someone brought you a private investment offering.

Many sellers focus entirely on the cash at closing, and treat the equity piece as an afterthought. That is a mistake. The rollover can be where even more wealth is created, but it can also be where it quietly disappears.

Begin with governance and information rights. You do not need operational control, but you do need visibility. Confirm you will receive regular financial reporting, key performance metrics, and meaningful insight into strategic decisions.

Next, clarify liquidity. Rollover equity is not a liquid security. You cannot sell at will or exit when you choose. Understand when the next liquidity event is expected and what determines the timing. If the buyer is a private equity firm, ask where they are in the life of their fund. If they are early in a fund cycle, they may have years to build value. If they are late in a cycle, they may be operating on a compressed timeline.

Protect yourself in the capital structure. Determine whether you will hold the same class of equity as the buyer or whether you sit below preferred investors who receive priority distributions or liquidation rights. Ask how future capital infusions, incentive pools, or recapitalizations will affect your stake. Quiet dilution is a common and painful outcome when sellers do not ask questions.

Approach the rollover like a disciplined investor. Request the operating agreement, capitalization table, waterfall model, and financial projections. Understand debt terms and covenants. If you are expected to remain in the business post-closing, confirm if and how your equity vests over time and what happens if your role changes or ends before you've fully earned it.

Key reverse due diligence questions and documents to request include:

- Fund age, expected exit horizon, and target returns

- Where the firm sits in its fund lifecycle

- Class of equity you will receive and its position relative to preferred units

- Operating agreement, capitalization table, and distribution waterfall

- Quarterly financial reporting and KPI reporting

- Debt structure and covenant requirements

- Tag-along rights and restrictions on transfers

- Track record of prior funds and realized returns

These requests are not adversarial. They signal sophistication and seriousness. A rollover can multiply the value of your exit, but only if you understand precisely what you are receiving, how decisions will be made, and how and when you can participate in the next liquidity event.

Cultural Fit: The Hidden Variable

Culture is the part of business that does not show up in the data room. It is not a line item on a spreadsheet or a paragraph in a term sheet. Culture is tone, values, attitude, and behavior. It is how decisions get made. It is the feeling you get when you walk into a room and talk with someone who will soon share the responsibility for your life's work.

If you are staying on for a transition period, this matters even more. You will be working with these people. You will be solving problems, reporting results, and making decisions together. If you sense misalignment, listen to that instinct. Culture friction is not a nuisance. It is a liability.

Ask yourself:

- Do I trust these people to run my business?
- Do I believe they care about the mission and the team?
- Do I feel respected and heard?
- Can I see myself working with them for two years or more?

If you pause on any of those questions, that is important data to consider. Culture impacts retention, integration, growth, morale, and your own fulfillment.

How do they talk about your team? Do they speak respectfully about your employees? Are they genuinely curious about your culture, or are they focused only on spreadsheets and synergies? How they treat you during negotiations is often how they'll treat your people afterward. The right buyer will be someone who values what you've built and will carry it forward with integrity.

How to Know If It's the Right Deal

The right deal is not an accident. It is built through clarity and discipline. You will know it is right when three elements lock into place:

Financial clarity. You understand exactly what you will receive, how you will receive it, and what risks or contingencies exist.

Cultural alignment. You trust the buyer and believe they will honor the business, care for your people, and build on what you created.

Emotional readiness. You feel complete, not conflicted. You can let go with confidence. You are not selling to escape something. You are choosing to move toward something.

When all three align, the deal is right. When even one is missing, a wise seller pauses. Deals succeed when founders lead with clarity, not adrenaline.

Choosing the right buyer is one of the most meaningful decisions of your life. It is not just the closing chapter of your journey, it is the bridge to the next one. Your company deserves a thoughtful transition. Your employees deserve a partner who respects what you've built. And you deserve a future shaped by intention, not pressure.

Take the time to evaluate buyers deeply, listen to other founders, trust your instincts, and choose alignment over urgency. You'll close the deal not only wealthier, but lighter, clearer, and proud of how you handled the most important decision of your business life.

The Emotional Marathon – Finishing Strong

Selling your company is one of the most demanding things you'll ever do: physically, mentally, and emotionally.

You'll need stamina, discipline, and a clear head to make it to the finish line without collapsing. Remember, you're not only running your company; you're also managing bankers, lawyers, accountants, and potential buyers, all while answering the relentless stream of "just one more" document requests that seem to never end.

At first, adrenaline and excitement carries you. But over time, the process wears you down. It's not the workload; it's the emotional grind. You're asked to justify decisions, explain expenses, and open up all corners of your business to scrutiny. It's invasive and exhausting. You can't approach the sale like a sprint. You need to train for the long race, by protecting your body and your mind.

Hitting the Wall

Here's what happens to almost every seller at some point: You hit the wall. Months into the process, you're exhausted. You've been working nights and weekends, running the company by day, and selling it by night. You've answered hundreds of questions, survived multiple rounds of diligence, and spent hours on calls dissecting each clause in the purchase agreement. You're worn thin.

When you finally reach what looks like the end, the definitive purchase agreement, you can see the light at the end of the tunnel. You can almost feel the relief. Could this finally be over?

Right then, when you are mentally and emotionally spent, that is when the hard conversations start. Post-sale employment terms. Earnout formulas. Non-compete provisions. Deferred compensation. The details that truly shape your financial future are negotiated after you are already exhausted.

And this is where many sellers stumble. They want it to be over, and they start saying yes too quickly, convincing themselves that pushing through the finish line means accepting whatever is put in front of them. They rationalize that a few small concessions won't matter, even though those "small" concessions can cost millions.

It's human nature. Fatigue changes perspective. When you are tired enough, peace feels more valuable than precision. That is why pace and emotional management are not soft skills in a deal. They are financial skills. The best founders do not win because they are the smartest. They win because they stay clear enough, long enough, to negotiate with strength instead of surrender.

Sometimes the strongest move a founder can make is to step back. I watched this play out firsthand with a client who was in the middle of a grueling diligence process. The buyer was pushing hard to calculate the earnout using a specific formula. On paper, it looked reasonable, but my client could not shake the sense that something felt off. His instinct told him the structure did not reflect how the business truly performed or how revenue would materialize.

For two weeks, the conversation dragged on. Every day brought new models, new legal edits, and new arguments from the buyer's side. The legal bill kept growing, his patience was disappearing, and his frustration was clear. "Why am I paying my attorneys this much to argue with me about how my own company works?"

He was worn down, frustrated by the time drain and furious about the mounting attorney fees. At one point, he told me he might give in to get it over with. That is the danger zone, when exhaustion disguises itself as reason. I could see he did not want to give up. He needed relief. So I told him I would take over for a bit. My goal was simple. I wanted to buy him time and space to take his mind off it.

I stepped in, handled communications for a few days, and kept the conversation moving without forcing decisions. That brief reset made all the difference, and, a few days later, he came back with energy, clarity, and conviction. He re-entered the negotiations with a steadier mindset and a stronger voice. Instead of caving, he secured terms that fairly protected his earnout.

Marathoners talk about hitting the "wall"—that point where their body screams to quit. The runners who push through it aren't superhuman. They just expect it. They've trained for it. Maybe we could all learn something from them.

Mental Fitness Is Financial Fitness

There is a reality many founders underestimate until they are in the middle of a sale process: Your mindset is not a side factor. It is a financial lever. The clearer and calmer you are, the better you negotiate. The more rested and grounded you feel, the more strategic and confident your decisions become. Emotional stability shows up in the numbers, in the terms, and in your ability to hold the line when it matters most.

Mental fitness during a sale is not about being stoic or pretending you do not feel the pressure. It is about protecting your sharpness. Your attention, emotional bandwidth, confidence, and resilience are not unlimited. If you drain them early, you will negotiate tired. And tired founders leave money on the table.

Do not treat stamina as optional. Invest in sleep, movement, nutrition, and quiet thinking time. Create space to decompress so you do not lose clarity. The deals that change lives are won in the final stretch, when 90 percent of people are too tired to advocate for the outcome they originally set out to achieve.

Your company has demanded determination from you for years. This final chapter will demand it again. Do not merely finish the race. Finish proud, clear-minded, and strong. That is where the difference between a good outcome and a life-changing outcome is decided.

Plan an Adventure

Selling your company can take months—sometimes more than a year—and that kind of effort inevitably wears you down. It's easy to lose perspective and feel buried in the process. This is why I encourage owners to plan something meaningful and restorative for immediately after the deal closes.

It gives you a psychological finish line to look forward to—something bright on the horizon that helps pull you through the darker moments. Visualizing what comes next—such as a beach or a mountain—can make all the difference.

One of my clients understood this perfectly. He was selling his logistics business, and the process was brutal: long, complicated, and emotionally draining. But he had a secret weapon: a plan to climb Mount Kilimanjaro right after closing. Whenever things got overwhelming, he'd talk about standing at 19,341 feet, looking out over Africa. That image kept him focused and calm. He used it as motivation when the buyer pushed back on terms or when fatigue crept in.

A few months after the sale, I got to join him at the top of that mountain. Standing there together, after everything he had been through, was a powerful reminder that the sale isn't the end. It's the summit of one chapter and the base camp of the next.

One of the biggest mistakes new retirees make is assuming they will instantly know how to fill their time. After years of constant motion, the stillness can feel unsettling. Having something planned for immediately after the sale prevents that shock, and gives you direction once the ink dries, reminding you that your story continues.

This matters even if you remain involved through an earnout. Many owners stay with their companies for a year or two after the sale, tied to performance targets. But your life no longer has to revolve around them. That period between ownership and full separation is an ideal time to begin building the habits of your next chapter. Having something outside the company that excites you, such as a trip, a course, or a creative pursuit, helps you stay balanced and keeps you from clinging too tightly when it's time to fully let go.

What big adventure, trip, or excursion could you do after you sell that gets you excited? A weekend road trip probably isn't emotionally captivating enough to get you through the tough times. You need something exciting. Something that gets your blood pumping. Something you would be thrilled to do. For some, it may be hanging out on a beach somewhere. For others, it could be doing something challenging and bold, like my adventurous mountaineering client. What do you want to do after you sell?

But here's the difficult reality. Sometimes, despite all your preparation and anticipation, the deal doesn't close. The adventure gets postponed. The summit you've been visualizing slips out of reach, not because you failed, but because deals fall apart for reasons beyond your control. When that happens, knowing how to respond can make the difference between a temporary setback and a lasting defeat.

When the Deal Falls Apart

If you've spent decades building a business, the sale can start to feel inevitable, almost preordained. The numbers line up, your banker is optimistic, and you can already picture yourself signing the deal. But here's a hard truth that all business owners need to hear: Sometimes the deal falls apart.

It can happen for a hundred reasons. Market conditions change. A buyer's financing collapses. Earnings dip at the wrong time. A key customer backs out. Maybe the buyer's investment committee simply gets cold feet. Whatever the reason, it's gutting, especially after months of emotional and financial investment.

But it's not the end. It's a setback—sometimes a devastating one—but it's also a source of intelligence. Every failed deal teaches you something about your business, your positioning, or the market. And often, the deal that falls apart leads to a better one down the road.

This section is about what to do when your deal collapses: how to process it emotionally, what to learn from it, and how to move forward without losing your mind or your company's momentum.

How to Process the Loss

When a deal collapses, you need to grieve it like any other major loss. Don't minimize what happened or tell yourself to "just move on." You invested months of your life into this. You made sacrifices and allowed yourself to hope. That deserves acknowledgment.

Here's how to process it constructively:

1. Take a break.

Don't make any major decisions for at least two weeks. No rushing into another deal. No pulling the company off the market out of spite. Just pause. Let your nervous system reset. You've been operating in fight-or-flight mode for months. Your body and mind need recovery time.

2. Talk to someone who gets it.

This is probably not your spouse (unless they've sold a business) or your employees (they're stressed enough). Talk to another founder who's been through a failed deal. They'll understand the specific flavor of this disappointment in a way others can't. If you don't have that person in your life, consider a therapist or executive coach who works with owners.

3. Debrief with your deal team.

Once the initial emotion settles, sit down with your investment banker, attorney, and advisors, and do a post-mortem. What did you learn? What could you have done differently? What signals did you miss? This isn't about assigning blame—it's about extracting intelligence for the next round.

4. Separate what you can control from what you can't.

Make two lists: things within your control (your company's performance, how you respond to diligence, your deal team, and your positioning) and things outside your control (buyer financing, macro conditions, and buyer's internal politics). Focus your energy on the first list. Let go of the second.

5. Protect your team.

Your employees likely knew a deal was in progress. Now it's not. They're confused, and maybe a bit worried. Communicate clearly and quickly. Reassure them that the company is stable. Don't overshare your frustration or blame the buyer publicly. Show leadership in the loss the same way you would have in the win.

Learning from the Failed Deal

Every failed transaction contains lessons. The owners who bounce back strongest are the ones who extract those lessons and apply them to the next attempt.

Ask yourself these questions:

About the buyer:

- Were there early warning signs we ignored?
- Did the buyer have the financial capacity they claimed?
- Was their interest genuine, or were they "shopping" without intent to close?

- Did their internal dynamics (leadership, strategy, portfolio) create instability?

About your business:

- What issues emerged during diligence that surprised us?

- Which concerns were legitimate vs. buyer's remorse?

- Are there structural problems we need to fix before going back to market?

- Did our financials, team, or operations hold up under scrutiny?

About the process:

- Did we move too fast or too slow?

- Did we maintain competitive tension, or did we put all our eggs in one basket?

- Did we negotiate effectively, or did we give up too much too early?

- Did our deal team perform well, or do we need to make changes?

About ourselves:

- Were we truly ready to sell, or were we ambivalent?

- Did fear or control issues sabotage the process?

- Did we communicate clearly and professionally throughout?

- Are we emotionally and psychologically prepared to try again?

Be brutally honest. This isn't about beating yourself up, it's about building self-awareness that makes the next attempt smoother.

Restarting the Process – When and How

The most common question after a failed deal is "When should I go back to market?"

The answer depends on why the deal failed and what you've learned.

Wait before restarting if:

- **You're still emotionally raw.** Don't negotiate your next deal from a place of desperation, anger, or exhaustion. Buyers can smell it, and it weakens your position.

- **Your business took a hit during the process.** If revenue dipped, key employees left, or operations suffered while you were distracted by diligence, stabilize first. You don't want to go back to market with declining metrics.

- **The market shifted dramatically.** If macro conditions caused the deal to fail and those conditions haven't improved, waiting might be wise. Selling into a down market rarely produces optimal results.

- **You discovered structural issues that need fixing.** If diligence exposed problems with customer concentration, financial reporting, or operational weaknesses, address them before reaching out to new buyers. Otherwise, you'll face the same objections again.

Restart quickly if:

- **The issue was buyer-specific, not company-specific.** If their financing fell through or their strategy changed, there's no reason to delay. Your company is still strong; you just need a different buyer.

- **You have other warm prospects.** If your investment banker kept other buyers engaged during the process, you might be able to pivot quickly to a backup. This is why maintaining competitive tension matters.

- **Market conditions are still favorable.** If your industry is hot and buyers are active, don't sit on the sidelines too long. Windows close.

- **You're financially and emotionally ready.** If you've processed the loss, learned from it, and still genuinely want to sell, there's no benefit to waiting. Get back out there.

Not every deal closes on the first try. Some owners go through multiple rounds before finding the right buyer at the right time. A failed deal is painful, but it's rarely fatal. Most owners who stay the course eventually get there. And when that moment arrives, everything you've learned along the way makes the outcome that much more rewarding.

Chapter Exit

You've learned that maximizing deal value isn't about getting the highest headline number. It's about getting the right deal, with the right structure, from the right buyer. You've seen how culture, alignment, and economics intersect. The true measure of success is walking away with confidence, knowing you didn't leave value on the table, but also knowing you didn't sacrifice your peace, your team, or your future for a few extra dollars.

The deal closes, the funds arrive, and suddenly the world feels different. The noise quiets, the adrenaline fades, and you're left with something you may not have felt in decades: space. For years you built wealth inside your company. Now you must learn to manage it as an investor, not an operator.

In the next chapter, we'll shift from selling to stewarding, from maximizing enterprise value to protecting and growing personal wealth. You'll learn how to turn a one-time liquidity event into lasting financial independence, how to structure your assets for security and freedom, and how to avoid the pitfalls that can erode a windfall. Because the sale isn't the finish line, it's the starting point for what comes next.

STAGE THREE:
AFTER

The wire hits your account. The deal is done! Champagne is poured, congratulations flood in, and everything feels perfect. Then the dust settles and reality arrives. Most sellers assume the hard part is over once the deal closes. They're wrong. The after stage is where the emotional weight finally lands. Identity shifts, relationships change, and the future you imagined suddenly feels uncertain. This is the stage most books ignore because it's messy, personal, and impossible to model in a spreadsheet. But how you navigate the months and years after the sale will determine whether you look back with pride or regret, whether your wealth becomes a tool for freedom or a source of anxiety, and whether you build something new or drift aimlessly. The deal may have ended, but your journey is just beginning.

CHAPTER 6:

MANAGE YOUR NEW WEALTH

*Turn a Liquidity Event
into Lasting Freedom*

When the offers started coming in, my client called me— not to celebrate, but to ask a question that caught me off guard. "Robert," he said quietly, "if one of these goes through, where do I even put all that money?"

He wasn't being arrogant. He was being honest. For twenty-five years, every dollar he had made went back into his business: hiring, equipment, marketing, and growth. The idea of suddenly holding tens of millions in cash wasn't exciting; it was unnerving. "I know how to build a company," he said. "But I've never had to manage this kind of money."

That moment captures the real turning point for most founders. Long before the money reaches your account, the smartest ones start thinking about what comes after—because selling your business and securing financial freedom are two completely different things. One is a transaction. The other is a transformation.

That's the irony of a liquidity event. The day you've dreamed about, the day when financial freedom becomes reality, can also be one of the most disorienting. You've spent decades building wealth through a business you could control, only to find yourself holding liquid assets that suddenly feel uncontrollable. Remember, the skills that made you a great business owner don't always translate cleanly into life after the sale.

This chapter is about that transition, from the moment you go from creating wealth to managing it. Because financial freedom isn't automatic; it's engineered. You'll learn how to turn a lump sum into a lifetime of stability, how to create a sustainable income strategy, and how to protect what you've built from taxes, volatility, and bad decisions. The sale gave you capital. Now, it's time to turn that capital into freedom.

The promise of this chapter is to "turn a liquidity event into lasting freedom." But how do you do that? Selling a business often creates a financial windfall overnight. Sure, many business owners had assets before the sale, but for most clients I've worked with, the vast majority of their net worth was tied up in their companies. Before the sale, it's hard to know how much a company is really worth. And that uncertainty can make it tough to do financial planning for clients. In fact, it almost got me fired…

Let me share one of my favorite client stories, because it highlights exactly why slowing down and planning with humility is so important, and why owners sometimes need a minute before fully appreciating the wisdom of conservative assumptions.

Years ago, I was sitting in a planning meeting with a business owner and his wife. I had spent days building their retirement and financial plan. I'd run multiple scenarios, stress-tested market returns, modeled taxes, and mapped out lifestyle spending. When I work with business owners, there is always one uniquely tricky variable: the company. I never truly know what the business will sell for, when it will sell, or if it will sell at all. Deals fall apart, markets shift, buyers disappear, and industries change. So in plans like this, I often assign the business a placeholder value of one dollar. This is not because I don't believe in the company, but because the plan needs to work even if the business never sells. It is a safeguard, a way to ensure the rest of the plan is strong enough on its own.

So there we are, reviewing the plan, and he suddenly points and says, "What the hell is that?" His finger was on the line where his business was listed at one dollar. Gulp. His wife gave me the kind of look that said I had royally screwed up.

I had to act fast, because the meeting was getting ugly. I walked him through my thinking. I explained that it wasn't about doubting him or the business, it was about building a plan that didn't require a liquidity event to work. If the business sold one day, great. If not, they were still on track. He understood the logic, eventually, but he was not thrilled. For years afterward, he'd remind me of that meeting, always half joking, half still annoyed that his life's work had been valued, even theoretically, at one dollar.

Fast-forward nearly a decade, and the client decides to sell. One morning, I open my inbox and see an email from him. No greeting. No explanation. Just two attachments: the original financial plan showing his business valued at $1 (yes, he had saved it after all those years!), and an LOI offering $78 million for that same company. The only line in the email read, "You were wrong."

I laughed, because technically, he was right, and that was the best possible outcome.

The goal for this chapter is to help you manage the new windfall from the sale of your business psychologically and financially. I've been helping clients manage sudden wealth for nearly thirty years. It's an area I fell into early on in my career, and it's one that I find fascinating. I get to work with people whose lives are changed overnight. They go from one socioeconomic stratum to another. As I've written and spoken about for years, the dynamics of sudden wealth are unique, and they are as much about psychology as they are about finances.

This chapter covers the emotional realities of sudden wealth, and the practical steps to convert your sale into lifetime income.

Emotional: The Psychology of Sudden Wealth

Selling your business can turn your life upside down. As someone with a master's degree in psychology and decades of experience working with sudden wealth recipients, I've seen this play out hundreds of times. Clients often describe it as being stripped of everything familiar—their routines, sense of purpose, and identity. Then they're dropped into a strange new world.

Imagine landing in a foreign country where you don't know the language, rules, or customs. The way people interact feels different. Even simple things like how decisions are made or what people value seem unfamiliar. You look around and realize that the world you knew, the one you built and understood, is gone. Exciting? Maybe. Unnerving? Absolutely.

I love to travel to new places. I thrive on the novelty, unfamiliar sounds, new smells, and energy. But when the wheels touch down back home, I feel a deep sense of relief. The thrill of the unknown gives way to the comfort of the familiar.

That transition happens quickly when I travel—I tolerate a plane ride and then I'm home again. But for business owners after a sale, that "return to normal" can take months, and even years. They've entered a new reality where their title, authority, and even daily purpose have changed.

If you're reading this chapter because the wire just hit and you're feeling something other than pure joy, let me say this clearly: You are not ungrateful, broken, or weak. You are experiencing one of the most disorienting transitions a human can face. I have worked with countless business owners post-sale, and almost all of them have described feeling some combination of relief, confusion, and a strange emptiness in the weeks after closing. Some feel guilty for not being happier. Others feel paralyzed by having too many options. A few even feel grief. All of it is normal. All of it is temporary. And all of it means you're human.

One of the key differences between those who adapt successfully and those who don't is how they see their role in this next phase. Business owners who take a passive role after the sale often struggle. They become spectators to their own new life, waiting for direction, leaning entirely on advisors, and letting others define what comes next. They feel hesitant to make decisions without the framework of their companies around them.

Those who thrive, by contrast, take an active role, engaging and making decisions. They see this next phase not as an ending, but as a new enterprise—one where they are once again the CEO, but this time of their wealth, time, and life.

In my book *The Sudden Wealth Solution*, I write about how you need to relax and breathe. That advice was never more important to me as it was a few years ago…

Have you ever choked or been unable to breathe? Imagine being in a small tent on the side of one of the world's tallest mountains in the middle of Africa and not being able to draw a breath. Medical help is days away. It's you and the mountain. Can you imagine the panic? What do you do?

This happened to me. I was two days into a seven-day climb up Mt. Kilimanjaro when I stopped breathing in the middle of the night. But I didn't panic. Instead, I smiled. Why? Because I knew what to expect. Before the trip, almost by accident, I had learned about a high-altitude phenomenon where your body intermittently stops breathing as it adapts to the thinner air. That knowledge changed it all for me. What could have been a terrifying experience, became a moment of calm awareness.

Fear often comes from not knowing what's happening or what's going to happen next.

Life after selling your business is no different. Much of the anxiety former owners feel isn't about money. It's about not knowing what comes next. The more you understand the emotional and financial stages that follow a sale, the more prepared you'll be.

When you can anticipate what's coming, you can approach the process with confidence instead of fear. Awareness replaces worry. Knowledge replaces panic.

And, like I experienced on that mountain, understanding what's happening gives you the power to breathe again.

The Sudden Wealth Paradox

You built a business for decades believing that once you sold, you'd feel secure. You'd have "enough". The stress would end. The nerves would lift. Money would finally solve the problem.

But when the money reaches your account, something unexpected happens. Instead of relief, you feel new fears. What if you lose it? What if you invest wrong? What if someone sues you? What if the market crashes? Suddenly, having wealth you've never had before creates new anxieties.

You went from concentrated confidence—all your eggs in one basket you controlled—to diversified uncertainty. You understood your business. You don't understand portfolio management. The numbers are bigger, but the comfort is less.

This is normal—expected, even. Sudden wealth creates new psychological challenges. The solution isn't ignoring these feelings or pretending they don't exist. It's building a plan that provides both growth and security, working with advisors you trust, and giving yourself time to adjust to your new reality.

You think money will give you security—but having it creates fears you didn't expect.

The Power of Slowing Down

Sudden wealth feels like being dropped into a foreign country without a map or a translator. Everything looks familiar, but nothing works the way it used to. Whether the wealth comes from selling a business, an IPO, a lawsuit, inheritance, or another windfall, the emotional experience is remarkably consistent. People describe it as exhilarating and terrifying at the same time. There is excitement, but also confusion. There is possibility, but also pressure. It feels like everyone expects you to know exactly what to do, yet inside you're thinking, "I've never done this before. Why does everyone else seem so sure?"

That emotional surge creates a dangerous paradox. The moment you have the most financial opportunity is also the moment you are most vulnerable to poor decisions. When the transaction accelerates—when lawyers, accountants, bankers, friends, and family all want answers and actions—the right move is often the opposite of what the world expects. Instead of rushing forward, you need to pause, breathe, and slow down.

Sudden wealth brings with it a rush of decisions, requests, and ideas. People feel pressure to act because they assume great wealth requires immediate movement. They believe they must invest quickly, buy quickly, give quickly, and change quickly. They feel a moral obligation to "do something" with their money right now. But urgency is the enemy of good judgment. When emotions are high, decision-making ability falls. Your brain is not built to handle joy and anxiety simultaneously while also analyzing complex financial choices. This is why lottery winners and athletes burn through fortunes, and why even highly intelligent executives can stumble after an exit.

Slowing down isn't about being passive; it's about regaining control. The goal is not to stop progress forever, just long enough for your head and heart to catch up with your personal balance sheet. Sudden wealth is overwhelming because life changes instantly, but your psychology lags behind. You are the same person, with the same habits and beliefs you had yesterday, suddenly asked to operate like someone with decades of wealth experience. That's unrealistic, and trying to force it only creates stress, fear, and mistakes.

One of the most powerful steps during this moment is to create space between impulse and action. Before you buy something new, invest in a private deal, fund a foundation, or make a major gift, give yourself time. Let the emotions settle. Give your brain room to process your new reality. This is not restraint born of fear, it is discipline born of wisdom. People get into trouble when they confuse motion with progress. You do not need to prove you deserve your success by immediately doing something with the money. You already earned it. Now you get to be thoughtful.

Part of slowing down means protecting your routine. Sudden wealth disrupts normalcy, and the more chaos you feel, the more you need familiarity. Keep exercising. Keep eating the way you usually do. Maintain your morning rituals, your social circles, and your hobbies. These familiar anchors stabilize your mind and body when everything else feels new and overwhelming. A simple walk, a workout, or lunch with a friend, are not luxuries right now; they are grounding mechanisms.

It also helps to stay connected to people who truly support you. Not everyone will. Some will be excited for you. Some will secretly be jealous. Some will suddenly have advice, business ideas, or needs. Others may act distant or uncomfortable. It's easy to isolate during this transition, or to rely too heavily on opinions from people who do not understand what you are going through. Reach out to grounded friends who can be present with you. Sometimes the most valuable thing they offer is perspective and normality.

Professional support matters, too. Not every advisor understands the emotional side of sudden wealth. If your attorney, accountant, or advisor pushes you to move faster than you feel comfortable, hit pause. Remember: They have seen these situations many times, and work in this world daily. You haven't. Your timeline does not need to match theirs. Financial decisions are important, but clarity and confidence are more important. When you slow down, you make better decisions and feel better about them.

Another powerful tool is to capture your thoughts before you act on them. In the early days after receiving significant wealth, ideas and possibilities come quickly. Write down everything, even the ideas that seem silly or extravagant. Don't evaluate yet. Just collect. The act of writing creates clarity and reduces emotional pressure. It turns swirling thoughts into grounded ideas. Later, when your emotions are steadier, you can look at your list and make intentional choices, as opposed to impulsive ones.

Exercise, journaling, talking to supportive people, meditating, and breathing practices all help settle your nervous system. Wealth changes circumstances overnight, but your physiology still needs time to adjust. These grounding activities keep you centered so you can think clearly instead of reacting to pressure.

Most importantly, whatever you're feeling is normal, be it confusion, excitement, fear, or guilt. You earned a life-changing opportunity, and now you must adjust to a new reality. Pause. Breathe. Get centered. Then move with intention, not adrenaline. And if you are still unsure what decisions you should or shouldn't make, play the stoplight game.

Green, Yellow, and Red Decisions

In *The Sudden Wealth Solution*, I introduced one of the simplest and most practical decision filters for the first phase after a windfall: the green, yellow, and red framework. It applies equally well after the sale of a business. When liquidity arrives, decisions rush in alongside it, and you feel a subtle pressure to "put the money to work." Without a disciplined filter, it becomes easy to rush, react, and regret. This framework slows decision-making to a pace that serves you rather than overwhelms you.

Green Decisions: Immediate and Safe

Green decisions are clear, necessary, and low-risk. They strengthen your foundation and provide stability during a period of transition.

Examples include:

- Paying off high-interest debt

- Ensuring adequate liquidity for living expenses

- Establishing a short-term cash and treasury-management plan

- Reviewing and updating insurance coverage

- Putting simple, temporary spending and gifting guardrails in place

Green decisions are about security and structure. They help create room to breathe, adjust, and think before making long-term choices. They do not move you forward rapidly, but they keep you safe while you get your footing.

Yellow Decisions: Pause, Evaluate, and Verify

Yellow decisions are meaningful and often highly beneficial, but they deserve planning, consultation, and intentional pacing. They are the decisions that shape the next chapter of your life, not just the next ninety days.

Examples include:

- Developing your long-term investment strategy

- Purchasing real estate or making lifestyle-influencing commitments

- Determining long-term asset allocation and wealth structures

- Evaluating business reinvestment or entrepreneurial opportunities

- Designing philanthropic or legacy strategies

- Having family financial conversations

Yellow does not mean "no." It means "not yet." You analyze, discuss, stress-test, and proceed thoughtfully and confidently instead of emotionally or impulsively.

Red Decisions: Avoid Early in the Transition

Red decisions are emotionally charged, pressured, irreversible, or rooted more in ego than strategy. These decisions tend to show up quickly after liquidity and often feel urgent, exciting, or validating.

Examples include:

- Funding other people's ventures merely because you can

- Starting a new business to fill a void or escape discomfort

- Making large luxury purchases for status or identity reassurance

- Entering private investments without deep due diligence and patience

- Making long-term promises before knowing what you truly want

Red decisions are where many post-sale regrets are created. Avoid them, not because they are always wrong, but because the early period after a sale is a vulnerable time. Your psychology is shifting, your identity is evolving, and rushing into big commitments can limit options and reduce negotiating power.

The color system is not meant to be restrictive. A liquidity event changes both your balance sheet and your psychology, and your early choices set the tone for what follows. The goal is to protect freedom, not limit it. When you master the timing of decisions, you protect your capital and future opportunities.

In this stage, being patient is not passive. Similarly, discipline is not austerity. It is power.

Do Not Spend the Money Before You Have It

One of the most dangerous mistakes an owner can make during a sale process happens long before the funds ever hit their account. They begin spending the money before the deal closes. This is human nature. The moment a promising term sheet appears or an LOI is signed, the mind races ahead. You start imagining the home you will buy, the trips you will take, the new chapter of life that suddenly feels guaranteed. Thinking about it is normal. Acting on it is something else entirely.

I call this "cashing the check before it clears." The fantasy becomes planning, and the planning quietly becomes spending. Sellers start rationalizing financial decisions as if the outcome were already certain. But nothing is certain until the wire arrives. Deals can fall apart for reasons that are unpredictable and sometimes unfair. Spending early creates financial risk, and that creates psychological risk.

There is a second, more subtle danger. When you commit to expenses you cannot comfortably support without a completed sale, you weaken yourself in negotiations. Instead of approaching the deal with confidence and patience, you enter with urgency. Urgency becomes pressure, and pressure becomes desperation. A desperate seller is a vulnerable seller. They push back less, accepting terms they would have rejected six months earlier. They want the deal to happen, not because it is the right deal, but because they need it to happen. Buyers can sense this shift immediately, and once they do, the balance of power moves in their direction.

I worked with a client who learned this the hard way. Early in the sale process, before anything binding was signed, he purchased a new oceanfront home. The property was stunning, but there was a problem: He could not afford it unless his company sold. I strongly advised against the purchase, but emotion (and a killer view!) won the day. The result was predictable. The distraction of acquiring and renovating the home pulled his time and attention away from both the business and the sale process. Then the financial pressure began to build. During the most complex phase of negotiations, he confided that he was losing sleep. He told me he felt a new sense of anxiety in meetings with the buyer, and he feared that, if the deal fell apart, he would be in real trouble. In his own words, "I lost my edge."

He ultimately closed, but the cost was stress, loss of leverage, and likely a reduction in final value. His lesson is clear. Discipline matters. Until the funds clear and you have full control of the proceeds, do not take on major new financial commitments. Do not buy the house. Do not lock in the yacht. Do not change your lifestyle based on money that has not arrived. Guard your financial power and your negotiating strength.

When Money Changes the Room

Money changes people, and relationships. Most owners notice shifts after sales. Some are positive; others aren't. I've heard versions of the same story for years. "We drifted." "They expected too much." "I changed." "They changed." It's noble to think nothing will be different when your net worth jumps, but it's not realistic.

Both sides feel it. Owners say friends and family who weren't there when needed, applied pressure to help them financially. Friends and family say the owner got distant or "let money change them." The result isn't just stress. It can be real loss: divorce, fractured friendships, and estranged relatives. That's why liquidity events get a bad rap.

The truth is that a big exit changes everyone. That doesn't necessarily doom your relationships, but it means you must manage them. Set expectations, communicate clearly, and take responsibility for how this new reality impacts the people you care about.

Common post-sale dilemmas (there are no perfect answers):

- Upgrade the house or car—how will close friends react?

- Group dinner—do you quietly pick up the check?

- A sibling asks for help; another doesn't—how do you stay fair and sane?

- Big trip you can afford—invite a friend who can't? Offer to pay?

- Party with mixed-income guests—do you scale it down or subsidize?

- Discretionary gifts such as tuition, rehab, debt payoff—how much, how often, and who decides?

Managing taxes, legal work, and investments can be straightforward compared to navigating expectations and feelings. There are rules for wealth, but there aren't rules for relationships. Your money doesn't have to be a divider, if you manage the relationships as intentionally as you managed your business.

If you are concerned about how your business sale proceeds will affect your most important relationships, I strongly recommend you read my book *The Sudden Wealth Solution*. It goes into much more detail about how to navigate your new wealth and your relationships.

Financial: Managing the Business Sale Proceeds

You built wealth by concentrating everything into one asset—your business. All your capital, effort, and risk were in one place. That concentration created asymmetric upside. It's how you won.

But the moment the wire reaches your account, every advisor tells you to do the opposite: diversify. Spread the wealth across stocks, bonds, real estate, and alternatives. Reduce concentration. Manage risk. Protect what you've built.

Intellectually, this makes sense. Emotionally, it feels wrong. You succeeded by going all-in. Diversification feels like dilution. You're shifting from a single bet you understood to a portfolio you don't. You're going from confidence to caution, from control to delegation.

I once explained this to a client by joking, "So you sold one company and now you have to manage 500!" The look on his face told me he got it immediately. He had spent his entire career building and running one business. That singular focus was the source of his success and ultimately his wealth. Then he sold it, cashed out, and invested the proceeds in an S&P 500 index fund. Overnight, he traded deep expertise in one enterprise for fractional ownership in hundreds of companies he would never understand with the same depth.

This transition is hardest right after your biggest win. You just proved that concentration works, and now you're supposed to abandon that strategy?

The reality is that the rules change when you're protecting wealth instead of building it. Concentration builds wealth. Diversification preserves it. Remember the Skill Shift Paradox? It applies to your money now, too. Call it the Reinvestment Paradox.

You win by concentrating everything into one asset and then must protect that win by diversifying into many.

And there's another shift happening simultaneously. Your wealth was previously locked inside your company. Your net worth grew every time the business expanded, hired, or reinvested, but most of that value was illiquid—it existed on paper, not in your checking account. You were asset rich but cash-flow dependent. After the sale, everything flips. Now you're sitting on liquid assets, but those assets must be converted into a reliable stream of income that can fund your life for decades.

You've gone from creator of value to allocator of capital. The game hasn't ended, but it most certainly has changed.

William Sharpe, a Nobel Prize-winning economist and one of the originators of the Capital Asset Pricing Model, described converting assets into income in retirement as "the nastiest, hardest problem in finance." That surprised the financial community. Of all the challenges in money and investing, nobody expected him to name this one.

Why is it so hard? Uncertainty. There are questions we just can't answer: How long will this wealth need to last? What returns will your portfolio produce, and in what order? What will taxes, inflation, and your own spending look like over the next thirty years? These unknowns make perfect planning impossible. But they don't make good planning impossible.

The Need for Escalating, Sustainable, and Predictable Income (ESP)

After a business sale, your financial life depends on one thing: income. But not just any income—it must be escalating, sustainable, and predictable.

Escalating because inflation quietly erodes purchasing power. If $10,000 a month covers your life today, it won't in twenty years. Sustainable because it needs to last as long as you do, balancing growth, preservation, and spending discipline across decades. Predictable because you need the same confidence you had when your business funded your life—knowing what's coming in this month, next month, and next year.

Achieving that balance is hard. Most owners move from one major source of wealth (their company) to relying on investment portfolios, installment payments, or passive income streams. Turning a portfolio into reliable income is deceptively simple to describe but extremely difficult to execute.

Post-Sale Financial Security

Post-sale financial security attempts to eradicate fear and uncertainty while providing a stable and predictable lifetime stream of income by focusing on five steps:

- Step 1: Calculate What You Can Spend Without Running Out

- Step 2: Structure Your Money So You Can Sleep at Night

- Step 3: Turn Your Assets Into Income That Never Stops

- Step 4: Stay on Financial Track

- Step 5: Build and Lead Your Post-Sale Advisory Team

Step 1: Calculate What You Can Spend Without Running Out

You may have heard of the "4 percent rule." Despite its popularity, it's widely misunderstood.

The idea began as an academic exercise, based on a specific and limited set of assumptions. Researchers looked back through historical market returns and asked, "What is the highest initial withdrawal percentage a retiree could take from a portfolio and still have it last at least thirty years?" They tested multiple market environments. Their finding: Withdraw 4 percent of your portfolio in year one, then adjust that dollar amount for inflation each subsequent year. This approach would likely provide sustainable income for thirty years or more. But that time horizon is crucial. The study only modeled three decades.

The second major misunderstanding is how the 4 percent is calculated. Many assume you pull 4 percent of the portfolio's balance each year. That is not the case. You calculate 4 percent only once, at the beginning. That dollar amount becomes your baseline, adjusted annually for inflation regardless of what markets do.

Here's how it works: Sell your business for $10 million, invest the proceeds, and withdraw $400,000 in year one. In subsequent years, you withdraw that same $400,000 (adjusted for inflation), not 4 percent of the current portfolio value.

The final foundational assumption was a standard portfolio composition: roughly half equities and half bonds. Researchers have since debated whether the safe rate should be higher or lower depending on market conditions, but that misses the point. There is no universally safe percentage. Anyone who treats 4 percent as a guarantee is misunderstanding its purpose.

Why the Order of Returns Matters

What makes withdrawal planning especially tricky is something called sequence of returns risk. The returns you experience are important, but the order in which you experience them can be even more important once you begin drawing cash from your portfolio.

Consider two founders who each sell their companies and invest identical amounts. They plan to withdraw the same dollar amount each year. Over thirty years, the average annual return on both portfolios is identical. On paper, it looks like a tie. In real life, it is not. If one founder gets strong returns in the early years and weaker ones later, the portfolio often holds up. Early growth builds a cushion, so later disappointments do less harm. If the other founder gets weak or negative returns in the early years, the portfolio can struggle to recover. Withdrawals continue while the asset base is smaller, so even a strong rebound later may not overcome the early damage.

This is why the first years after a sale deserve special protection. The goal is to avoid being forced to sell growth assets at depressed prices to fund lifestyle spending. If you can keep your income flowing from stable reserves while markets recover, you give your long-term investments the time they need to do their job.

Flexibility Is the Real Safeguard

For a business owner entering this new stage, the better perspective is to treat the withdrawal rate question as a flexible planning tool, not a rigid rule. If your asset base is large enough and your spending needs are moderate, a lower withdrawal rate may give you extraordinary longevity and peace of mind. If you require a higher withdrawal rate, then you must build flexibility into your life so you can adjust spending in difficult market periods. This might mean choosing not to increase your withdrawals in years when markets decline, or temporarily reducing discretionary expenses if conditions warrant. The danger lies not in spending, but in rigidity. Portfolios fail not because they support a lifestyle, but because they are asked to support one without adaptation.

The most powerful way to think about this is with a simple metaphor that a client once shared with me after listening to my long technical explanation of withdrawal theory. She smiled and said, "So what you are really saying is, do not kill the chicken." Your portfolio is the chicken and the income it produces are the eggs. If you become too aggressive in taking from the nest, you impair the thing that generates your livelihood. That simple idea has guided many clients more effectively than any mathematical formula ever could.

In short, the goal is not to find a magic percentage. It is to create a rational, flexible system for turning your life's work into lasting financial freedom.

Step 2: Structure Your Money So You Can Sleep at Night

The most effective method I have found for building a portfolio with confidence is what I call a tiered portfolio (sometimes also referred to as a bucket strategy). Think of this as rebuilding the dependable paycheck your business once provided, but through thoughtful investment design.

Your portfolio is divided into three conceptual pools of capital, each with a distinct purpose. The first is your long-term growth engine: the equities, real estate securities, and longer-duration investments intended to grow wealth over time and keep you ahead of inflation. The second is a stability reserve, typically consisting of low-volatility instruments such as short-term bonds or certificates of deposit, with enough set aside to cover several years of living expenses. The third is pure liquidity—cash held specifically to fund monthly spending needs.

At the start of each year, you hold roughly two years of living expenses in cash and another three years in low-volatility investments. This means that, no matter what markets do, you have a five-year runway of spending already secured. As you draw from the cash portion each month, you replenish it annually from the low-volatility pool, which in turn is replenished periodically from the growth portfolio. The flow moves in one direction: long-term growth assets feed the stability reserve, which feeds your spending account. You are always refilling from strength, not panic. In good market years, the process feels routine. In difficult markets, it becomes invaluable. You have already planned for uncertainty, which means you are never forced to sell assets at the wrong time to fund your lifestyle.

Risk Capacity vs. Risk Tolerance

Even with a solid structure, you will still need to choose how much risk to take. Two related ideas can help. Risk capacity is your financial ability to absorb losses without jeopardizing your plan. Risk tolerance is your emotional ability to remain invested when values fall. A founder with significant guaranteed income or modest spending needs has higher capacity. A founder who knows a 20 percent decline will cause sleepless nights has lower tolerance. If capacity is high and tolerance is low, the portfolio must be built to respect the lower number, not the higher one. If capacity is low and tolerance is high, restraint is vital because enthusiasm does not add dollars when markets disappoint.

There is also a paradox that trips up many sellers. What feels safest now is often riskiest later. A portfolio stuffed with cash and short-term bonds may feel secure, but it can struggle to support withdrawals over decades. A portfolio that owns a healthy share of equities may feel jumpy in the short term, but over long periods it tends to support higher sustainable income. The task is not to eliminate discomfort, but to choose the right discomfort. Choose the day-to-day wiggles that buy you long-term growth rather than the day-to-day calm that leaves you vulnerable to inflation and longevity.

Protecting Your Mindset

This structure does more than protect your finances. It also protects your psychology. Former owners often find themselves staring at market headlines more than they ever checked industry reports. Declines in equity markets may feel like declines in personal security. The instinct, especially for someone accustomed to control, is to act.

Yet reacting impulsively to market swings is often the greatest risk to long-term wealth. A tiered system removes the pressure to respond emotionally. You already know your next several years of expenses are secure. You do not need to liquidate assets when markets are down. You have engineered calm into the process.

There will always be more complex strategies, more elegant models, and more academically optimal theories, but what matters most in this stage of life is alignment between your money and your psychology. You built a company by making countless decisions under pressure. You do not need that kind of pressure in your financial life after a sale. What you need is clarity, confidence, and the ability to enjoy the rewards of your work without fear that the next downturn will derail your future.

A well-built portfolio lets you ignore the market on the days when the market wants your attention most.

Step 3: Turn Your Assets Into Income That Never Stops

There is a specific moment in almost every liquidity planning meeting when I see the tension leave a founder's face. It happens the instant we talk about recreating a predictable paycheck after the sale. Shoulders drop. Eyes relax. People lean back in their chairs and exhale. It is as if their nervous system finally gets permission to believe, "I am going to be okay." That moment matters, because selling a business means stepping out of the one system that has always paid you, and that psychological shift is enormous.

To soften that transition and create stability that feels familiar, we automate income again, only this time your portfolio provides the monthly deposit instead of your company. The mechanics are simple. Your custodian, whether it is Schwab, Fidelity, or another firm, transfers a predetermined amount from your portfolio to your checking account at the start of each month. It looks and feels exactly like the payroll deposits you have received throughout your career. You can plan around it, build a spending rhythm around it, and maintain the same sense of financial continuity you had when your business funded your life.

A structured monthly income restores order and supports smart financial behavior. It also gives your long-term investments time to grow, because your lifestyle draws from stable reserves while growth assets compound undisturbed.

For larger or irregular expenses, such as buying a car, taking a major trip, or covering unexpected medical bills, funds flow from your liquid reserve. This keeps your spending strategy clean and intentional. It also ensures that large expenses do not derail your daily financial rhythm. The idea is not to constrain your life, but to support it with structure so that your wealth works for you, rather than the other way around.

I often encourage founders to begin this system before the sale closes. Even one or two months of seeing the automatic transfer hit your account builds trust in the process. When your salary stops, the paycheck from your portfolio continues. There is no gap, no moment of panic, and no uncertain adjustment period. It becomes a smooth handoff from business income to wealth income—and that continuity matters, especially for someone who has spent a lifetime relying on performance and production as the source of their security.

This is as much an emotional bridge as it is a financial tool. When you sell, your identity, routine, and income all shift at once. A lifetime paycheck stabilizes one of the most important parts of that transition.

It allows you to focus on your next chapter with confidence instead of worry. You built something that provided for you and your family. This system allows your wealth to do the same, quietly and consistently, long after the business is no longer yours.

Step 4: Stay on Financial Track

It would be wonderful if you could set your post-sale plan once and then ignore it while you enjoy life, but that is not how durable wealth works. Managing your portfolio and your cash flows is an ongoing process that protects the engine of your freedom. The portfolio must be kept alive and healthy. That does not require staring at screens all day, but it does require a steady cadence of maintenance. You can run this cadence yourself, or you can outsource most of it to a capable advisor.

Start with rebalancing. During your working years, every paycheck bought into your portfolio automatically. When markets dropped, your contributions scooped up shares at a discount. When markets rose, you bought fewer shares at higher prices. That steady discipline did a lot of quiet work, and you probably never noticed. In retirement, the paychecks stop but the need for discipline doesn't. Rebalancing takes over. When markets surge, you trim winners and add to the safer side. When markets fall, you harvest from stable assets and buy equities on sale. On paper, this is obvious. In practice, it means selling what feels good and buying what feels terrible. That's not a flaw. That's the entire point. Put dates on the calendar, define your guardrails, and execute regardless of what your gut tells you.

Next, watch your spending relative to the income the plan is designed to produce. The danger that shows up quietly in both retirement and post-sale life is expense creep. People begin with withdrawals that match their plans, then, over time, allow fixed costs and discretionary habits to expand. They do not notice the change from month to month, but they feel its weight years later, when flexibility is gone. You do not need a line-item household budget to stay ahead of this, but you do need visibility. Track monthly withdrawals and compare them to your target. If you see several months trending higher, address the drift before it becomes the new normal. If you use bookkeeping software, let it produce a simple spending report so you or your advisor can spot patterns early, especially the slow rise of fixed obligations that are hard to unwind.

Layer in a light reporting rhythm. Review current net worth snapshots at regular intervals and look for trends rather than reacting to each wiggle. If liabilities are rising, or if ongoing withdrawals are larger than the plan anticipates, the net worth line will reveal it. In the same review, glance through your investment accounts. You will see the normal ups and downs, but familiarity breeds calm. Clients who once felt anxious about markets often relax once they can see, month by month, how reserves fund their paychecks while the long-term bucket does its compounding in the background. If impulse purchases are a habit, create a cooling-off rule with your advisor for large outlays so that big decisions are aligned with the plan instead of eroding it.

Finally, patrol what I call the snowball effect. A $1 million portfolio with $40,000 in annual withdrawals is a 4 percent rate. If markets drop that portfolio to $800,000 while withdrawals continue, the rate climbs to 5 percent. Another decline pushes it higher still. Left unchecked, the withdrawal rate can climb into a zone where recovery becomes nearly impossible. The antidote is awareness. Monitor the ratio of withdrawals to current portfolio value. Below 4 percent, you're comfortable. Mid-single digits for more than a brief spell, consider adjustments. Above 6 percent, act decisively. The earlier you respond, the easier it is to stop the snowball.

Staying on track is not about obsessing over the portfolio or reacting to daily market noise. It is about building a simple operating system and running it with discipline. Rebalance on a schedule. Watch whether your spending matches your projections. Review a small set of reports that make trends visible. Monitor your effective withdrawal percentage. These habits are not glamorous, but they are the engine behind quiet compounding, the kind that funds the rest of your life. A good advisor can handle most of this for you, freeing you to focus on what matters most. That freedom to spend your days on what actually matters is the most valuable thing you won in the sale. Protect it.

Step 5: Build and Lead Your Post-Sale Advisory Team

Once the wire clears, you step into a world of new tax rules, legal considerations, investment responsibilities, and long-term planning decisions. This is not a time to rely on instinct or assume you can figure things out as you go. The smartest clients I have worked with over the years do the opposite and build a team around them.

If you followed the guidance in Chapter 4, you already have a financial advisor in place. That relationship should continue and deepen. Your advisor now shifts from helping you prepare for the sale to helping you manage its outcome. They become the personal CFO for your financial life, building the plan, overseeing the moving parts, holding the entire picture in their mind, and helping you make smart decisions over time. When you ran your business, your CFO saw the big picture, coordinated advisors, managed cash flow, and ensured that decisions aligned with long-term strategy. Now, you are the business. Your portfolio, tax plan, estate plan, insurance structure, philanthropic

ROBERT PAGLIARINI, PH.D., CFP®

strategy, and cash flow all must work in concert. Without someone managing that integration, important decisions become fragmented, blind spots appear, and opportunities are missed.

Your legal and tax advisors, however, will likely change.

The M&A attorney who guided you through the transaction was essential during the deal. But their job is done. Post-sale, you need a different kind of legal expertise. An estate and asset-protection attorney will help you with ownership structures, trust planning, gifting strategies, charitable vehicles, and risk protection. These are not one-time conversations. They require ongoing attention as your life evolves. A generalist will not do. The right specialist often saves many multiples of their fee.

The same shift may apply to your CPA. The accountant who prepared your business returns or even advised on deal structure may not be the right fit for post-sale wealth management. You now need a CPA who does tax planning, not just preparation. Estimated payments, income structuring, investment entity formation, multi-state issues, charitable planning, and coordination with your attorney are all ongoing responsibilities. A CPA who only files your returns once a year is not enough. The right CPA becomes a strategic partner in preserving wealth.

Think of this as the post-sale version of your leadership team. In your business, success came from the right people in the right seats, working toward aligned goals. The same is true here. Your financial advisor provides continuity and coordination. Your estate attorney and CPA are new hires for a new chapter.

Remember, your role is not to execute every detail. Your role is to lead the team. Assemble excellence. Insist on communication between advisors. Stay involved, but don't try to do everything yourself. You did not sell your business to take on a new full-time job managing your wealth. You sold it to build the life you have earned. Your advisory team is how you protect it.

Beyond the Five Steps – The First Ninety Days After the Wire

You have the team. You have the structure. Now what? The first ninety days after the sale are the most critical and most confusing period of your post-exit life. What you do in this window sets the tone for everything that follows.

Focus on three things. First, get your financial house in order. This does not mean making permanent investment decisions. As I mentioned earlier, rushing into a long-term portfolio strategy is one of the biggest mistakes new liquidity holders make. What it does mean is making sure your money is safe, properly held, and not sitting in a place where it could be exposed to unnecessary risk or oversight gaps. Meet with your wealth manager to confirm the funds are positioned appropriately for now, that a thoughtful plan is taking shape, and that nothing is left unresolved. Finalize any outstanding tax strategies with your CPA. The goal is stability and clarity, not speed.

Second, protect your time and energy. Say no to everything that isn't essential. Decline the investment opportunities, the speaking requests, the "quick coffee" meetings with people who suddenly want your advice. You need space to breathe, not a packed calendar.

Third, begin experimenting with what life could look like. Take the trip, sleep in, spend unstructured time with your family and try the hobby you've been putting off. Test what it feels like to not be the business. The first ninety days aren't about having all the answers.

They're about asking better questions and giving yourself permission to find them slowly.

Chapter Exit

Managing your wealth after the sale isn't about chasing the highest returns. It's about designing a financial life that supports the kind of human life you truly want. The numbers matter, but they're only half the story. The real goal is confidence, not complexity. When your income is stable, your risks are controlled, and your plan is built to last, you can finally shift your focus away from money and toward meaning.

At some point, every seller realizes something profound: You may have sold your purpose when you sold your company. The meetings, decisions, pressure, and victories that once gave structure to your days are suddenly gone. The spreadsheets are quiet, but so is the phone. That silence can be disorienting. Managing wealth is the technical part; rediscovering who you are without the business is the human part.

In the next chapter, we'll explore what happens when the deal closes and the adrenaline fades. We'll talk about the identity vacuum that follows a sale, the danger of drifting, and how to rebuild purpose that's bigger than profit. Because true wealth isn't just what you keep, but what you create next.

CHAPTER 7:

DISCOVER YOUR IDENTITY AND MEANING

*Rebuild Yourself
After the Sale*

A few months before selling his company, a client pulled me aside and asked a question I've heard many times. "Robert," he said, "I'm a little nervous about selling. I'm not sure what I'll do all day. What if I'm bored out of my mind? I don't want to regret this."

He wasn't afraid of losing money or the deal falling through. He was afraid of losing himself. For decades, he'd been the business. All the decisions, hires, and successes had his fingerprints on them. The idea of no longer being "the guy" and losing his identity was deeply unsettling.

So before the deal closed, we worked through the ideas you'll find in this chapter: uncovering his values, identifying what gave him energy, and designing a vision for what his next chapter could look like. We prepared his balance sheet and his new identity.

A couple of years later, we were hiking the Grand Canyon together when he said, "Robert, remember how nervous I was before I sold my company? I haven't regretted selling for a minute." That's when I knew he hadn't just sold his company. He'd also successfully built a new life—but it didn't happen overnight.

In the previous chapter, we tackled the practical question of how you manage your new wealth. Now, we address the deeper question that haunts many successful sellers: Who am I now? That's the surprising part of the business sale. You sell the company, but it can feel like you've sold part of yourself in the process. It can leave a void, and if you don't intentionally fill that void, it fills itself with uncertainty, restlessness, and sometimes regret.

But the good news is that identity isn't something you lose; it's something you create. When I talk about reinvention, I'm not talking about abandoning who you are. I'm talking about expanding it. And the even better news? You can use what made you successful in business, such as your vision, discipline, leadership, and grit, to make your post-sale life extraordinary. You just have to apply them differently.

The Freedom Void

You've done what few people ever will. You built something from nothing, you sold it, and you won. You've joined the small, elite group who got a deal done and walked away with not just congratulations, but also cash in the bank.

And yet, for all the celebration and success, something feels off.

You tell yourself you should feel nothing but relief and joy. But now that the deal is done, you find yourself feeling something you didn't plan for: emptiness.

You wake up, check your phone out of habit, and realize there are no fires to put out. No problems to solve. No team waiting for your direction.

The business that demanded everything from you is gone. The systems you built run without you. The company has a new owner. Your name might still be on the paperwork, but your role, identity, and daily purpose are all gone.

This is what I call the freedom void.

The very thing you worked for becomes disorienting. The problem isn't that you lack opportunity, it's that, for the first time in years, nothing is required of you.

Founders describe this sensation as the void after victory. It's the sudden stillness that follows decades of motion.

This isn't depression; it's displacement. Your internal compass was tuned to urgency: growth targets, strategy sessions, deals, and deadlines. Those markers gave each day gravity. Remove them, and you lose the magnetic pull that once guided you.

The human brain craves meaning. When we stop pursuing, we start drifting. In small doses, leisure feels rewarding; in large doses, it becomes a mirror. It reflects questions you postponed for decades: Who am I without this company? What now deserves my full effort?

The void after victory isn't a mistake to fix; it's a transition to honor. It's the decompression chamber between the person who built and the person who will become. If you rush through it, you'll miss the lessons embedded in the silence.

The Identity Gap

For years, your business card wasn't an introduction; it was an identity. "Founder." "CEO." "Owner." Those words were shorthand for your value in the world. When people asked, "What do you do?" your answer came instantly. You were the business, and the business was you.

Then you sell, and suddenly, that clarity evaporates. The next time someone asks what you do, you hesitate. You might say, "I used to run..." or "I recently sold my company..." but each answer carries an echo of the past tense. You're describing who you were, not who you are.

Psychologists call the space between roles an identity gap. It's not unique to founders. Retired athletes feel it when the cheering stops; veterans feel it when they take off the uniform. When something that once defined you disappears, you face a quiet identity crisis.

In business, identity and performance are intertwined. The business needed you, and that need reinforced your importance.

After the sale, that validation vanishes. No one's waiting on your decision. Your name isn't at the top of the org chart, and what remains is the uncomfortable question: If I'm not leading, am I still valuable?

The answer, of course, is yes, but it takes time to believe it. And the gap between knowing intellectually that you're still valuable and feeling it emotionally is where most post-sale founders live for months. If you're in that gap right now, it's not a character flaw. It's a predictable stage of transition. I have watched some of the sharpest, most confident founders I know question their worth after selling. These are people who built massive businesses, led hundreds of employees, and made bold decisions under pressure. And yet, six months after the sale, they were asking themselves what the point was. That question doesn't make you weak. It makes you someone who tied their identity to their work, which is exactly what made you successful in the first place.

The first step in bridging the identity gap is separating role from essence. You're not defined by your title. You're defined by the qualities that earned it: creativity, resilience, discipline, empathy, and courage. Those attributes didn't get sold with the company; they're still yours to deploy.

What many founders discover is that their businesses were both amplifiers and filters. They magnified certain traits, such as competitiveness, drive, and focus, while suppressing others, such as patience, curiosity, and vulnerability. Post-sale, you have the rare chance to rebalance.

This period can feel like an audit of the self. You're reassessing values that were once obscured by velocity. What did you sacrifice to build success? Which parts of you have been waiting to re-emerge?

Reclaiming identity is less about reinvention than reclamation. The goal isn't to become someone new, but to recover the fuller version of who you've always been: the parts that existed before the business, the passions that fell dormant under deadlines, and the relationships that deserve more of you now.

Many founders tell themselves they'll "figure it out later," after some time off or a long vacation. But time doesn't automatically create clarity. In fact, unstructured freedom can amplify uncertainty. Without something meaningful to replace your company's demands, you can feel like a bystander in your own life.

This is why some founders rush back into another venture immediately after selling. It's not greed; it's gravity. They crave the validation loop that the business once gave them. But jumping too quickly into a new company, investment, or "project" often masks the deeper issue: You've lost the role that defined your worth.

The goal now isn't to find another business to run. It's to rediscover who you are when you're not running one.

The irony is that this phase requires the same skill that made you successful in the first place: vision. The difference is that the vision now has to turn inward. Instead of designing a company, you're designing a life. Instead of optimizing KPIs, you're optimizing fulfillment. And that requires something you may not have exercised in years: reflection.

The Grief You Didn't Expect

We rarely talk about it this way, but selling a business can create a form of mourning. You do not grieve only people. You grieve roles, relevance, and the sense of being needed. For years, you have been the person everyone looked to for answers. Every problem passed through you. Every win reflected back to you. When that ends, even if you initiated it, your system feels the loss. It is not weakness. It is the human response to detachment from something that once defined you. The habits, pace, and constant demand all stops at once, and your mind and body need time to catch up.

This is the part of the sale that surprises even the most disciplined and rational founders. They expect stress during the deal, but they do not expect sadness after it. They prepare financial statements, not emotional ones. They are told to focus on post-sale tax strategy, not post-sale identity repair. I often tell clients that a successful exit is 50% financial, 50% psychological, and 10% being good at math. They usually laugh. Then they sell and stop laughing. The psychological part turns out to be the hardest. Yet almost every owner I have worked with feels it to some degree. Some describe it as a fog. Others say it feels like standing still after running at full speed for years. There is pride and gratitude, but also an ache they cannot quite name. That ache is grief. It deserves to be acknowledged, not ignored.

The way forward is not to fight it, but to move through it. The same qualities that helped you build your company—resilience, self-awareness, and the ability to adapt—help you navigate this transition. You built something extraordinary once, and you can build again. But first you have to honor what you are letting go. Grieving the sale is not a failure of gratitude. It is a sign that what you created mattered deeply. You invested your time, energy, and imagination into something real. Let yourself feel that loss. When you do, space opens for what comes next.

Sometimes, though, the grief lingers longer than it should. It can start to feel heavy and unrelenting. You may lose motivation, struggle to find interest in new pursuits, or feel detached from the people around you. This is when it helps to talk with someone trained to guide you through it. A therapist or coach can help you separate who you are from what you built, so you can move forward without guilt or confusion. In *Badass Retirement*, I wrote that seeking professional help is not about weakness; it is about performance. The same way you once hired experts to grow your company, you can bring in an expert to help you grow through this next stage. Sometimes, you need a space to process what you have lost before you can fully see what you have gained.

How to Process Seller's Remorse Constructively

If you're experiencing seller's remorse, here's how to work through it without letting it consume you.

1. Name it and normalize it.

First, stop beating yourself up for feeling this way. Seller's remorse is not a sign of weakness, ingratitude, or failure. It's a predictable response to a major life transition. You're allowed to feel complicated emotions about a complicated decision.

Say it out loud. "I'm experiencing seller's remorse, and that's normal." Just naming it reduces its power.

2. Separate the decision from the transition.

Often, the regret isn't about the sale itself, it's about how hard the transition has been. You can make a good decision and still struggle with the aftermath.

Ask yourself this question. "Am I regretting selling, or am I regretting that life after the sale is harder than I expected?" If it's the latter, the solution isn't to undo the sale, it's to build a better post-sale life.

3. Give it time (but not forever).

Grief and adjustment take time. Most experts suggest giving yourself at least twelve to eighteen months before drawing firm conclusions about whether you made a mistake.

But don't use "giving it time" as an excuse to avoid doing the work. Use the time to actively build your next chapter—don't just wait for clarity to arrive on its own.

4. Talk to someone who's been there.

The best antidote to seller's remorse is talking to other founders who've sold and felt the same way. Their perspective will give you something no book or advisor can: proof that what you're feeling has a path through it.

If you don't have access to that network, work with a therapist or coach who specializes in transitions and identity. This isn't a problem you can think your way out of. You need to process it with someone who understands.

5. Build something new (but not immediately).

The urge to "fix" seller's remorse by jumping into a new business or buying back your company is understandable. Give yourself space to grieve and recalibrate before making another big move.

That said, if, after twelve to eighteen months, you're still miserable and genuinely believe you made a mistake, explore your options. Maybe you do start something new. Maybe you consult or invest in other founders. Maybe you negotiate a role with the buyer.

Make that decision from a place of clarity, not desperation.

6. Focus on what you can control.

You can't undo the sale (in most cases), but you can control what you do with the freedom it gave you. You can:

- Design a daily routine that gives your life structure.

- Invest in relationships that matter.

- Pursue new challenges that energize you.

- Contribute your experience to causes you care about.

- Take care of your physical and mental health.

Regret keeps you focused on the past. Action moves you toward the future.

7. Reframe the narrative.

Instead of "I made a terrible mistake," try "I made the best decision I could with the information I had at the time, and now I'm learning how to live with it."

You're not a victim of your decision. You're a person navigating a complex transition. That reframe shifts you from powerless to empowered.

The Sale That Felt Like Failure Until It Didn't

I worked with a business owner who was a co-founder of a nutrition company, but held only a minority interest. When the majority owner decided to sell, my client would have preferred to keep building. He believed the company still had tremendous runway, but, as a minority shareholder, he had no vote. The deal went through, and it was brutal. The new buyers made it clear they didn't want him around. Despite his being instrumental to the company's success, they saw him as part of the old guard rather than an asset. He walked away with millions of dollars, but money didn't erase the sting of being forced out of something he had built from nothing.

I remember a distinct conversation we had not long after the sale closed. He was angry. The new buyers were making terrible decisions, he told me. They were contradicting everything that had made the company successful. Cutting costs in the wrong places, alienating key retail partners, trying to scale too fast without understanding the nuances of the brand. I could hear the defeat in his voice, but I also heard something else: He still cared deeply about what he had built. The passion hadn't disappeared. It had just been redirected into frustration.

That's when I told him the story of Snapple. In 1994, Snapple sold to Quaker Oats for over a billion dollars. It seemed like a massive win. But Quaker didn't understand the brand. They tried to apply corporate strategies that had worked for Gatorade, but destroyed everything that made Snapple special. Sales plummeted, the brand lost its identity, and a few years later, the company was sold again for a fraction of what Quaker had paid. Eventually, some of the original team found ways to get involved again and help restore what had been lost.

I looked at him and said that if these new buyers were as inept as he believed, he might get the same opportunity. If they continued down their current path, the company's value would crater. When it did, he could be the one positioned to step back in. He could buy it back, or launch something even better. Rather than cashing out and retiring to a beach somewhere, he could stay sharp and in the game.

That conversation changed everything. He stopped mourning and started preparing. He invested in smaller nutrition companies that weren't direct competitors, but that allowed him to stay connected to the industry. He started speaking at conferences, writing articles, and building his personal brand. He cultivated relationships with investors who respected his track record and wanted to back his next venture. With each step, he gained more credibility, influence, and optionality. He was no longer defeated. He had his edge back. He wasn't waiting for permission or nursing his wounds. He was positioning himself for the moment when opportunity returned.

And just recently, that moment arrived. He got a call from the buyers. The very people who had pushed him out, who had dismissed his expertise and treated him like dead weight, now realized they were in over their heads. Sales were declining and retail partners were frustrated. The brand was losing its soul and they needed his help. He's not sure yet what he'll do. He's weighing his options carefully, consulting with advisors, and exploring whether this is the right opportunity, or just a distraction. But what is certain is that this time, he's negotiating from strength. He's not the minority shareholder being dragged into a sale he didn't want. He's the expert they need, the one with the knowledge and relationships they can't replace. And if the terms aren't right, he'll walk away and build something new on his own. Either way, he wins.

The Truth About Seller's Remorse

After thirty years of watching business owners sell, here's what I know: Of all the clients I've worked with, only one actually regretted the decision long-term. One.

Many regret how they handled the transition. Some regret not preparing emotionally. Others regret rushing into (or away from) the next thing. Some regret not giving themselves permission to grieve. But the sale itself? Almost all of them eventually realize it was the right call.

If you're feeling remorse right now, give yourself grace. You're not broken. You're not ungrateful. You're human, and you're in the middle of one of the hardest transitions a person can face. The business sale was the end of a chapter. Seller's remorse is part of the bridge to the next one. It's uncomfortable, but it's also temporary. And on the other side of it? There's a life waiting for you that you haven't built yet.

The Identity Paradox

You built a business that could run without you. You hired strong leaders, documented processes, and created systems. You made yourself less essential on purpose, because that's what makes a business sellable. And it worked. You sold. The business continues without you. But now you face an uncomfortable question: Who are you without it? For years, your business card answered that question. Your title was your identity. After the sale, that clarity evaporates. The business you built successfully became independent of you. Now you must become independent of it.

You spent years making your business work without you—now you must figure out who you are without it.

The Problem with Endless Leisure

Leisure sounds like the ultimate prize. For years, you imagined the freedom to golf on Tuesdays, travel without limits, or finally relax without guilt. And for a while, it feels great. But eventually, leisure loses its luster, because it lacks stakes.

Leisure without meaning becomes anesthetic: pleasant but numbing. The same mind that once thrived on complex decisions and creative pressure now faces a void of stimulation.

This is why so many post-sale founders find themselves busier than ever, but not necessarily happier. They chase distractions such as new projects, investments, and hobbies not because they're passionate about them, but because they fear stillness.

The truth is, you can't relax your way into fulfillment. Fulfillment comes from engagement and the sense that what you're doing today connects to something that will matter tomorrow. Redefining work is essential. You must reintroduce meaningful challenge, but on your terms. You've earned the right to choose what you struggle for.

Freedom is not the absence of work. It's the ability to choose work that aligns with your deepest values.

Beyond the Deal: Creating New Meaning

Before the sale, you had context. Every day was shaped by responsibility: to clients, staff, family, or the mission itself. After the sale, responsibility dissolves, and you confront the unsettling truth that motivation built on obligation doesn't survive liberation.

This paradox has been studied across professions. When retirees or high-achieving individuals step away from careers that defined them, they often experience a decline in satisfaction and health. The problem is a lack of engagement. Humans are wired for contribution. Remove that, and meaning evaporates.

Meaning doesn't arise from comfort; it arises from challenge. The same fire that once kept your business alive still burns inside you, but without a target, it scorches inward. This is exactly why so many post-exit founders feel restless, anxious, and even guilty for not feeling happier. They mistake peace for meaning, but the two are different currencies.

To rebuild meaning, you must design it intentionally. Meaning isn't discovered; it's constructed through alignment of what you value with where you invest your time and energy.

You already possess all the tools! You know how to plan, test, iterate, and execute. The only difference is that, this time, the project is you.

There's a question almost all owners eventually face, but few ever say out loud: Who am I now that the business no longer needs me?

This moment isn't a crisis; it's an invitation. It's a chance to rebuild your sense of self—not around performance, but around meaning. The first step is acknowledging that this gap exists.

Busy Isn't the Goal: Why Motion ≠ Meaning

The weeks and months following a business sale often bring an unexpected emotional vacuum that catches even the most prepared sellers off guard. Many successful entrepreneurs find themselves wrestling with fundamental questions about identity, purpose, and what comes next. Before the sale, your time wasn't fully yours. Clients, employees, banks, vendors, audits, payroll—you ran your day, but the day also ran you. Since you can do anything after the sale, the reflex might be to do it all, to say yes to any and all invitations, trips, or roles that come your way. Your calendar refills because a full calendar feels familiar.

That's the trap. Busyness imitates importance. It scratches the itch of being needed without actually feeding the deeper need to matter. When owners tell me they're worried about being bored, what they actually mean is they can't imagine something that will be as meaningful or exciting as running their company. The instinct to "stay busy" after the sale is the same instinct that drives people into what I call "average retirement" in my book *Badass Retirement*. They fill their calendar, but not their soul, confusing activity with meaning. It's easy to stay distracted; it's harder to sit with the question of what truly matters.

The temptation during this transition is to retreat to the opposite extreme, to sit quietly and think deeply about what you want to do with the next chapter of your life. You might believe that through careful contemplation and analysis, you will arrive at clarity about which activities will bring you fulfillment and meaning. This approach feels logical and prudent, particularly for people who have built successful businesses through careful planning and strategic thinking. However, staying in your head and theorizing about what might bring you joy is actually one of the least effective ways to discover what will make you happy in this new phase of life.

I recently sat down with a client who had just closed a substantial sale of his manufacturing business. He was wrestling with what to do next, and true to form as the analytical CEO who had built a successful company through data-driven decisions, he showed me a detailed spreadsheet. It contained dozens of potential activities such as volunteering opportunities, hobbies, travel destinations, educational pursuits, with each having multiple columns scoring factors like time commitment, cost, social interaction level, physical demand, and his estimated interest level on a scale of one to ten. He had color-coded cells and weighted averages. It was impressive in its thoroughness and completely paralyzing in its effect. After watching him agonize over whether kayaking should score a seven or an eight on the "outdoor experience" dimension, I finally stopped him. "Just do anything," I said. "Pick three things on that list at random and go try them this week. Look, trying something once doesn't mean you're locked in for life. These are experiments, not lifetime contracts."

The reality is that we are remarkably poor predictors of what will make us happy, a phenomenon psychologists call affective forecasting. If you reflect on your past, you can likely recall situations where something you thought would be amazing and fulfilling turned out to be disappointing, or conversely, where an activity you expected to dislike became a source of unexpected pleasure. The best way to predict what will genuinely engage you and provide meaning is not to think about it endlessly but to get out and try as many things as you can. Writing and performing your own poetry at open mic night? Worth a try. Improv classes? Worth a try. Off-roading? Worth a try. Learning about the history of famous art? Worth a try. Cooking Filipino dishes? Worth a try. Sometimes we need to get out of our heads and just go for it. Engagement is the only way we can truly know if we enjoy something or not.

The practical application of this principle is straightforward but requires nuance. Say yes more often than feels comfortable, but say yes with intention. This might seem to contradict earlier advice about protecting your calendar and avoiding motion for its own sake. It doesn't. The distinction matters. Say no to obligations that serve other people's agendas. Say yes to experiments that might reveal your own. One fills your calendar. The other fills your life.

When we had full-time jobs running our businesses, we had so little time to say yes to anything outside of work demands. If a friend invites you somewhere you would not normally go or asks you to do an activity you would not normally do, say yes. Being bold and discovering what brings you meaning often requires doing things you have never done, even things you think you might not enjoy. Keep testing and experimenting with an open mind, and if you try enough activities, you will find several to which you gravitate and several that you cannot stand. Do not let the disappointing experiments deter you. Each experience, whether positive or negative, provides valuable data about your preferences, energy levels, and what genuinely engages you. The goal is not to find the perfect activity through analysis, nor is it to purely fill your calendar with random commitments. The goal is to build a portfolio of experiences that collectively reveal what gives your life meaning and purpose after the sale. You have to slow down long enough to feel the void, then design something worthy of filling it. Jumping out of bed with renewed meaning doesn't happen by accident. It's constructed deliberately, like a business. The raw materials are your needs, values, interests, and passions, the same elements that drove your success, but that now must be redirected.

Freedom Without Direction Isn't Freedom

Sergey Young, founder of the Longevity Vision Fund, once wrote, "We've created technologies to extend our life, but we haven't created a life we want to extend."

That quote carries more weight after you've sold your business, because for the first time in decades, you have the freedom to do anything, but still struggle to find something worth doing.

For most of your life, meaning wasn't something you searched for; it was something built into the architecture of your work. You didn't have to "find meaning." It found you every morning at 7:00 a.m. in the form of employees, clients, and goals. Even the stress had purpose, because it was attached to progress.

When the business goes away, that scaffolding disappears. You wake up with time, money, and freedom, but without the frame that gave your life shape. The same thing you thought you wanted can quickly feel like emptiness.

You finally have control of your time, yet you no longer know what to do with it.

Some respond by filling the void—buying property, joining boards, funding startups, or traveling the world. It all feels productive, but it's often a distraction. Being busy is easier than being bored, and boredom can feel like failure to someone who's always been in motion.

The good news is that boredom is fertile ground for rediscovery.

Part I: What's Important to You (Needs and Values)

The fastest way to design a life you love is to understand the internal forces that have been steering you all along. Two lenses matter most: your needs and your values.

The Six Human Needs

In my work with owners post-sale, I often use a model from human needs psychology. It outlines six universal needs that drive all human behavior:

Certainty. The desire for stability, safety, and predictability. You once had control over outcomes, people, and decisions. When you sell, you trade that for ambiguity. The solution isn't to recreate control. It's to build confidence in a new system—your life system.

Variety. The craving for change, novelty, and surprise. Entrepreneurs thrive on change. Too much sameness feels like suffocation. Inject new challenges: travel, learn, mentor, or build something new.

Significance. The need to feel important, valued, and unique. You've been the center of gravity for years. Post-sale, you can feel invisible. Find new ways to matter: teaching, philanthropy, or leadership in causes that align with your values.

Love / Connection. The need for belonging, closeness, and community. You may lose daily camaraderie with your team. Rebuild connection intentionally: with peers, family, and people who share your stage of life.

Growth. The need to evolve, learn, and improve—the ultimate fuel. You've outgrown your business; now grow yourself. Learn, explore, and evolve.

Contribution. The need to give beyond oneself and impact others. More than making money, this is about making a difference. Consider mentorship, community impact, or helping others succeed.

These needs shape all that we do, but we each prioritize two above the rest. Before the sale, you likely met your needs for significance and growth through your company. You mattered because you built something that mattered. You grew because the business grew.

After the sale, the vehicles that once met those needs disappear. The trick is not to suppress them, but to fulfill them differently.

If your primary need is significance, find it not in titles, but in impact: mentoring, philanthropy, teaching, or thought leadership. If your primary need is growth, channel it into mastery: learning, health, creativity, or relationships.

The owners who stay fulfilled after selling are those who design a life that meets all six needs consciously.

To identify your top two needs, begin by reflecting on the six universal human needs. Although we all share these needs, two tend to dominate and guide most of your decisions and emotions. The process starts with honest self-observation: noticing what consistently motivates you, what brings satisfaction, and what triggers frustration. Read through the descriptions of each need and pay attention to which two resonate most strongly. Often, they "fly off the page," feeling unmistakably true. If you're uncertain, you can find several short assessments online that can help you rank the six needs and clarify which two dominate your decision-making.

Understanding your top two needs is a practical framework for designing a more fulfilling life. These needs determine what you move toward and why, influencing the vehicles you use to meet them. Once you identify your dominant needs, you can align your time, relationships, and post-sale pursuits around them, creating a life that feels meaningful instead of reactive.

Pause here and identify your top two needs.

The Vehicles of Fulfillment

One of the most powerful insights from human needs psychology is that while our core needs remain the same throughout life, the ways we meet those needs evolve. We are driven by familiar forces: the desire to matter, to grow, to create, to contribute, to feel connected, and to experience control over our world. Those needs do not vanish when a business is sold. They do not retire just because you did. They merely look for new outlets. The challenge is that the primary vehicle that once satisfied them is gone.

Owning a company is one of the most comprehensive fulfillment vehicles a person can experience. It provides structure, challenge, community, accountability, creativity, leadership, status, control, and the ability to directly see the impact of your decisions. It is a powerful container for meaning. When you sell that container, the needs do not disappear but become unanchored. That is where many clients stumble. They feel restless or unsettled without fully understanding why. It is not because they made the wrong choice to sell. It is because they have not yet chosen the new vehicles through which their needs will be met.

Consider significance. During your ownership years, significance may have shown up through authority, recognition, industry respect, the ability to build something from scratch, or maybe just being needed by your team and clients. You mattered in visible ways. After the sale, that same need can be fulfilled through mentorship, strategic board roles, investing in founders, philanthropy, creative pursuits, or building something new entirely outside of business. The need stays constant. The vehicle changes.

Or consider contribution. Entrepreneurs tend to be wired for service. They wake up thinking about customers, employees, products, and problems to solve. Each day is a chance to create value. Contribution in the next chapter might look like supporting younger people, volunteering your expertise, funding innovation, building a foundation, serving your community, or even contributing to your family in ways that work never allowed. Again, the need remains, but the vehicle shifts.

Growth follows the same pattern. Business ownership forces growth. You rarely get to coast. The market pressures you, competition sharpens you, and the next phase of the company constantly demands new skills. Post-sale, growth becomes optional, which is why so many former owners feel an internal void once the adrenaline settles. When growth is no longer automatic, it must become intentional. Learning a new skill, exploring a field outside of business, tackling a personal challenge, diving deeper into health or creativity, or building a completely different kind of enterprise are all new ways to honor that need.

None of this happens by accident. Fulfillment requires conscious re-engineering in the post-exit world. When you understand your core drivers and intentionally redesign the vehicles that satisfy them, you move from drifting to directing your life again. You regain momentum and purpose. You shift from feeling like you lost something to recognizing that you are gaining new dimensions of yourself.

The Success Paradox

You spent decades chasing goals and building a valuable company. You worked longer hours than anyone else. You sacrificed weekends, vacations, and time with family. You bet everything on this outcome. And then you won. The deal closed. The money hit your account. You're financially free. And now you feel lost. The goal that drove you for years is gone. The scoreboard that measured success no longer exists. The challenge that got you out of bed every morning has disappeared. What should feel like triumph feels strangely empty. Achievement without direction creates a vacuum. Meaning doesn't come from reaching the destination. It comes from choosing a new mountain to climb.

You achieve everything you worked for—and discover that success without purpose feels hollow.

Values and Direction

Needs drive us, but values steer us. Needs are universal, and every human shares them. Values are personal. They shape how we choose to live, what we pursue, and what we refuse to compromise. Before the sale, your values were often filtered through the lens of the business. Priorities such as growth, achievement, competition, and financial security may have dominated because they had to. The business demanded those values to thrive, and you rose to the challenge.

After the sale, many owners experience a shift. Freedom may rise where ambition once sat. Family may replace expansion as the dominant priority. Impact may take the place of income as the primary scorecard. Peace may suddenly matter in a way intensity once did. You are not losing your edge, but reclaiming choice.

This is why the period after a sale should be intentional, reflective, and grounded. It is a reorientation. The question is not merely, "What will I do now?" The deeper question is, "What matters to me now?" Too many owners jump immediately into new projects because they are uncomfortable sitting in the space between identities. But clarity is found in reflection, not reaction.

Spend time identifying what truly animates you at this stage of life. Look back at your most meaningful moments, not your biggest achievements. Success and fulfillment are not always the same thing. Ask yourself when you felt deeply at peace, proud in a way that had nothing to do with numbers, energized by possibility, or grounded by purpose. Those moments reveal your values more clearly than any financial goal ever could.

Then, notice the common threads. Perhaps they involved learning, mentoring, creating, building relationships, solving complex problems, serving others, or experiencing adventure. Those patterns form a compass and guide your next chapter. When values become your navigational instrument, you build a life rather than fill time.

Selling a company creates space, but space can feel like freedom or disorientation. It depends on whether values fill that space with direction. The business owners who build extraordinary post-exit lives are not necessarily the ones who start the next big venture. They are the ones who choose with intention, design with awareness, and honor who they have become, not who they were required to be.

Part II: Where You Get and Give Energy (Interests and Passions)

Owners who thrive after the sale pay close attention to energy. They track what gives it and what drains it, and then they allocate their calendars accordingly.

Interests: The Breadcrumb Trail

These are the things you naturally read, watch, buy, and talk about: health tech, aviation, private lending, music producing, conservation, classic cars, culinary schools, workforce housing, STEM education, etc. Interests are signals, so don't judge them. Make a messy list and then test them. Affective forecasting, which is our ability to predict what will make us happy, is famously inaccurate. You cannot think your way into certainty here. You have to run experiments. Try new things. Take classes. Volunteer. Create. Engage.

One of the most revealing ways to discover your true interests is to pay attention to where your energy naturally rises and falls. Energy is the body's truth detector. When you're engaged in something meaningful, time disappears and you feel alert and alive. When you're doing something that drains you, even simple tasks feel heavy.

Too often, we chase what we think we should enjoy instead of what genuinely energizes us. The trick is to notice, without judgment, the moments when you feel most curious, creative, or present. Those flashes of engagement are clues pointing toward activities that align with your authentic interests.

Instead of trying to reason your way to an answer, become a quiet observer of your days. At the end of each day, ask yourself these questions. What gave me energy today? What drained it? The answer might surprise you. Maybe it was a deep conversation with a younger entrepreneur, a few hours spent researching a new technology, or organizing something chaotic into order. These seemingly small bursts of energy are signals from your deeper self, reminders of what excites you at a cellular level. Don't dismiss them because they don't fit a familiar category like "work" or "hobby." Energy doesn't lie.

Once you begin tracking what gives and takes your energy, patterns will emerge. You'll start to see themes: curiosity around certain topics, joy in specific kinds of problem-solving, or fulfillment in particular environments. For example, you might notice that mentoring founders lights you up more than investing in their companies, or that creative expression gives you more energy than operational control ever did. This awareness becomes your compass. It's your most reliable guide to discovering interests that will sustain you long after the excitement of the business sale fades.

Finally, think of energy as both a measure and a resource. Spend it where the return feels highest, where you leave an activity feeling more alive than when you started. That's the sweet spot between enjoyment and meaning. As you design the next chapter of your life, your goal isn't simply to fill your time, but to fill it with pursuits that recharge you.

Passions: Your Flow States

Most founders have a dozen interests, but few have passions. The difference is intensity and alignment. Interests entertain you; passions engage you. Interests pass time; passions expand it.

You know you've found a passion when time disappears. Psychologists call this "flow," that state where you're so absorbed in what you're doing that hours feel like minutes. You forget to check your phone. You skip meals without noticing. You look up and realize the afternoon is gone. Flow is what made building your company addictive, even when it was hard. The challenge matched your skill level just enough to demand your full attention without overwhelming you. That's the sweet spot.

After a sale, many founders struggle because nothing produces flow the way the business did. They try golf, but it doesn't grab them. They travel, but the novelty wears off. They tinker with investments, but it feels like a pale imitation of the real thing. The problem isn't that they're broken. The problem is that they're searching for interests when they need to be searching for passions.

In the early months after a sale, it's easy to chase excitement: new toys, new trips, new deals. But excitement fades. Passion, on the other hand, sustains. Excitement is a sugar rush. Passion is a slow burn. One gets you out of bed for a week. The other gets you out of bed for a decade.

Those who thrive after selling their companies are the ones who intentionally build a portfolio of passions and activities that challenge and stretch them. They don't wait for passion to find them. They experiment until they find it. And when they do, they protect it the way they once protected their most important client relationships.

Part III: Designing Your Future (Vision and Purpose)

The hardest part about selling your business isn't letting go of control; it's learning to lead yourself again.

Before the sale, your company gave you structure. It organized your day, your decisions, and your sense of progress. After the sale, all of that disappears. The challenge now isn't to manage money, but to manage meaning.

Vision: Redefining Success

In business, your vision was external: revenue, valuation, market share. You could measure it on a dashboard. In life after the sale, your vision must turn inward. The metrics change. The questions become harder. What does success look like when no one is keeping score but you? What kind of person do you want to become? How do you want to spend the years you just bought back?

Ask yourself:

- What does success look like for me now, not five years ago, not what my peers expect, but right now?

- What would an extraordinary life actually look like, day to day, not just on paper?

- Who do I want to grow into over the next decade, and who do I need to stop being to get there?

Vision turns freedom into direction. Without it, you drift. And drift, over time, becomes regret.

Think of your next chapter as a company you're founding again, but this time, the product is your life. You're the CEO of your time, energy, and legacy. No board to answer to. No investors to please. Just you, deciding what gets built.

Write your vision on one page. Not a vague list of hopes. A declaration. If it doesn't make you a little nervous and a lot excited, it isn't big enough or true enough. Edit until it does.

Meaning: What Will I Build Now?

Money gives you options, but meaning gives you direction. And after selling your business, meaning is what separates those who thrive from those who fade. You didn't build your company by accident. You built it by waking up each day with a mission. That instinct doesn't vanish just because you sold. It sharpens. And eventually, one question drowns out all the others: What am I building now?

Without a mission, too much possibility becomes paralyzing. You're used to a narrow lane with high stakes, not an open field with none.

Meaning answers the question, "What now?" It gives structure to your days, momentum to your decisions, and depth to the freedom you've earned. It's about staying useful, not because you owe the world, your employees, or anyone else, but because being useful keeps you alive in the biggest way. Humans are wired for contribution, particularly people who've successfully started and run companies.

So how do you find it? Start with what's already pulling you:

- What kinds of problems still interest you?
- Who do you enjoy helping?
- What conversations energize you?
- What did you love long before the business existed?

You don't need a grand revelation. You just need to notice what's already there.

The most fulfilled founders aren't the ones who escaped work entirely. They're the ones who graduated into a different quality of work, one fueled by meaning instead of necessity.

Chapter Exit

You came into this chapter with a question most sellers are afraid to ask out loud: Who am I without the business?

Now you have the beginning of an answer. You've mapped your core needs and values. You've tracked what gives you energy and what drains it. You've started to build a vision for who you want to become. And you've begun asking the question that will guide everything that follows: What am I building now?

This was the inner work, and I know for some readers, that was neither easy nor fun. I get it. Most people skip this part because it's uncomfortable and doesn't show up on a net worth statement.

But understanding yourself is only half the equation. Clarity without action is just philosophy. The next step is turning what you've discovered into a life you're proud of. That's what the final chapter is for.

CHAPTER 8:

CREATE A RICHER LIFE

Design What Comes After the Exit

A few years ago, I watched a documentary series called *Lockup*. It followed life inside some of America's toughest prisons. Most episodes blended together, except one. It wasn't about an inmate; it was about a guard.

A year before filming, this woman had been brutally attacked by a prisoner. She was beaten nearly to death, suffering multiple broken bones, a shattered jaw, and months of painful recovery. Even as her body healed, the trauma lived on: nightmares, flashbacks, panic attacks. Yet, when the cameras rolled, she was back in uniform, walking through the same prison gates that almost took her life.

Through tears, she explained that she had no choice. She'd run out of money. No one would hire her. She needed to pay rent and buy groceries. She went back because she had to survive.

She's not alone. Billions of people endure jobs that drain their spirit simply because they have no alternative. Survival is a powerful instinct, but the cost can be devastating. I've counseled people who stayed in toxic relationships or abusive situations because they couldn't afford to leave.

Money doesn't erase every problem. Everyone faces challenges, no matter their wealth. In fact, sudden wealth brings its own set of issues. But it also brings something extraordinary: options. Money gives you freedom—the ability to shape your life on your own terms. It provides stability, security, and a voice.

Most of us live by default. Our finances dictate what's possible. But when you sell your business, that bar disappears. You're no longer limited by what you *have* to do; you can decide what you *want* to do. That freedom can feel both exhilarating and disorienting.

Money itself doesn't improve happiness. Watching numbers on a screen get larger won't change your life. A growing bank account feels good for a moment, but then the feeling fades, because those numbers, by themselves, don't *do* anything. They just sit there.

The real value comes from knowing how to *convert* those digits into something meaningful—experiences, connection, growth, joy, and a life that feels as rich as your investment account looks.

In the last chapter, you discovered who you are after the sale. This final chapter is about designing what comes next, and building a life that's financially secure and deeply fulfilling.

Your new job isn't to maximize your portfolio's return; it's to maximize your *life's* return. If you want fulfillment, you have to build it with intention. So how do you do that? You invest—but differently this time…

From ROI to ROL: Return on Life

For decades, your professional instincts were trained around a single governing metric, and that metric was return on investment. Every major decision was justified or rejected based on how efficiently it converted effort into financial gain. That mindset served you well. It helped build your company, protect your margins, and create wealth.

But after a sale, the equation changes. You move out of the world of ROI and into the world of ROL: return on life. The numbers still matter, but they are no longer the central scoreboard. The most valuable returns you will earn in this next chapter are not denominated in dollars. They are measured in how you spend your time, with whom you spend it, and what you choose to pursue when you no longer have to chase anything.

Return on life asks better questions. Instead of "What will this investment return financially?" the questions become "Does this choice energize me or drain me?" and "Is this commitment aligned with who I am now, not who I used to be?" You are no longer allocating capital. You are allocating hours, presence, and passion.

This transition requires clarity. Without it, freedom quickly becomes fragmentation. After their exits, many owners suddenly have more opportunities than ever: invitations from founders, investment pitches, advisory roles, nonprofit boards, and projects that all sound interesting. In the absence of purpose-driven criteria, it is easy to agree to too many things and end up with a portfolio of obligations instead of a life of intention.

The goal is to build a life where the things that matter most get the space to breathe. Instead of measuring success in revenue or headcount, measure it in alignment, impact, joy, and contribution. That's the mindset. Now you need the method.

The 6-P Framework: The Blueprint for a Life That Gets Better After the Sale

You didn't sell your business to slow down. You sold it to step into a life with more possibility, freedom, and meaning. But freedom alone is not a plan, just like wealth alone is not fulfillment and time alone doesn't automatically create purpose.

To build a life after the sale that's richer, you need a framework. A design. A way to channel your ambition, energy, curiosity, and independence into something that lifts you up rather than leaves you restless.

That's where the **6-P Framework** comes in. In Chapter 7, you identified your core needs and values. The 6-P Framework translates those discoveries into daily life.

This isn't the typical "retirement checklist." It's not about withdrawal rates, downsizing, or filling time so you don't go crazy. This is a performance model for life after the exit, one that ensures you grow, thrive, and feel fully alive long after the deal closes.

Here's your new operating system:

- **Physical health.** Your body carried you through the grind, and now it's time to invest back into it. This isn't about vanity or chasing youth; it's about building strength, energy, and capacity for everything ahead.

- **People.** These are the relationships that make life meaningful. Strengthen family connections, rebuild friendships, and design a circle that energizes you for the future instead of anchoring you in the past.

- **Positive impact.** Financial success is powerful, but personal significance is better. Trade "What did I build?" for "What will I contribute?" and design the next mission you care about deeply.

- **Pace.** You've been sprinting for years; now you get to choose your speed. Pace is about owning your time, not filling it. It's trading urgency for intention and constant motion for movement that matters. Build a rhythm that fuels you instead of drains you, and live life at the speed of meaning.

- **Pursuit.** Growth, challenge, adventure, self-improvement, and bold experiences. This is oxygen. Build a path of continual development and seek the impossible, because that is where fulfillment lives.

- **Play**. You deserve joy without justification and activity without agenda. The hobbies, interests, and creative outlets that bring joy and spark curiosity are what keep you vibrant. This is where you give yourself permission to do things just because they feel good and accept that not everything needs to matter. Ironically, that's what makes it matter most.

Master these six areas and your life doesn't just stay good after the sale; it gets better. Not smaller or slower. Bigger and deeper. More interesting. More fun. With that in mind, let's look at where to invest your most valuable resources, starting with the foundation that makes everything else possible.

Physical Health: Protect the Machine That Powers It All

The Asset You Can't Afford to Lose

Everything you have built—your company, your wealth, and your freedom—depends on one piece of infrastructure: you. If your body fails, the rest unravels. You can sell your company for eight figures, design the perfect post-exit life, and check every box of success, but if you are sick, weak, or chronically tired, none of it feels like winning. Physical health isn't one of the Ps just because it fits neatly in the sequence. It is the one that supports all the others.

Physical health magnifies or diminishes everything else in your life. You cannot be fully present with your family if you are distracted by pain or fatigue. You cannot travel, explore, or pursue new challenges if your body is unreliable. You cannot make a positive impact if you are constantly managing symptoms or recovery. Every other P—people, positive impact, pace, pursuit, and play—depends on the energy you bring to it.

I have seen too many owners step out of the boardroom and into retirement only to realize they are living in a body that is falling apart. Years of pressure, stress, travel, poor sleep, skipped meals, and endless urgency have taken their toll. They have traded their health for performance, assuming they could buy it back later. But you cannot outsource vitality. You can buy comfort, convenience, and access to care, but you cannot purchase strength, flexibility, or energy. Those have to be earned.

The truth is harsh: If your body is broken, the rest of your life becomes smaller. Relationships shrink. Curiosity fades. Joy loses its sharpness. You are living inside a house with cracks in the foundation, and no amount of wealth can make it feel steady.

Retiring into a Broken House

You have likely met people who built empires but retired to poor health. They are not lazy or undisciplined. They merely spent decades prioritizing everyone and everything else. They ran on caffeine and adrenaline, skipped workouts because "today was too busy," and numbed stress with late-night work. They told themselves they would focus on health "once the deal closes" or "once things settle down." Those moments never arrived.

Then, suddenly, the sale happens. The adrenaline fades, and their bodies collapse under the weight of deferred maintenance. Their blood pressure is high, their joints ache, their energy is gone, and their mind feels foggy. They finally have time, but no capacity. They retire into a house that looks beautiful on the outside but is crumbling inside.

I call this "retiring into a broken house." It is the reality for too many founders. They did not run out of time; they ran out of health. The good news is that it is not too late to rebuild. The human body is remarkably adaptable. You can restore function, strength, and vitality at any age. I have watched former CEOs and entrepreneurs in their sixties and seventies become stronger and more energized than they were in their forties. It takes intention, consistency, and humility—but that is a familiar formula for you.

Becoming an Athlete Again

In *Badass Retirement.* I wrote about the idea of becoming an athlete again. That phrase resonated deeply with readers because it reframes health from punishment to performance. You do not have to compete or wear a jersey. You need to approach your body with the same intentionality you once brought to your business.

Athletes have coaches, routines, and goals. They measure progress and make adjustments. They rest strategically and fuel their performance. They understand that recovery is as important as effort. You can apply that same mindset now. Your business once required constant optimization. Now your body deserves that same focus.

Becoming an athlete again means taking ownership of your energy. It means moving every day, lifting something heavy, sleeping deeply, eating clean food, and staying curious about your own biology. It is not about chasing youth. It is about building capability for the next chapter of your life. You invested years in building external assets. Now you are the asset.

The Best Investment You'll Ever Make

Here's something most people won't tell you, but I will: Now that you have wealth, spend it on your health. Not cautiously. Not sparingly. Aggressively.

I encourage clients to invest as much as they can reasonably afford in things that improve their physical and mental health. Personal trainers. Gym memberships. Weekly massages. Physical therapy. High-quality supplements. A nutrition coach. A sleep specialist. Whatever it takes to optimize how your body functions and how you feel every day.

You just sold your company for millions of dollars. You spent decades building wealth. Now is not the time to cheap out on the one asset that determines whether you can enjoy that wealth. What good is financial freedom if you're too tired to travel, too sore to play with your grandkids, or too sick to pursue the things that matter?

Think about the ROI differently now. A $200-per-hour personal trainer who keeps you strong and injury-free for the next twenty years is worth exponentially more than any stock pick. A $150 massage every week that helps you recover, sleep better, and move without pain is a bargain. A $10,000 annual investment in longevity-focused health care that catches problems early is the smartest money you'll ever spend.

Most people can't afford these investments. You can. Don't let frugality born from your building years prevent you from living well in your freedom years. You've already proved you can build wealth. Now prove you can invest it wisely, starting with yourself.

This isn't indulgence. It's strategy. Every dollar you spend extending your vitality, energy, and capacity multiplies the value of every other dollar you have, because money without health is just a number on a screen. Money with health, on the other hand, is freedom, adventure, presence, and joy.

The Mindset Shift

Business owners often think in extremes. If they cannot go all in, they hesitate to start. Health does not work that way. You do not need to train like a professional athlete. You just need to show up consistently. Small, repeated actions build extraordinary results. Walking daily, stretching, improving nutrition, and sleeping better can transform how you feel within weeks.

This requires a shift in mindset. In business, success comes from output—doing more, producing more, and grinding harder. In health, success comes from balance—knowing when to push and when to recover. The habits that helped you win in business can hurt you in longevity. You must unlearn the idea that exhaustion equals effectiveness. The next stage of your life is not about grinding harder. It is about sustaining better.

The moment you stop seeing health as optional and start seeing it as essential, everything changes. Energy becomes the baseline, not the exception. You wake up with curiosity again. You start to feel possibility in your body instead of limitation.

When you commit to becoming strong, flexible, and resilient, you reestablish a sense of progress, and rediscover purpose. You have something measurable to work toward. You reintroduce challenge into your life, but this time the challenge serves you rather than drains you. Physical health becomes the new scoreboard, but it is a scoreboard that measures quality, not quantity.

You can still set goals, but now they are rooted in vitality. Run a 5K. Hike a mountain. Hit a certain body fat percentage. Sleep eight hours a night. Lift your grandchild easily. These are milestones that matter because they directly improve your experience of living.

Rebuilding the Foundation

If your health has declined, start by rebuilding the foundation. Movement, sleep, and nutrition are the pillars. Move daily, even if it is just a short walk. Sleep consistently, aiming for quality, not just quantity. Eat food that fuels rather than numbs. Do not aim for perfection; aim for consistency.

You do not need a personal trainer to begin. You need a reason, something that makes the effort meaningful—a trip you want to take, a hobby you want to return to, or a grandchild you want to keep up with. Tie your health to something emotional, and it becomes sustainable.

Your body does not care how many companies you sold or what your net worth is. It responds only to how you treat it today. That truth can be sobering, but it is also empowering. Every day gives you another chance to move the needle. The compounding effect of daily effort is staggering. A year of consistent movement, sleep, and mindful nutrition can transform your physical and mental landscape.

In the end, health is freedom.

Physical health is not the final P—it's the first P. It is the foundation of all the others. People, positive impact, pace, pursuit, and play depend on the energy you bring to them. You can have deep relationships, meaningful work, and endless adventure, but without strength and stamina, you are a spectator in your own life. Take care of the machine that powers it all.

Once that foundation is built, turn your attention to what makes it all worthwhile: the people who give your life meaning. Because health creates capacity, but connection creates purpose. The second P is where freedom becomes fulfillment.

People: The Relationships That Make Life Rich

For years, your life has been built around people: your team, your customers, your partners, and your advisors. You were constantly surrounded by conversations, decisions, collaboration, and momentum. Whether you realized it or not, your business created your social world. When the sale closes, that world evaporates almost overnight. For a while, that silence feels like a reward—a long-overdue exhale. But eventually, the quiet becomes noticeable. Time expands, but meaning doesn't, unless you rebuild it intentionally. That's where the second P (people) becomes the foundation of a richer life after the sale.

Money improves life, but people give it meaning. You dedicated years building financial capital. Now, your focus becomes relational capital: the people you love, trust, respect, and want in your life moving forward. Selling your business frees your attention. You no longer have the excuse of being "too busy." You now have the ability to choose who you spend your time with and how deeply you invest in those relationships. Those who thrive after an exit aren't the ones who just have more free time. They're the ones who turn that time into deeper family bonds, richer friendships, and a more connected life.

Rebuilding Your Inner Circle

Think of this phase as rebuilding your founding team—not for a company, but for your life. The people who surround you shape how you think, how you feel, and how fast you grow in this next chapter. But unlike the business stage, this time is more personal, and the criteria are different. You're not selecting for skill sets; you're selecting for energy, integrity, curiosity, humor, loyalty, and shared values.

Ask yourself:

- With whom do I want to spend more time?

- Who brings energy into my life, rather than drains it?

- Who challenges me to think bigger or live better?

- Who cares about me, and not just what I've achieved?

Now that you have time, your relationships don't default to whoever happens to be near you. Instead, you choose them. That's the difference between passive association and intentional connection.

Family: The Foundation That Outlasts the Business

For many owners, family quietly absorbed the cost of ambition: late nights, stress spillover, distracted dinners, and postponed plans. They supported you through the mission; now you have the rare chance to truly support them back. That doesn't mean suddenly hovering or overcompensating; it means showing up fully. You are no longer the person who "drops in" between meetings.

Real presence isn't measured in hours; it's measured in attention. Put the phone down. Ask questions that invite real conversation. Be curious about their world as much as they were curious about yours. If you have adult children, this can be an extraordinary time, as your relationship evolves from parent-child into adult-to-adult partners in life. Talk openly about values, lessons, and life.

If you are married or partnered, this transition is just as significant for them as it is for you. You once shared a life paced by the demands of the business; now you get to co-design a life paced by shared intention. Build rituals—weekly breakfasts, evening walks, travel plans, and shared classes—small anchors that strengthen connection. In business, you learned that consistency compounds. The same is true here. This chapter of life allows you to be the partner you wanted to be when time and pressure made it hard.

Friendships: Fuel for Fulfillment

This is where the need for connection you identified in Chapter 7 becomes concrete. Family grounds you. Friends expand you.

During the building years, friendships often survive through proximity: neighbors, industry peers, and parents of your kids' friends. After the sale, that casual cluster disappears. Your friendships now require intention, and that's a good thing. You get to choose friends for who they are, not where they happen to be. Prioritize the people who bring life into your life. These are the ones who make you laugh and challenge you.

Ask yourself:

- Who do I always leave feeling better than when I arrived?

- Who inspires curiosity or laughter?

- Who sees me, not my success?

Friendships aren't merely social interactions. They are emotional infrastructure. After the exit, they become one of your strongest predictors of meaning and well-being. Don't wait for invitations; create them. Reach out, schedule dinners, plan trips, and start traditions. Entrepreneurs are great at initiating, so use that skill here.

But keep in mind that you don't need more people; you just need the right people. Success can attract the wrong attention. After your exit, more people may suddenly want your time. Be generous with your time, but also be discerning. Protect your attention the way you once protected company resources. In business, you learned to prevent scope creep; in life, prevent relationship creep. The people you choose determine the emotional ROI of your days.

Consider this filter:

- Does this person expand or shrink my world?

- Do I feel more or less myself around them?

- Would I still value this relationship if money and success were removed from the equation?

This isn't harsh; it's healthy. You're not cutting people out; you're choosing who enters the next chapter. A smaller circle of meaningful relationships beats a crowded room of shallow ones.

Community: Belonging by Design

Work once gave you belonging. Now you create it. Community is not accidental; it's constructed. Join groups that challenge you, inspire you, and make you feel part of something bigger than yourself. These can include:

- Travel or adventure groups

- Philanthropic or service organizations

- Mastermind for post-exit founder groups

- Fitness and training communities

- Learning cohorts or book clubs

- Faith-based groups

- Youth mentoring programs

- Clubs based around hobbies or pursuits

These aren't hobbies; they're identity anchors. They give you context, connection, and continuity. They replace the social ecosystem the business once created. When you show up somewhere consistently, you start to build a community. And if you're fortunate, you become part of one.

The Real Return on Life

Money gives you freedom. People give you meaning.

The relationships you build and rebuild after the sale determine whether the next chapter becomes the richest one of your life. Selling your company was the economic exit. Strengthening relationships is the emotional entrance into the life you earned.

The business was your vehicle. People are your destination. When you invest in family, deepen friendships, seek new circles, and show up with presence instead of distraction, you create a life not just of success, but of significance.

You now have something rare. The wealth to live freely and the time to live fully with the people you love. Don't waste it.

This is the second P, and it builds directly on the first. People aren't just another priority. They are what makes the foundation meaningful.

Strong relationships make life rich. But connection alone isn't enough. Once you're physically capable and surrounded by the right people, the next step is to aim that energy outward. That leads us to the third P. Positive impact means using your experience, wisdom, and resources to make a meaningful difference beyond yourself.

Positive Impact: Make a Difference Beyond the Business

I once met with an engineer who had just sold his company and was trying to figure out what came next. He told me he wanted to help others, to do something that mattered more than just another business venture. He was a natural leader, so I suggested that he consider joining a local nonprofit board. "Are you kidding? I never want to see another boardroom in my life." He laughed, but he meant it. For him, the thought of agendas, committees, and endless meetings felt like a return to everything he had just escaped.

Instead, he goes to his local library once a week, where they host a few hours for people to bring in broken appliances and electronics. He sits at a folding table with a small toolkit and a cup of coffee, and he fixes whatever shows up—a lamp, a toaster, even an old radio. He told me it's the best part of his week. There's no pressure, politics, or hierarchy—just helping real people and solving real problems, one repair at a time.

You may be wondering why I didn't name this the more obvious P-word: philanthropy. Philanthropy, for many, feels institutional and formal. What I'm talking about is positive impact—something smaller, more personal, and often more meaningful. Making a positive impact doesn't have to mean joining a board, launching a foundation, or funding a headline-worthy initiative. It can be as simple as using your skills, time, or presence to make life better for someone else. Helping a neighbor. Tutoring a student. Teaching the boy down the street without a dad how to throw a curveball. It's not about scale or structure, it's about intention.

The engineer at the library wasn't chasing recognition or status. He just wanted to stay useful and keep creating, fixing, and contributing in ways that felt human. That's the essence of positive impact. If contribution ranked among your top needs in Chapter 7, this is where you design the vehicle for it. It's not about giving back from a distance. It's about staying close to the work of life, where you can see and feel the difference you make.

Positive Impact Through Mentorship and Knowledge Transfer

As a business owner, you carry one of the most valuable forms of capital on the planet. It's called experience. You earned that education in the real world through risk, resilience, trial by fire, hard calls, and challenging lessons. There are seasoned executives who couldn't replicate your instincts in a PowerPoint if they tried.

This knowledge is scarce. It is also powerful, and the world is hungry for it.

You can mentor formally or informally. You can advise founders, coach executives, speak at schools, or quietly pull someone aside who reminds you of your younger self. You can help someone take a five-year leap by telling the truth about your journey. We underestimate the impact of wisdom, because we're used to measuring success in revenue and scale. But in this chapter of your life, you measure it in lives shaped, perspectives shifted, and paths accelerated.

You built a business. Now you can build people.

Consider the leverage in offering:

- Strategic guidance to a nonprofit that needs direction
- Negotiation coaching to a grassroots leader
- Operational advice to a mission-driven founder
- Leadership development to a youth organization
- Fundraising knowledge to someone doing meaningful work

Writing a check is generous. Sharing capability is transformational.

Positive Impact Through Personal Influence

Impact doesn't always require a stage. Sometimes it's quieter and more personal. You can become a north star in your family. A grounding presence for your spouse. A mentor to your children—not about business, but about life. You can start modeling how to live well and achieve well. You can share the parts of your story that matter most, including the mistakes, lessons, failures, resilience, and beliefs that shaped you. Money gives them comfort. Your wisdom gives them direction.

You don't have to make an impact on the world to make an impact on *your* world. The deepest legacy you leave might not be public. Instead, it might be in people who carry a different standard because of you.

When Positive Impact Evolves

One final truth about post-sale positive impact is that you don't have to pick one thing and stick to it forever. Impact isn't a title or a lifelong commitment. You can explore multiple paths. You can try something, learn from it, and pivot. You can have one mission for a year and a different one after that.

Give yourself permission to experiment.

- "Let me advise two startups this year and see how it feels."

- "Let me spend time mentoring young people before deciding if I want to formalize a program."

- "Let me support this cause locally before I consider launching my own initiative."

People think making a difference has to be big, but just like the engineer in the library, small actions beat inaction. When you sold your business, you may have lost your engine and the track it was running on. Start again with one commitment that lights you up. One person you want to help. One cause that resonates. One challenge that uses your skills.

Positive impact fuels meaning, but even meaning needs rhythm. Once you step into work that matters, you need to design how you show up for it—and for everything else. That takes us to the next P:

pace. This refers to choosing your speed instead of letting life choose it for you. Here, you trade urgency for intention and build a cadence that sustains you for the long haul.

Pace: Re-Shaping Your Relationship with Time After the Sale

When you sell your business, something fascinating happens. For years, your time has been defined by your company. You woke up thinking about it, solved problems in the shower, and measured your days by deals closed, clients served, fires put out, and milestones hit. You lived by calendars, deadlines, and the steady hum of responsibility.

And then one day the clock stops running your life, and that can be disorienting.

I've seen this over and over. Clients who fought for every inch of progress wake up post-sale and find themselves oddly anxious. They should feel joy and relief, but instead they feel uneasy. Why? Because they've lost the pace that once gave their days shape. Before the sale, your time wasn't your own, but it was full. After the sale, your time is yours, but it can feel empty.

This is why I often say the most important post-exit investment isn't financial; it's psychological. You have to rethink your relationship with time. You have to learn to set your own pace again: intentionally, not reactively.

Redefining the Clock

When you ran your business, your calendar was your scoreboard. You could look at your week and instantly see what mattered. Meetings, production cycles, investor calls, payroll—your time was accounted for. But now, that same calendar can become a blank page staring back at you.

This is where many former owners make a common mistake. They try to fill the vacuum the same way they filled their company calendar—by doing more. But unless your time aligns with your new purpose, you're only recreating activity.

Time is not just a resource; it's your most valuable currency. And after the sale, you have more control over it than ever before. But unless you consciously choose how to spend it, someone else will.

Here's something few people tell you: Unlimited freedom can be paralyzing. When every door is open, it's hard to choose which one to walk through. You can travel anywhere, invest in anything, and structure your days however you want, and that can feel liberating for a while. But soon, it can turn into restlessness.

That's why you need structure—not the rigid kind you escaped from, but the kind that supports your pace and channels your energy toward what fulfills you. Freedom without focus leads to frustration.

So ask the most important question of this phase: What does my ideal day look like now?

Not your ideal life—your ideal day. Great lives are built one intentional day at a time. If you can't define a great day, you'll struggle to design a great life.

Most former owners don't truly want to stop working. They just want to stop doing what drains them. They want to engage, build, and contribute, but on their terms, at a pace that feels aligned but not obligated.

That's the sweet spot, where freedom meets focus, rhythm, and pace.

Buying Time

One of the greatest advantages of selling your business is buying back time. It's the most irreplaceable asset you have. Money is powerful not because of what it can buy, but because of what it returns to you—time to think, rest, explore, reconnect, or build something new. During your business years, you invested capital to generate more capital. Now the equation shifts: You invest capital to generate a more meaningful life.

That may mean hiring help for tasks you don't enjoy or saying no to commitments that feel obligatory. It may mean giving yourself permission to take six months to travel, reflect, and design your future with intention, not because you're lost, but because you refuse to rush back into the grind for the sake of motion. The point is not to pack your time full, but to elevate the quality of how you spend it.

Time, not money, is the truest form of wealth. That's why I often ask former business owners a simple question: "If I gave you one hour every day that belonged entirely to you, how would you use it?" The answers are always revealing. Some say they'd read more. Others want to learn something new, train their bodies, deepen relationships, or pick up passions long deferred. Some realize they've never truly asked themselves this question before.

That single hour is symbolic. How you would use it tells you what matters. It tells you where fulfillment lives. And it tells you how you want to pace your life moving forward.

The New Definition of Time Well Spent

After you sell your company, your hours become a blank canvas. You get to paint your days again. But if you don't decide what matters, someone else will.

Reclaim your time not by scheduling each minute, but by choosing your pace on purpose. The point isn't to do less; it's to do what matters more, at the rhythm that supports who you are becoming.

As I wrote in *Badass Retirement*, wasted time never returns, but time invested intentionally compounds. That principle isn't exclusive to retirement, but it is even more important after selling your business.

Pace gives you control again—the freedom to design your days and the power to live on your own terms. But once you regain that control, it's time to aim it outward. Rhythm creates space, but boldness fills it. This leads us to the next P: pursuit. This is not chasing deals or growth targets anymore, but instead seeking adventure, exploration, and experiences that stretch you. Travel that challenges you. Physical feats that test you. New environments that wake you up and remind you what it feels like to be fully alive.

Pursuit: Keep Growing, Live Boldly, and Seek the Impossible

Selling your business creates a rare moment in life, where you finally have control over your time, energy, and priorities. But freedom alone does not create fulfillment. Freedom is merely the raw material. What you do with that freedom determines whether the next chapter becomes your greatest yet or you slowly drift into complacency.

For decades, your life ran on goals, pressure, deadlines, and progress. You had a target to hit, a competitor to beat, a team to support, customers to serve, and a mission to chase. Progress wasn't optional; it was what kept you going. And that rhythm shaped you. The entrepreneurial nervous system runs on advancement, momentum, striving, and waking up with a reason to move.

So, what happens when suddenly nothing requires you to move?

Some people think the answer to "What now?" is rest—permanent rest. But rest without motion eventually becomes stagnation. The problem after selling isn't burnout, it's softness. Too much ease erodes the edge that made you exceptional. Too much stillness dulls the instincts that made you strong.

To thrive after the sale, you must embrace progress not as pressure, but as practice. You don't need to grind. You don't need to compete with younger founders or prove yourself anymore. This is no longer about survival or significance. It's about continuing to become; to pursue your potential with the same intensity you once pursued success.

This section isn't about productivity hacks or performance metrics. It's about preserving the fire that built your business and redirecting it toward something deeper: mastery, growth, confidence, capability, and the courage to live boldly again.

Pursuit doesn't end when you sell. It just shifts direction.

Become a Beginner Again

One of the most powerful ways to stay alive and awake in this chapter of life is to return to curiosity. Step back into the arena not as a master, but as a learner. Do something unfamiliar, humbling, and challenging, and commit to it.

Clients often forget how energizing it is to not be the expert. For years, people looked to you for answers. Now you get to be the one asking questions again. Learning a language, taking voice lessons, training in a new sport, studying philosophy, practicing woodworking, or exploring music—whatever sparks curiosity, follow it.

Most owners I've worked with hate being bad at things. My guess is you're used to competence, mastery, and control. What happens when you start something new? You can feel uncomfortable. But mastery isn't the goal here, aliveness is. The willingness to be a beginner again is one of the most powerful skills in your post-exit life.

New experiences rewire the brain. They generate excitement. They build humility and curiosity. They remind you what growth feels like from the start. Pick things that interest you, not things you're already good at. Try activities that stretch you. Let "fun" and "interesting" be the metrics, not "successful" and "efficient." If you've always been the expert, challenge yourself to be the student. If you've always been the one teaching, put yourself in environments where you're learning again.

You became successful by leaning into discomfort. That hasn't changed. Becoming a beginner again isn't regression; it's rebirth. It wakes up the parts of your mind that have been dormant. It keeps you honest, humble, and hungry.

Humility and ambition are a powerful combination. They are the ingredients of greatness in business, and in life after business.

Live Boldly Again

Now that you have time, freedom, and resources, what do you do with them?

This question is not philosophical; it is urgent. It's easy to fall into routines that feel comfortable but slowly shrink your world. You did not build a business to one day live a life so quiet that nothing stirs you. You didn't earn this freedom so you could coast through your days. You earned it so you could chase what excites you, explore the world, learn new skills, take risks again, and build a life defined not by safety, but aliveness.

Running a company demanded boldness, and that boldness didn't disappear when you sold. When boldness goes unused, it calcifies into caution. Post-exit life can quietly seduce you into smaller choices: routines that are predictable, social circles that feel safe, travel that is comfortable, and hobbies that don't challenge you.

But inside, you still know how to be bold. That instinct is still alive. It needs a reason. Pursuit gives it one.

Boldness isn't reckless. It is intentional courage. It's saying, "I'm not done growing," and proving it with your actions.

Comfort is wonderful—in doses. It restores you. But make no mistake, too much comfort slowly narrows your life. When every day becomes predictable, you start to soften at the edges. When nothing feels unfamiliar, your world stops expanding. Comfort is not the goal; aliveness is.

Your goal now is not to avoid discomfort, but to choose the right kind of challenge. The challenges you seek now shouldn't feel like work; they should feel like curiosity. Pursuit isn't grinding; it's exploring. It isn't pressure; it's possibility.

Ask yourself regularly:

- What would make me feel fully alive right now?
- What new environment would wake up a different part of me?
- What challenge would be exciting, not stressful?
- What experience have I always imagined but never prioritized?

Your business demanded responsibility. Your next chapter demands adventure.

Seeking the Impossible

Most people spend their lives avoiding struggle. Business owners are often wired differently. You don't need struggle, but you do need stretch—not for ego or significance, but for vitality. In *Badass Retirement*, I talk about "seeking the impossible," not because you expect to achieve every impossible goal, but because pursuing them pulls the best out of you. Impossible goals have a way of sharpening your thinking, raising your energy, and reminding you what you're capable of. When the bar is low, life becomes dull. Raise the bar, and life expands again.

Impossible is a moving target. For some, it means running a marathon. For others, it's writing a book, learning a language, or launching a nonprofit. What matters isn't the size; it's the stretch. The moment you commit to something bigger than your comfort, life snaps back into focus. You feel that hum again—the hum of purpose, courage, and forward motion.

The paradox of success is that once you can do anything, it becomes dangerously easy to do nothing. That's why seeking the impossible isn't about achievement; it's about orientation. It gives you "juice," as one client phrased it—a reason to train, learn, show up, and compete again.

Consider the times you tackled something that made no sense on paper, but ultimately changed you. That's the energy you're looking for now. Seeking the impossible keeps you dangerous in the best way: curious, alive, and engaged with life instead of retired from it. It gives you an edge again. It brings back fire.

So ask yourself what scares you enough that it excites you? What challenge requires a stronger version of you? That's the one. That's your next impossible.

Pursuit brings back your edge—your energy, boldness, and aliveness. But adventure needs balance, a counterweight to all that intensity. And that's where the final P comes in. Play is joy without justification and activity without agenda. It's the hobbies, interests, and creative outlets you do purely because they feel good, not because they build toward anything. Play is proof that some things matter precisely because they don't have to.

Play: Rediscover Joy Without Purpose

After years of endless commutes, meeting deadlines, and grinding, you didn't think I'd forget about having some fun, did you? Owners spend decades optimizing every hour for output. Every meeting has an agenda. Every activity has a goal. Every minute is measured against ROI. Play is the antidote to all of that. It's activity without agenda, joy without justification, and time spent for no reason other than it feels good.

Play isn't frivolous; it's essential. It resets your nervous system, sparks creativity, and reminds you that life isn't only about achieving, but about enjoying. After years of high-stakes performance, play teaches you something radical: Not everything needs to matter.

These are the only metrics that matter: Did you lose track of time? Did you smile? Did you forget to check your phone?

Why Play Feels Unproductive (and Why That's the Point)

After years of disciplined focus, play can feel unproductive, even to the point of being uncomfortable. You might catch yourself thinking, "What's the point? What am I accomplishing here?" That internal resistance is exactly why play matters. It teaches you that value isn't always measured in outcomes. Sometimes, the experience itself is the reward.

One of my clients, a medical doctor, rediscovered woodworking after his sale. This wasn't to build furniture to sell or launch a side business or YouTube channel about craftsmanship. It was just to create. He'd spend Saturday mornings in his garage workshop, losing himself in the smell of sawdust and the satisfaction of shaping something with his hands. There were no deadlines, goals or needles—just flow.

He told me, "For the first time in thirty years, I'm doing something that doesn't need to matter!"

Another client started playing golf again. Not business golf or networking golf, but actual play. He joined a group of guys who teed off at dawn on Wednesdays, and the rule was absolutely no shop talk. Just golf, trash talk, and bad jokes. He'd been playing golf for twenty years as a business tool. Now, for the first time, it was just fun.

Here's what I hear from clients constantly when I suggest they add play back into their lives. "I don't know how." They're not being dramatic. After decades of optimizing every hour for productivity, the idea of doing something purely for joy feels foreign. If that's you—if play feels awkward, pointless, or like something you've forgotten how to do—you're in good company. Most high-achievers struggle with this. The good news is that play is like a muscle. It atrophies from disuse, but it comes back with a little practice.

The Science and Soul of Play

There's neuroscience behind this. Play activates different parts of your brain than work does. It lowers cortisol, increases dopamine, and creates what researchers call "psychological safety"—the feeling that it's okay to experiment, fail, laugh, and try again without consequence. This is the opposite of the high-pressure, high-stakes environment you lived in for years. Your nervous system needs this reset.

Play also connects you to others in ways that work never could. Shared play—whether it's a game, sport, or creative project—builds bonds faster than any business relationship because it's rooted in joy, not transaction. You're not trying to get something from each other. You're just enjoying being together.

I've watched serious, intense founders transform when they give themselves permission to play. The guy who wouldn't take a vacation because "the company needed him" suddenly spends three hours every Sunday building elaborate LEGO sets with his son. The woman who optimized every minute of her day now spends entire afternoons painting in her studio, covered in acrylics, grinning like a kid.

This isn't regression. It's reclamation. You're not becoming less serious; you're becoming more whole.

For years, you've lived in a world where everything had to justify itself. Play inverts that logic. It doesn't need to be useful. It doesn't need to teach you a skill that transfers elsewhere. It doesn't need to make you better at anything. It just needs to make you happy.

Finding Your Form of Play

Some of the most fulfilled post-sale founders I know have at least one activity in their lives that is pure play. It might be absurd to an outsider. One client collects and restores vintage pinball machines. Another teaches himself magic tricks. Another joined a community theater group and performs in local productions. None of it advances their wealth, status, or legacy. All of it makes them come alive.

If you're struggling to identify what play looks like for you, start with this question: "What did I love doing before I had to be productive?" Maybe it was drawing, skateboarding, playing an instrument, building things, exploring the woods, or playing cards. Somewhere in your past, before ambition took over, there were activities you did simply because they felt good. Go back there. Rediscover them. Or find new ones.

Schedule it, and protect it like you once protected your most important client meetings. Tuesday mornings are for woodworking. Thursday nights are for poker. Sunday afternoons are for playing with the grandkids. Treat play with the same seriousness you treated board meetings, because in this new chapter, play is just as essential to your well-being as any strategic decision you'll make.

Some owners struggle a little with play because for the decades they spent in business, it was the reward they got after being productive. But post-sale, that changes. Now play isn't something you earn by checking off your to-do list. Play is what makes life worth living. It's the laughter, joy, and moments when time disappears and you're fully present, fully yourself, and fully free. That can take some time to adjust to, though.

You spent decades proving you could build something that mattered. Now you get to spend time doing things that don't matter at all—and discover that they matter more than you ever imagined.

Ask yourself:

- What did I love doing before I started a company?
- What fun things did I drop because "I didn't have time"?
- What activities made me lose track of time when I was younger?
- What fascinated me long before money mattered?

These aren't nostalgic questions; they're signals. Following those early clues reconnects you with parts of yourself that got overshadowed by performance for far too long.

Your younger interests weren't immature; they were evidence of identity. They were who you were before the world rewarded you for productivity. Some of those passions are ready to come back to life.

Physical health. People. Positive impact. Pace. Pursuit. Play. These are the building blocks of a life that gets better after the sale. Master them, and you won't just survive the transition. You'll thrive in it. But there's another way to make sure these lessons stick. Instead of asking what to build, ask what would destroy it.

How to Guarantee Misery After Selling Your Business

You now have the 6-P Framework. You understand what to build. But sometimes the clearest path forward comes from looking at the problem in reverse.

The Stoics practiced something called premeditatio malorum, which translates roughly to "the premeditation of evils." It sounds dark, but the purpose was practical. By imagining what could go wrong, they prepared themselves to handle adversity and avoid preventable mistakes. Charlie Munger, Warren Buffett's longtime partner, used a modern version he called inversion thinking. Instead of asking how to succeed, he asked how to fail, and then avoided those behaviors.

The principle is simple. If you want to know how to thrive after selling your business, first figure out how to guarantee misery. Then do the opposite. Some people respond better to warning signs than destination markers. They're more motivated by what to avoid than what to pursue. If that sounds like you, the next few paragraphs are for you.

Let's invert the 6-P Framework. If your goal were to be as unhappy as possible after your exit, here's exactly what you'd do.

Neglect your physical health. You've earned a break. Sleep poorly. Drink more. Skip the gym. Tell yourself you'll get back in shape once things settle down. Treat your body like it's separate from your mental state. Run on the fumes of decades of stress and adrenaline. Discover too late that wealth without energy is just a number on a screen.

Abandon your people. Convince yourself that no one understands what you're going through. Pull away from the friends and family who supported you during the build. Decide that your problems are too unique or too privileged to share. Let relationships atrophy while you figure things out alone. Wonder why success feels so lonely.

Forget about positive impact. Focus entirely on yourself. Hoard your expertise instead of sharing it. Assume that writing checks is the same as making a difference. Never mentor, never teach, never use what you've learned to help anyone else. Let your experience die with your title.

Ignore your pace. Fill your calendar with obligations instead of interests. Say yes to every board seat, advisory role, investment pitch, and coffee meeting that comes your way. Mistake hustle for purpose. Let other people's agendas dictate your time. Never ask whether something energizes you, only whether it sounds impressive. Sprint until you collapse again.

Stop all pursuit. You've already made it. There's nothing left to prove. Avoid new challenges because you might fail. Stay comfortable. Stop learning. Let your skills atrophy and your curiosity fade. Watch as the world moves forward without you.

Eliminate play. Everything must have a purpose. Every activity must produce a return. Never allow yourself joy without justification. Dismiss hobbies as frivolous. Forget what it felt like to do something simply because it was fun. Become someone who has everything but enjoys nothing.

No one chooses this path on purpose. But it's easier to drift into than you think. Small compromises compound. One skipped workout becomes a year without exercise. One declined invitation becomes a pattern of isolation. One busy month becomes a life lived for other people's priorities.

You now have two tools. The 6-P Framework shows you what to build. The inversion exercise shows you what happens if you don't. One is a compass. The other is a warning light. Use both.

Chapter Exit

The sale of your business was never really about the money. It was about possibility. You devoted years building something extraordinary, a company shaped by your grit, your judgment, your ambition, and your refusal to settle. Now you face a challenge far fewer will ever master. You must build a life that is as intentional and proud as the business you created.

The 6-P Framework is your blueprint. After the exit, your greatest returns don't come from spreadsheets. They come from investing in physical health, deepening connections with people, creating positive impact, setting the right pace, living in bold pursuit, and rediscovering play. These aren't retirement ideas. They're human performance principles for the most liberated phase of your life.

Your deal may be done, but your greatest work is not behind you. You've already proven you can build wealth. This stage is about building worth, and the most meaningful, fullest, and richest life you can.

CONCLUSION:
THE REAL EXIT

You've reached the end of this book, but you're just getting started. You've got a whole new deal to work on, and it starts now.

Selling your business wasn't the finish line, it was the starting gun. You didn't exit something. You entered something far bigger, far more demanding, and infinitely more important. *The rest of your life.*

You've learned that success in a sale isn't measured only by valuation multiples or tax savings. It's measured by peace of mind, alignment, and freedom. The kind that lets you wake up and want to attack the day. The mechanics of the deal matter, but what matters *most* is what you do after the funds arrive. That's where life stops being theoretical and starts being lived.

Remember the business sale paradox and the 98 percent trap? Most sellers obsess over the during—the transaction itself—and wonder why they feel empty afterward. You now know why. The 1 percent before and the 1 percent after aren't footnotes. They're everything. Preparation protects your wealth, but purpose protects your soul.

You've mastered all three acts by preparing before the sale, executing during the sale, and designing a portfolio and a life after the sale. That's how you avoid the trap. That's how you maximize value and live richer.

You built something incredible once. Now you get to do it again, this time with more wisdom, more freedom, and nothing left to prove. The world doesn't need another business from you. It needs the next version of you, the one who knows that wealth without vitality is poverty, success without connection is loneliness, and freedom without purpose is just expensive boredom.

You built something worth buying. Now build something worth living.

CONTINUE THE JOURNEY

You've read the book. Now let's put it to work.

At BusinessSaleParadox.com you'll find free tools and resources to help you prepare for, navigate, and thrive after your business sale.

Free downloads include:

- **The Business Sale Readiness Scorecard** — Assess where you stand across the Four Pillars and identify what needs attention before you go to market.

- **The Why Letter Template** — The single most important document you'll write before selling, with prompts to help you clarify your motivation, vision, and non-negotiables.

- **The Deal Team Interview Guide** — Questions to ask when vetting investment bankers, M&A attorneys, CPAs, and wealth advisors so you build the right Core Four.

- **The Post-Sale Life Design Worksheet** — Start designing what comes next using the 6-P Framework from Chapter 8.

- **And much more...**

Want to go deeper?

If you're preparing to sell or have recently sold and want help navigating what comes next, I'd welcome the conversation. I work with a small number of business owners each year, but if I'm not the right fit, I'm happy to help you find an advisor who is.

Visit BusinessSaleParadox.com to learn more, access the free resources, or schedule a conversation.

ABOUT THE AUTHOR

Hi, I'm Robert Pagliarini. For over 30 years I've helped business owners navigate the most consequential financial event of their lives—selling their company. If you're reading this, you've probably spent years, maybe decades, building something valuable. Now you're thinking about letting it go and realizing a successful sale isn't just about maximizing value—it's about setting yourself up for what comes next.

I get it. I've sat across from countless owners in exactly your position. They've built something real, and they want to make sure they don't screw it up at the finish line. They want to know they're getting what they deserve, that they won't get crushed on taxes, and that life after the sale will actually be worth living. This is where I can help.

My wealth management practice focuses on sudden wealth and retirement planning. I work with business owners before, during, and after the sale—helping them maximize value, minimize taxes, and create real financial security. I also work with retirees who want more than an average retirement—people who, like business owners after a sale, are navigating a major identity shift and want what comes next to actually matter. Whether clients are exiting a company or exiting a career, my focus is the same. Helping them navigate big financial transitions while building lives with more meaning, freedom, and purpose.

I have a Ph.D. in financial and retirement planning, I'm a Certified Financial Planner™, and I have a master's degree in psychology. That last one matters more than you might think. Early in my career, I realized that the riches-to-rags stories you hear are rarely caused by one bad investment. The real cause is how money changes people— and the people around them. So I went back to school, trained in counseling, and learned how to help clients make sound decisions in the middle of chaos.

This is my sixth book. I've also written Badass Retirement, The Sudden Wealth Solution, Get Money Smart, The Other 8 Hours, and The Six-Day Financial Makeover. I've written columns for Forbes and CBS, and I've appeared on Dr. Phil, CNBC, 20/20, Good Morning America, The Today Show, Fox Business, and many others.

I try to live the kind of life I encourage my clients to design after the sale. I've climbed Kilimanjaro, trekked through Patagonia, and completed an Ironman—all with clients because some conversations are better on a mountain than in a conference room!

If you're thinking about selling your business and want someone in your corner who's been through this for over three decades, I'd love to talk.

I'm on this journey with you.

INDEX